GOLD

GOLD

Firsthand Accounts from the Rush That Made the West

JOHN RICHARD STEPHENS

TWODOT®

Guilford, Connecticut
Helena, Montana
An imprint of Globe Pequot Press

To buy books in quantity for corporate use
or incentives, call **(800) 962–0973**
or e-mail **premiums@GlobePequot.com**.

A · T W O D O T® · B O O K

TwoDot is a registered trademark of Morris Book Publishing, LLC.

Project Editor: Lauren Brancato
Layout: Chris Mongillo
Maps: Melissa Baker © Morris Book Publishing, LLC

Library of Congress Cataloging-in-Publication data is available on file.

ISBN 978-0-7627-9150-7

Printed in the United States of America

10 9 8 7 6 5 4 3 2 1

This book is dedicated to Joanne and Monte Goeller.

Contents

ACKNOWLEDGMENTS

I would like to thank Elaine Molina; Martha and Jim Goodwin; Scott Stephens; Marty Goeller and Dorian Rivas; Terity, Natasha, and Debbie Burbach; Brandon, Alisha, and Kathy Hill; Jeff and Carol Whiteaker; Christopher and Doug Whiteaker; Gabriel, Aurelia, Elijah, Nina, and Justin Weinberger; Rachel, Roxanne and Lotus Nunez; Jayla, Anthony, Sin, and Bobby Gamboa; Pat Egner; Baba and Mimi Marlene Bruner; Anne and Jerry Buzzard; Krystyne Göhnert; Eric, Tim, and Debbie Cissna; Norene Hilden; Doug and Shirley Strong; Barbara Main; Joanne and Monte Goeller; Irma and Joe Rodriguez; Danny and Mary Schutt; Les Benedict; Dr. Rich Sutton; SK Lindsey; Jeanne Sisson; Michael and Roz McKevitt; Carmen and Danny Shafer; and my agent, Charlotte Cecil Raymond.

A Note on the Text

I have fixed typographical errors, modernized punctuation and paragraphing, and have removed a few instances of racism. I have not changed nonstandard or unusual spellings, as I did not consider these to be typos.

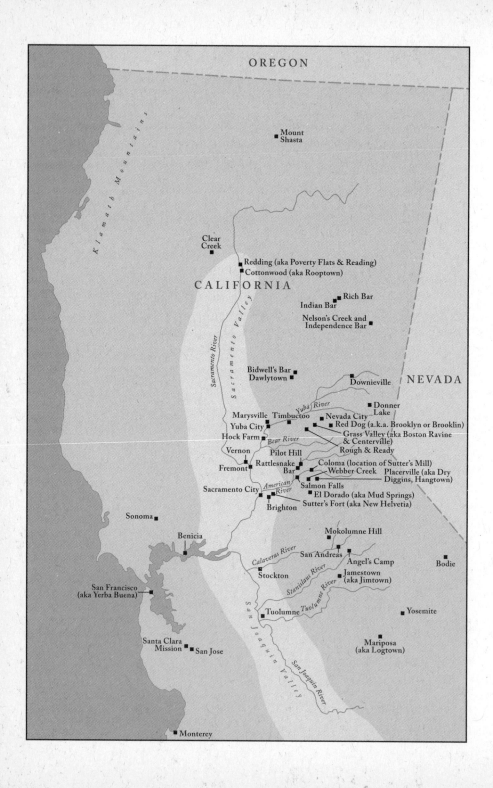

OREGON

Mount
Shasta

Clear
Creek

Redding (aka Poverty Flats & Reading)
Cottonwood (aka Rooptown)

CALIFORNIA

Rich Bar
Indian Bar
Nelson's Creek and
Independence Bar

Bidwell's Bar
Dawlytown

Downieville

NEVADA

Sacramento River

Sacramento Valley

Yuba River

Donner
Lake

Marysville Timbuctoo   Nevada City
Yuba City   Red Dog (a.k.a. Brooklyn or Brooklin)
Hock Farm *Bear River*   Grass Valley (aka Boston Ravine
                            & Centerville)
Vernon   Pilot Hill   Rough & Ready
           Rattlesnake   Coloma (location of Sutter's Mill)
Fremont   Bar   Webber Creek   Placerville (aka Dry
                                           Diggins, Hangtown)
Sacramento City *American Salmon Falls
                 River*   El Dorado (aka Mud Springs)
           Brighton   Sutter's Fort (aka New Helvetia)

Sonoma

Benicia

Mokolumne Hill

Calaveras River   San Andreas

                    Angel's Camp   Bodie
Stockton *Stanislaus River* Jamestown
                              (aka Jimtown)

San Francisco
(aka Yerba Buena)

San Joaquin Valley

Tuolumne *Tuolumne River*   Yosemite

Santa Clara
Mission San Jose   Mariposa
                                 (aka Logtown)

San Joaquin River

Monterey

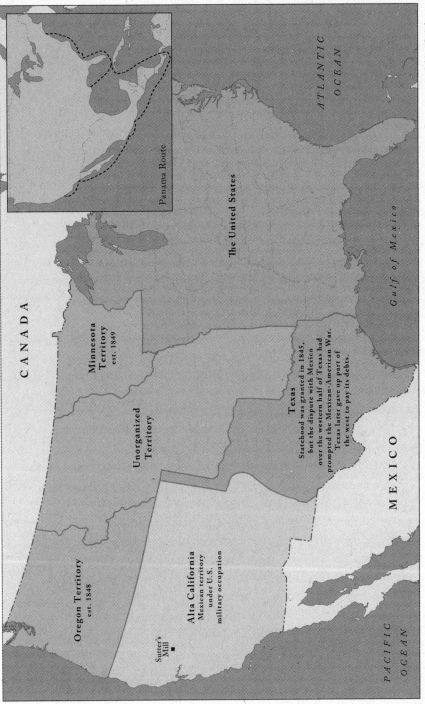

The United States at the time gold was discovered. As part of the treaty with Mexico that ended the Mexican-American War, the occupied territory of Alta California was handed over to the United States in July 1849. California became a state in 1850, while the remainder of Alta California became the Utah Territory.

Introduction:
The World's Most Humongous Treasure Hunt

THE MIDDLE OF NOWHERE

The discovery of gold in California in 1848 was a momentous event that completely altered the nature of the West, generated major changes in the entire United States, and economically affected every developed country. It was an event that eventually shook the world.

Oddly, no one took much notice of it at the time. Most of the participants didn't believe the discovery had actually taken place. They thought it couldn't really be gold, or else someone would have found it long before. Subsequently, those involved weren't even sure what day the first nuggets were found on. To them the discovery was a minor curiosity, but the rush slowly built momentum until it reverberated around the globe, its effects felt for many years to come.

The discovery site was an unlikely spot for such a monumental event. About two dozen men were building a sawmill alongside a river in a quiet valley dotted with pines, oaks, willows, buckeyes, and manzanitas. This little valley sat in the rolling foothills below the snow-peaked Sierra Nevada, thirty-five miles from the nearest frontier outpost—Sutter's Fort—which in turn was fifty-five miles from the nearest town and military camp at Sonoma. All of this was in the sparsely populated province of Alta California, which had just been taken from Mexico and was occupied by the United States military. The nearest US border, not counting the remote territory of the Louisiana Purchase, was about 850 miles away at the far-flung edge of the newly ratified state of Texas. The nearest US city was St. Louis, Missouri, and it was 1,650 very rough miles away. As far as the world was concerned, gold was discovered at an unknown place in the middle of nowhere. But Alta California didn't remain unknown for much longer.

At the time of the US occupation, Alta California—then a Mexican department, a step up from a territory—included what is now California, Arizona, Nevada, and Utah, along with parts of Colorado and Wyoming. The part that became the state of California was very remote and sparsely populated, and contained only four presidios—military outposts that were each responsible for their district—at Santa Barbara, Monterey, Yerba Buena (San Francisco), and Sonoma. In addition to the pueblos, or towns, near each of the presidios, there were pueblos at San José, Villa de Branciforte (Santa Cruz), San Diego, and El Pueblo de Nuestra Señora la Reina de los Angeles del Río de Porciúncula (Los Angeles). By this time California's string of missions were all in private hands. The Mexican government had sent the Franciscan friars back to Spain, converting the missions into ranchos. By the time of the war, there were about 800 scattered ranchos, each generally consisting of thousands of acres. The missions didn't really exist, as such, at this time. When they did exist, there were just a handful of friars and a large number of Native Americans. When the missions were converted into ranchos, most of the Indians returned to their rapidly changing native lands.

Except for Native Americans, almost the entire population lived in those pueblos along the coast. The Los Angeles pueblo was by far the largest, with an 1846 population of about 3,500 residents. One historian's census for that same year listed the population of Yerba Buena at 149, with an additional 102 at the mission, and 30 in the presidio. Mexico was trying to increase the area's population by encouraging immigration.

Unfortunately, most population figures for this time don't include Native Americans, and some don't even include Californios (Spanish-speaking Californians). Before the American invasion, mortality from diseases dropped the Indian population from approximately 310,000 to around 150,000. It's difficult to figure out how many Indian communities there were or where they were located. The primary role they played in the events at the time of the war and the gold rush was as the victims of massacres. Two years into the gold rush their population was down to about 70,000.

THE MEXICAN-AMERICAN WAR

When the Mexican-American War broke out in 1846, because the US annexed Texas, around thirty settlers seized the presidio at Sonoma in the Bear Flag Revolt. The Mexican commander consolidated his forces in Los Angeles, enabling Commodore John Sloat, with 250 men, to walk in and take over Monterey, Alta California's capital, unopposed. The

Mexicans couldn't have defended Monterey anyway, since they didn't have any gunpowder for their few cannons. Yerba Buena was similarly captured, with a force of seventy men. Los Angeles was also eventually occupied, after a few minor skirmishes.

US Army lieutenant colonel and explorer John Frémont and about 160 men then took San Diego unopposed. Leaving forty men behind to hold the town, Frémont headed for Los Angeles. Fearing they were about to be overrun, the forty men holding San Diego fled, allowing Francisco Rico and Serbulo Varela, with fifty men, to recapture the pueblo unopposed. Three weeks later US forces recaptured San Diego after a brief skirmish. Then Captain Leonardo Cota and Ramon Carrillo, along with 100 men, laid siege to the town. The siege lasted several months, with daily skirmishes and several deaths.

The largest battle of the Mexican-American War in California was the Battle of San Pasqual. General Stephen Kearny, who had marched overland from Santa Fe with a force of from 179 to 200 men, was lured into a trap by 160 Californios led by Major Andrés Pico. Kearny's men were weakened by the 850-mile march through the Sonora Desert. The situation was desperate when Kit Carson, accompanied by another man, snuck through the Californio line in the middle of the night, and ran 35 miles barefoot to San Diego for reinforcements. Commodore Robert Stockton sent 200 men to rescue Kearny's forces, and the Californios dispersed. Kearny had twenty-one men killed, while the Californios lost about half a dozen.

By comparison to other battles in the Mexican-American conflict, in California it wasn't much of a war. Overall, the locals were largely neutral. The rest were divided, with many Californios siding with the United States.

THEN THE WORLD WENT CRAZY

When gold was discovered, the world went crazy, but it was a slow process. Jim Marshall found the first nuggets on or about January 24, 1848, but it was seven weeks before the first small article about the discovery appeared in a San Francisco newspaper. It was another ten months before people on the East Coast began to believe the reports. It took the rest of the world a bit longer to catch on. The gold rush began in earnest in 1849; the name "Forty-Niners" was given to those pioneers who headed for California during that and subsequent years. Because of the difficulties endured in getting to the state, the pioneers were also called the argonauts.

Once the residents of San Francisco realized they could find gold themselves, practically the entire population of the city headed for the hills. Businesses locked their doors, schools closed, sailors abandoned ship, and California's military governor sought the public's help in finding and arresting Army and Navy deserters. Then men began flooding in from all over the world, including Australia, which at the time was still a British penal colony. This created a tremendous shortage of supplies, and the prices of commodities shot sky high. For example, in early 1848, lots in San Francisco were priced from $16 to $50; by the end of that year they were selling for $10,000 each.

Gold country was inhabited by an unusual population. There were almost no women, children or old people. Practically the entire population was young men. This was largely because of the difficulty and dangers of getting to the gold fields, and because the lifestyle was so hard. Miner William Swain wrote, in a letter dated January 6, 1850, from the South Fork of Feather River: "George, I tell you this mining among the mountains is a dog's life. A man has to make a jackass of himself packing loads over mountains that God never designed man to climb, a barbarian by foregoing all the comforts of civilized life, and a heathen by depriving himself of all communication with men away from his immediate circle."

AN INFLUX OF PIONEERS

Pioneers, hearing great things about California—not all of them true—began making the difficult journey to the state, mainly traveling overland. In 1848, right before the gold rush began, the *California Star* reported that San Francisco's nonnative population—probably not including Hispanics—was 575 males, 177 females, and 60 children. Within just two years, the city's population went from around 1,000 to 25,000, and by 1870 it was 150,000.

In the seven years before the gold rush, 2,700 settlers arrived in California, mainly in covered wagons. By 1854, more than 300,000 pioneers had made the long journey. Almost all of them were men between the ages of twenty and forty. Of course, many of these men tried their luck and then returned to the East.

It's estimated that, in 1848, California's entire nonnative population totaled no more than 15,000. Two years later, according to US Census Bureau data, the state's population was 92,597. Ten years later, in 1860, the population had increased by 287,379, and by 1870 the state had gained an additional 180,253 residents, to a total population of 560,247. Since then the population has continued to rise, usually at greatly increasing rates.

On the other hand, as with the rest of the country, the Native American population was dropping precipitously due to disease, starvation, and massacres, which were much more common than most people realize. During the gold rush, the aboriginal population dropped from around 100,000 to 30,000. The treatment of California's tribes by the government and the general public has been described by some scholars as genocide, and there is considerable evidence to support this. Unfortunately, prejudice, racism, intolerance, and ignorance were rampant in those days.

GETTING THERE

When the gold rush began, getting to California was very difficult. There were essentially three ways to get to the state. The easiest and most popular route was to sail from New York City or St. Louis, Missouri, to Central America, then hike over the isthmus of Panama to the Pacific Ocean. Sometimes small boats or canoes could be taken part of the way over the isthmus. While the distance across the isthmus was only about thirty-five miles, the roads were very bad and in some places nonexistent. They also weren't direct, making the journey an estimated fifty to seventy-five miles by foot or mule. Besides being exposed to the dangers of the jungles, pioneers often caught diseases, such as malaria. Once on the Pacific side, so many people were waiting for passage up the coast that it could take months to catch a ship headed for San Francisco.

Another way to reach the state was to take passage on a ship sailing to San Francisco by going around Cape Horn, at the southern end of South America. This, too, was dangerous, primarily because of the sudden, violent storms at the cape, which occasionally sank ships. Storms could appear at any time of year, and gale force winds struck up to 5 percent of the time during the summer and up to 30 percent of the time during the winter. Once the fresh food ran out, passengers and crew were stuck eating things like salt pork and hardtack, essentially a large unsalted saltine cracker that was hard as a brick. Of course, diseases including scurvy were problems, and the trip generally took six months.

The third route to California was traveling the two thousand miles overland at the rate of about three miles per hour. This was the most difficult and dangerous way to get to the state. While there were three main trails, there were no roads for parts of the journey, and there were large rivers to cross, not to mention the Rocky Mountains and the Sierra Nevada to scale. Wagons literally fell apart, while horses, mules, and oxen dropped dead from hunger and exhaustion. Travelers had to cross wide deserts, sometimes encountered snow in the mountains, and occasionally confronted hostile native tribes that often considered it honorable to capture an enemy's livestock. And again there were diseases, along with sunstroke, exposure to extreme temperatures, dehydration, and starvation, in addition to myriad other dangers stemming from wild and domestic animals, and nature in general. Those who made it were sometimes damaged for life, and many died along the way.

TONS AND TONS OF GOLD

There were other gold rushes—in Australia, the Black Hills of the Dakotas, Canada's Klondike, and Alaska—but the one in California was the biggie. The California gold rush lasted two decades, ending about the time the first transcontinental railroad was completed, in 1869. The amount of gold mined peaked in 1852, but gold was still being found in very large quantities well into the 1860s. On average, seventy-six tons of gold were mined each year. In ten years, $550 million worth of the stuff was pulled out of the ground, which would be roughly equivalent to $187 billion in today's dollars.

"The whole world felt a beneficent influence from the great gold yield of the Sacramento basin," journalist and prospector John S. Hittell noted in *Mining in the Pacific States of North America* (1861). "Labor rose in value, and industry was stimulated from St. Louis to Constantinople.

The news, however, was not welcome to all classes. Many of the capitalists feared that gold would soon be so abundant as to be worthless, and European statesmen feared the power to be gained by the arrogant and turbulent democracy of the New World."

. The gold rush also occurred before and during the Civil War. Some historians have suggested that the gold flowing out of California played a major role in enabling the Union to defeat the Confederacy. In addition, it probably did contribute greatly to America's becoming a world power.

The region where gold was found is six hundred miles long and forty-five to sixty miles wide, and is known as the Gold Country and the Mother Lode Country. It extends from central through northern California and is mainly on the western slope of the Sierra Nevada, although a few spots are on the eastern slope.

Gold is a very rare element in the universe. While many elements are formed in stars, those heavier than iron aren't. After stars explode as supernovas they leave behind dead cores called neutron stars. Evidence indicates gold is formed when two neutron stars collide and become a black hole. The gold and other heavy elements are ejected with about 3 percent of the two neutron stars by the brief gamma-ray burst, while the rest of the stars are sucked into the black hole. These events are rare so the amount of gold in the universe is small. Scientists estimate that a single collision would produce up to ten moon masses of gold. They believe that every bit of gold on earth was created by one of these tremendous collisions. The resulting gold was eventually mixed into the earth's crust, scattered about as atoms or microscopic particles.

Gold deposits are made by earthquakes. During an earthquake, the two sides of a fault grind past each other under great pressure, but where the fault zigzags there are places where the two sides can quickly move apart, creating a rapid drop in pressure. Within a few tenths of a second, very hot, mineral-rich water flowing along these separating parts of the fault vaporizes, causing quartz and gold to precipitate out, forming a tiny vein. Repeated earthquakes add more to the vein. The size of the earthquake doesn't matter; small ones can create a deposit just as well as large ones, although large ones probably create more deposits. It's not uncommon for a single fault to produce hundreds of thousands of earthquakes a year; when this goes on for many millennia, tiny quartz and gold veins can slowly build up into large veins. Mountain-forming processes and volcanoes eventually push some of the veins to the surface, where erosion creates placer gold—gold that is no longer in its quartz matrix—in the form of nuggets and gold dust.

Gold is found in a variety of forms. Gold dust, also known as fine gold, falls into seven basic categories: flour, grain, fine shot, shot, scale, thread, and spangle. Coarse gold comes in eight types: crystalline, coarse shot, pea, bean, cucumber seed, pumpkin seed, moccasin, and miscellaneous coarse. Most of these forms were found in California during the gold rush, but many of them were rare. Gold is also found as large nuggets. The vast majority of gold found in California was gold dust, miscellaneous coarse gold, and nuggets. Collecting gold from surface dirt and sand, usually in riverbeds, was called placer mining. This yielded gold dust and some nuggets. Mining deep into the ground usually turned up gold embedded in quartz and miscellaneous coarse gold, smooth, irregular-size particles that tended to be somewhat flat.

The methods of mining progressed with time. Initially, a single man with a shovel, rocker and gold pan could do very well for himself. Then, groups of men were needed to work a sluice or long tom. These progressed to flumes. By the mid-1850s, the phase of pick-and-shovel mining was coming to an end and mining by small groups of men fell to the wayside. Mining companies took over, able to search for harder-to-access gold. Quartz and hydraulic mining, which required heavy equipment and large mills, dominated the era of corporate mining. Within a short space of time, the gold-mining process progressed from small to large, from simple to complicated, and from individual to corporate.

It was mainly during the early years that any man could make his fortune. This possibility is what inspired the rush and captured people's imaginations. And the incredible success stories are what led to the greatest treasure hunt in history.

Part One: Nonfiction

Discovering Gold

James Marshall

James Marshall discovered gold at Sutter's Mill in January 1848. The exact date is unknown because those involved placed such little significance on it at the time, but based on the sequence of events, diaries, and the various conflicting accounts it had to be sometime between the 17th and the 28th—most likely on the 24th. At the time, no one realized the implications of the discovery. Marshall thought what he'd found was gold, but had difficulty believing it was true. Marshall's firsthand account of his discovery appeared in the November 1857 issue of *Hutchings' Illustrated California Magazine.*

Looking down on the American River from Cape Horn in the early 1860s

"I HAVE FOUND IT"

Being a millwright by trade, as there was a ready cash sale for lumber, I concluded to seek a location in the mountains and erect a mill, to supply the valley with lumber. Some time in April 1847, I visited New Helvetia, commonly known as the "Fort," where I made my resolution known to John A. Sutter, sen., and requested of him an Indian boy, to act as an interpreter to the mountain Indians in the vicinity of the American river—or Rio del los Americanos, as it was then called.

At first he refused, because he said that he had previously sent several companies, at various times, and by different routes, for that purpose, all of whom reported that it was impossible to find a route for a wagon road to any locality where pine timber could be procured, and that it was the height of folly to attempt any such thing.

Capt. Sutter at length, however, promised me the desired interpreter, provided I would stock some six or eight plows for him first, of which he was in immediate want, which I readily agreed to do. [...]

Sutter's sawmill after the tailrace was filled in. It's usually said that the man is James Marshall. While this is not certain, the man in the picture does resemble him. Various dates are given for the photograph, but 1852 appears to be the most common.

The report which I had made on my first trip having been fully confirmed by observations on the second, the co-partnership was completed, and about the 27th of August we signed the agreement to build and run a saw-mill at Culluma. [. . .]

The sawmill was to be powered by a diverted stream of water from the river. This side stream that flowed under the mill was called a tailrace. As they built the mill, they needed to deepen the tailrace, but rather than dig it by hand, they deepened it by allowing water from the river to flow through it each night, carrying away dirt, sand, and rocks. In effect, it acted sort of like a giant sluice, carrying away lighter rock and leaving the heavier gold nuggets behind.

While we were in the habit at night of turning the water through the tailrace we had dug for the purpose of widening and deepening the race, I used to go down in the morning to see what had been done by the water through the night; and about half past seven o'clock on or about the 19th of January—I am not quite certain to the day, but it was between the 18th and the 20th of that month—1848, I went down as usual, and after shutting off the water from the race I stepped into it, near the lower end, and there, upon the rock, about six inches beneath the surface of the water, I discovered the gold.

I was entirely alone at the time. I picked up one or two pieces and examined them attentively; and having some general knowledge of minerals, I could not call to mind more than two which in any way resembled this—sulphuret of iron, very bright and brittle; and gold, bright, yet malleable; I then tried it between two rocks, and found that it could be beaten into a different shape, but not broken. I then collected four or five pieces and went up to Mr. Scott (who was working at the carpenters bench making the mill wheel) with the pieces in my hand and said, "I have found it."

"What is it?" inquired Scott.

"Gold," I answered.

"Oh! no," returned Scott, "that can't be."

I replied positively, "I know it to be nothing else."

Mr. Scott was the second person who saw the gold. W. J. Johnston, A. Stephens, H. Bigler, and J. Brown, who were also working in the mill yard, were then called up to see it. Peter L. Wimmer, Mrs. Jane Wimmer, C.

Bennet, and J. Smith were at the house, the latter two of whom were sick; E. Persons and John Wimmer (a son of P. L. Wimmer) were out hunting oxen at the same time.

About 10 o'clock the same morning, P. L. Wimmer came down from the house, and was very much surprised at the discovery when the metal was shown him; and which he took home to show his wife, who, the next day, made some experiments upon it by boiling it in strong lye, and saleratus; and Mr. Bennet, by my directions, beat it very thin.

Four days afterwards I went to the Fort for provisions, and carried with me about three ounces of the gold, which Capt. Sutter and I tested with nitric acid. I then tried it in Sutter's presence by taking three silver dollars and balancing them by the dust in the air, then immersed both in water, and the superior weight of the gold satisfied us both of its nature and value. [...]

The *first piece of gold* which I found *weighed about fifty cents*. Mr. Wimmer, having bought a stock of merchandise some time about May or June 1848; and Mrs. Wimmer being my treasurer, used four hundred and forty dollars of my money to complete the purchase; and among which was the first piece of gold which I had found. Where that went, or where it is now, I believe that nobody knows.

Actually, Jennie Wimmer kept the nugget that she had tested in the boiling lye, eventually donating it to the University of California, Berkéley. There is conflicting testimony as to whether the Wimmer nugget is actually the first one found, but if it wasn't *the* first one, it was definitely one of the first. Marshall found several nuggets that first day and might not have been sure himself which was the first one he picked up.

My Great Plans Were Destroyed

John A. Sutter

FOUNDING A UTOPIA

Johann Suter, as was his name before he Americanized it, fled his home in Switzerland in 1834. After going deeply into debt and facing trial, at the age of thirty-one he left his wife and four children in Switzerland and sailed for America, changing his name to John Sutter to sound more American. For several years he was a merchant and innkeeper on the Santa Fe Trail, before moving on to Fort Vancouver, in what is now Washington State. With great difficulty, he made his way to Monterey, which was the capital of Alta California.

At that time, California was very remote and sparsely populated. Mexico was trying to boost its population, and one method was by offering land grants to foreigners. When Sutter told the governor at Monterey that he intended to build a settlement in the interior of northern Alta California, in an isolated area populated only by what were assumed to be hostile Native Americans, the governor probably believed Sutter was insane or foolish, but gave him permission to settle. With the help of eight Hawaiian men and two Hawaiian women who had joined Sutter when he passed through Hawaii on his way to Alta California, he traveled up the Sacramento River and built his fort.

John Sutter, probably in the 1840s

Sutter intended to start a Utopian agrarian community, which he named New Helvetia—Helvetia being the Swiss name for Switzerland—but most people called it Sutter's Fort. After making peace with the native tribes, he quickly became the head of his own little empire.

To get a land grant Sutter had to become a Mexican citizen, convert to Catholicism, serve as a Mexican government official, and get the Native Americans under control. He also had to have twelve nonnative settlers join him, build a permanent settlement, and survive in the settlement for a year. On completing these requirements, he received a grant of eleven square leagues—48,712 acres. With the help of the Native Americans, he soon had wheat fields, orchards, vineyards, and 13,000 cattle. Then, in 1844, Sutter was made a captain in the Alta California militia and was given another land grant of twenty-two square leagues, for a total of 146,136 acres. He was eventually able to bring his family over from Switzerland to join him.

Frémont Describes Sutter's Fort

When John Frémont was exploring the West, he stopped at Sutter's Fort. In his book *The Exploring Expedition to the Rocky Mountains, Oregon and California* (1852), Frémont described Sutter's Fort as it was in March 1844:

[Sutter] had, at first, some trouble with the Indians; but, by the occasional exercise of well-timed authority, he has succeeded in converting them into a peaceable and industrious people. The ditches around his extensive wheat-fields; the making of the sun-dried bricks, of which his fort is

Sutter's Fort in 1846 by Norton Bush

constructed; the plowing, harrowing, and other agricultural operations, are entirely the work of these Indians, for which they receive a very moderate compensation—principally in shirts, blankets, and other articles of clothing. In the same manner, on application to the chief of a village, [Sutter] readily obtains as many boys and girls as he has any use for. There were at this time a number of girls at the fort, in training for a future woolen factory; but they were now all busily engaged in constantly watering the gardens, which the unfavorable dryness of the season rendered necessary. [...]

A few years since, the neighboring Russian establishment of [Fort] Ross [on the coast about 120 miles west of Sutter's Fort], being about to withdraw from the country, sold to [Sutter] a large number of stock, with agricultural and other stores, with a number of pieces of artillery and other munitions of war; for these, a regular yearly payment is made in grain.

The fort is a quadrangular adobe structure, mounting twelve pieces of artillery (two of them brass), and capable of admitting a garrison of a thousand men; this, at present, consists of forty Indians in uniform—one of whom was always found on duty at the gate. As might naturally be expected, the pieces are not in very good order. The whites in the employment of Capt. Sutter, American, French, and German, amount, perhaps, to thirty men. The inner wall is formed into buildings, comprising the common quarters, with blacksmith and other workshops; the dwelling-house, with a large distillery-house, and other buildings, occupying more the centre of the area.

It is built upon a pondlike stream, at times a running creek communicating with the Rio de los Americanos [the American River], which enters the Sacramento [River] about two miles below. The latter is here a noble river, about three hundred yards broad, deep and tranquil, with several fathoms of water in the channel, and its banks continuously timbered. There were two vessels belonging to Capt. Sutter at anchor near the landing—one a large two-masted lighter, and the other a schooner, which was shortly to proceed on a voyage to Fort Vancouver for a cargo of goods.

A New Country

For pioneers making their way into Alta California in the seven years before the gold rush, Sutter's Fort was the first stop in Mexico on the main branch of the California

Trail heading west to Yerba Buena (later renamed San Francisco). During the winter of 1846, the Donner Party became trapped by snow in the Sierra Nevada; thirty-nine of the eighty-seven pioneers died and some were forced to resort to cannibalism to survive. It was Sutter who sent the five relief parties that rescued the survivors and brought them back to his fort.

Sutter's main business was growing wheat. Native Americans worked the fields in exchange for clothes and blankets, and Sutter exported many tons of grain for several years. Wheat was his primary source of income.

Overall, things were going very well for Sutter when the western border of the United States suddenly jumped from Texas, Arkansas, Missouri, and Iowa to the Pacific Ocean. Since he had provided assistance to Captain Frémont leading up to and during the Mexican-American War, it was likely the new government would look favorably on him.

Then the gold rush destroyed everything he had built. While Sutter was probably the one man in the best place to profit by the rush, he ended up losing just about everything. In 1857, he wrote about his travails in *Hutchings' California Magazine.*

When things began to go wrong Sutter was in the middle of constructing two mills: the sawmill where gold was discovered and a large flour mill at Brighton. He tried to keep the gold discovery a secret until his mills were finished, but within a few weeks the story found its way into the newspapers.

THE WINDS CHANGE DIRECTION

So soon as the secret was out my laborers began to leave me, in small parties first, but then all left, from the clerk to the cook, and I was in great distress; only a few mechanics remained to finish some very necessary work which they had commenced, and about eight invalids, who continued slowly to work a few teams, to scrape out the mill race at Brighton.

The Mormons did not like to leave my mill unfinished, but they got the gold fever like everybody else. After they had made their piles they left for the Great Salt Lake. So long as these people have been employed by me they have behaved very well, and were industrious and faithful laborers, and when settling their accounts there was not one of them who was not contented and satisfied.

Then the people commenced rushing up from San Francisco and other parts of California, in May 1848. In the former village, only five men were left to take care of the women and children. The single men locked their doors and left for "Sutter's Fort," and from there to the El Dorado. For some time the people in Monterey and farther south would not believe the news of the gold discovery, and said that it was only a "Ruse de Guerre" of Sutter's, because he wanted to have neighbors in his wilderness. From this time on I got only too many neighbors, and some very bad ones among them.

What a great misfortune was this sudden gold discovery for me! It has just broken up and ruined my hard, restless, and industrious labors, connected with many dangers of life, as I had many narrow escapes before I became properly established.

From my mill buildings I reaped no benefit whatever, the mill stones even have been stolen and sold [for use in crushing rocks in quartz mining].

My tannery, which was then in a flourishing condition, and was carried on very profitably, was deserted, a large quantity of leather was left unfinished in the vats; and a great quantity of raw hides became valueless as they could not be sold; nobody wanted to be bothered with such trash, as it was called. So it was in all the other mechanical trades which I had carried on; all was abandoned, and work commenced or nearly finished was all left, to an immense loss for me.

Even the Indians had no more patience to work alone, in harvesting and threshing my large wheat crop out; as the whites had all left, and other Indians had been engaged by some white men to work for them, and they commenced to have some gold for which they were buying all kinds of articles at enormous prices in the stores; which, when my Indians saw this, they wished very much to go to the mountains and dig gold.

Taking Up Prospecting

At last I consented, got a number of wagons ready, loaded them with provisions and goods of all kinds, employed a clerk, and left with about one hundred Indians, and about fifty Sandwich Islanders (Kanakas) [Hawaiians] which had joined those which I brought with me from the Islands. The first camp was about ten miles above Mormon Island, on the south fork of the American River.

In a few weeks we became crowded, and it would no more pay, as my people made too many acquaintances. I broke up the camp and started on the march further south, and located my next camp on Sutter Creek (now in Amador County), and thought that I should there be alone. The work was going on well for a while, until three or four traveling grog-shops surrounded me at from one and half to two miles distance from the camp; then, of course, the gold was taken to these places for drinking, gambling, etc., and then the following day they [the workers] were sick and unable to work, and became deeper and more indebted to me, and particularly the Kanakas.

I found that it was high time to quit this kind of business, and lose no more time and money. I therefore broke up the camp and returned to the Fort, where I disbanded nearly all the people who had worked for me in the mountains digging gold. This whole expedition proved to be a heavy loss to me.

At the same time I was engaged in a mercantile firm in Coloma, which I left in January 1849—likewise with many sacrifices. After this I would have nothing more to do with the gold affairs. At this time, the Fort

Looking north across Coloma Valley in the summer of 1858. The American River is to the right, while the arrow indicates the approximate location of Sutter's Mill, where gold was first discovered.

was the great trading place where nearly all the business was transacted. I had no pleasure to remain there, and moved up to Hock Farm, with all my Indians, and who had been with me from the time they were children. The place was then in [the] charge of a Major Domo [boss of the fort].

A Country Rich in Gold

[Referring back to before Marshall's discovery:] It is very singular that the Indians never found a piece of gold and brought it to me, as they very often did other specimens found in the ravines. I requested them continually to bring me some curiosities from the mountains, for which I always recompensed them. I have received animals, birds, plants, young trees, wild fruits, pipe clay, stones, red ochre, etc., etc., but never a piece of gold.

Mr. [James] Dana of the scientific corps of the expedition under Com. [Charles] Wilkes' Exploring Squadron, told me that he had the strongest proof and signs of gold in the vicinity of Shasta Mountain, and further south. A short time afterwards, [Swedish naturalist] Doctor [G. M. Waseurtz af] Sandels, a very scientific traveler, visited me, and explored a part of the country in a great hurry, as time would not permit him to make a longer stay.

He told me likewise that he found sure signs of gold, and was very sorry that he could not explore the Sierra Nevada. He did not encourage me to attempt to work and open mines, as it was uncertain how it would pay and would probably be only for a government. So I thought it more prudent to stick to the plow, not withstanding I did know that the country was rich in gold, and other minerals.

An old attached Mexican servant who followed me here from the United States, as soon as he knew that I was here, and who understood a great deal about working in placers, told me he found sure signs of gold in the mountains on Bear Creek, and that we would go right to work after returning from our campaign in 1845, but he became a victim to his patriotism and fell into the hands of the enemy near my encampment, with dispatches for me from Gen. [Manuel] Micheltorena [the governor of Alta California from 1842 to 1845], and he was hung as a spy, for which I was very sorry.

Ruined

By this sudden discovery of the gold, all my great plans were destroyed. Had I succeeded for a few years before the gold was discovered, I would have been the richest citizen on the Pacific shore; but it had to be different. Instead of being rich, I am ruined, and the cause of it is the long delay of the United States Land Commission of the United States Courts, through the great influence of the squatter lawyers. Before my case will be decided in Washington, another year may elapse, but I hope that justice will be done me by the last tribunal—the Supreme Court of the United States. By the Land Commission and the District Court it has been decided in my favor. The Common Council of the city of Sacramento, composed partly of squatters, paid Adelpheus Felch, (one of the late Land Commissioners, who was engaged by the squatters during his office), $5,000, from the fund of the city, against the will of the taxpayers, for which amount he has to try to defeat my just and old claim from the Mexican Government, before the Supreme Court of the United States in Washington.

When Sutter's employees abandoned him, squatters took chunks of his land. New arrivals and bandits stole everything, his cattle were slaughtered, and his crops were destroyed. Sutter instantly became famous, but was left bankrupt and had to sell his fort to pay his debts. His family had come over from Switzerland to join him; what little he had left, he gave to his son and retired to Hock Farm, his ranch in Marysville. He lived there for a few years until squatters once again took his land and rustlers stole his cattle. Then some men set his house on fire. When that burned down, he moved to Pennsylvania.

After California became part of the United States, he spent thirty-two years in court fighting to get some of his land back, or at least compensation for it, but failed. Shortly before he died in 1880, the government began making monthly payments to reimburse him for taxes he had paid on the land that was taken from him.

"Gold! Gold!!!"

General William Tecumseh Sherman

William Tecumseh Sherman was one of the Union's top generals during the Civil War and is primarily remembered for his famous March to the Sea, from Atlanta to Savannah, Georgia. After the war he replaced General Ulysses S. Grant as Commanding General of the Army and became the country's second full, or four-star, general. Grant was the first.

When the gold rush kicked off, Sherman was a lieutenant stationed in Monterey, working as assistant to Colonel Richard Mason, who was the acting military governor of California. His office received a letter and samples of some of the first gold from John Sutter. Sherman later wrote down his recollections of that incident and the reports that followed.

THE FIRST GOLD MINING CLAIM

I remember one day, in the spring of 1848, that two men, Americans, came into the office and inquired for the Governor. I asked their business, and one answered that they had just come down from Captain Sutter on special business, and they wanted to see Governor Mason *in person*. I took them in to the colonel, and left them together. After some time the colonel came to his door and called to me. I went in, and my attention was directed to a series of papers unfolded on his table, in which lay about half an ounce of *placer*-gold. Mason said to me, "What is that?"

I touched it and examined one or two of the larger pieces, and asked, "Is it gold?"

Mason asked me if I had ever seen native gold. I answered that, in 1844, I was in Upper Georgia, and there saw some native gold, but it was much finer than this, and it was in phials, or in transparent quills; but I said that, if this were gold, it could be easily tested, first, by its malleability, and next by acids. I took a piece in my teeth, and the metallic lustre was perfect.

I then called to the clerk, Baden, to bring an axe and hatchet from the back yard. When these were brought, I took the largest piece and beat it out flat, and beyond doubt it was metal, and a pure metal. Still, we attached little importance to the fact, for gold was known to exist at San Fernando, at the south, and yet was not considered of much value.

Colonel Mason then handed me a letter from Captain Sutter, addressed to him, stating that he (Sutter) was engaged in erecting a saw-mill at Coloma, about forty miles up the American Fork, above his fort at New Helvetia, for the general benefit of the settlers in that vicinity; that he had incurred considerable expense, and wanted a "preemption" to the quarter-section of land on which the mill was located, embracing the tail-race in which this particular gold had been found. Mason instructed me to prepare a letter, in answer, for his signature.

CLAIM DENIED

I wrote off a letter, reciting that California was yet a Mexican province, simply held by us as a conquest; that no laws of the United States yet applied to it, much less the land laws or preemption laws, which could only apply after a public survey. Therefore it was impossible for the Governor to promise him (Sutter) a title to the land; yet, as there were no settlements within forty miles, he was not likely to be disturbed by tres-passers. Colonel Mason signed the letter, handed it to one of the gentle-men who had brought the sample of gold, and they departed.

That gold was the first discovered in the Sierra Nevada, which soon revolutionized the whole country, and actually moved the whole civilized world. About this time (May and June 1848), far more importance was attached to quicksilver [mercury]. One mine, the New Almaden, twelve miles south of San Jose, was well known, and was in possession of the agent of a Scotch gentleman named Forbes, who at the time was British consul at Tepic, Mexico. Mr. Forbes came up from San Blas in a small brig, which proved to be a Mexican vessel; the vessel was seized, con-demned, and actually sold, but Forbes was wealthy, and bought her in.

His title to the quicksilver-mine was, however, never disputed, as he had bought it regularly, before our conquest of the country, from another British subject, also named Forbes, a resident of Santa Clara Mission, who had purchased it off the discoverer, a priest; but the boundaries of the land attached to the mine were even then in dispute. Other men were in search of quicksilver; and the whole range of mountains near the New Almaden mine was stained with the brilliant red of the sulphuret of mercury (cinnabar). [. . .]

FABULOUS DISCOVERIES

As the spring and summer of 1848 advanced, the reports came faster and faster from the gold-mines at Sutter's saw-mill. Stories reached us of fabulous discoveries, and spread throughout the land. Everybody was talking of "Gold! gold!!!" until it assumed the character of a fever. Some of our soldiers began to desert; citizens were fitting out trains of wagons and packmules to go to the mines. We heard of men earning fifty, five hundred, and thousands of dollars per day, and for a time it seemed as though somebody would reach solid gold.

Some of this gold began to come to Yerba Buena [San Francisco] in trade, and to disturb the value of merchandise, particularly of mules, horses, tin pans, and articles used in mining. I, of course, could not escape the infection, and at last convinced Colonel Mason that it was our duty to go up and see with our own eyes, that we might report the truth to our Government. As yet we had no regular mail to any part of the United States, but mails had come to us at long intervals, around Cape Horn, and one or two overland.

KIT CARSON BRINGS THE MAIL

I well remember the first overland mail. It was brought by Kit Carson in saddle-bags from Taos in New Mexico. We heard of his arrival at Los Angeles, and waited patiently for his arrival at headquarters. His fame then was at its height, from the publication of Fremont's books, and I was very anxious to see a man who had achieved such feats of daring among the wild animals of the Rocky Mountains, and still wilder Indians of the Plains.

At last his arrival was reported at the tavern at Monterey, and I hurried to hunt him up. I cannot express my surprise at beholding a small, stoop-shouldered man, with reddish hair, freckled face, soft blue eyes, and nothing to indicate extraordinary courage or daring. He spoke but little, and answered questions in monosyllables. I asked for his mail, and he picked up his light saddle-bags containing the great overland mail, and we walked together to headquarters, where he delivered his parcel into Colonel Mason's own hands.

The *Californian* Ceases Publication

The Californian

As news of the discovery spread, everyone was seized with gold fever. Closing up their businesses, they headed for the foothills to seek their fortunes. Among those businesses was a local newspaper, the *Californian*.

GONE GOLD-HUNTING
May 29, 1848
To Our Readers:

With this slip ceases for the present the publication of the *Californian*—
   "Othello's occupation's gone!"
   The majority of our subscribers and many of our advertising patrons have closed their doors and places of business and left town. . . . We really do not believe that for the last ten days, any thing in the shape of a newspaper has received five minutes attention from any one of our citizens. This, it must be allowed, is decidedly encouraging—*very*. The whole country, from San Francisco to Los Angeles and from the sea shore to the base of the Sierra Nevada, resounds with the sordid cry of "*gold!* gold!! GOLD!!!" while the field is left half planted, the house half built, and everything neglected but the manufacture of shovels and pickaxes, and the means of transportation to the spot where one man obtained $128 worth of the *real stuff* in one day's washing, and the average for all concerned is $20 per diem;—for such in fact are the reports which have reached us, and from apparently reliable sources.

In consideration of this state of affairs, and the degeneracy of the taste for reading so naturally consequent upon the rush for gold, where the word is "every man for *himself*," and a total disregard for his neighbor, it would be a useless expenditure of labor and material to continue longer the publication of our paper.

The *Californian* reappeared on August 14, 1848.

Official Report to the US Government

Colonel Richard Mason

After the United States took Alta California from Mexico in the Mexican-American War, a series of six military governors and one military acting governor headed the newly forming state, while the US government negotiated a treaty with Mexico, and up until California was admitted into the Union. Because of all the gold, California was rushed into statehood in 1850, without first becoming a territory.

Richard Mason was a colonel in the US Army and the acting governor of Califor-

nia, a position he held from 1847 to 1849. As acting governor, Colonel Mason needed to send a report to Washington, DC, on the extraordinary circumstances brought on by the gold rush. With all the sensational and false stories that were floating around, Mason had to discover the true extent of the gold discoveries, estimate how much gold had yet to be found, and provide samples of the various types of gold that the prospectors were finding. While his official report was addressed to Brigadier General R. Jones, it actually went straight to President James Polk.

Colonel Richard Mason

A Tour of the Gold Mines
Headquarters Tenth Military Department
Monterey, August 17, 1848

Sir: I have the honor to inform you that, accompanied by Lieut. W. T. Sherman, 3rd Artillery, acting Assistant Adjutant-General, I started on the 12th of June last to make a tour through the northern part of California. My principal purpose, however, was to visit the newly-discovered gold placer in the valley of the Sacramento.

I had proceeded about forty miles when I was overtaken by an express, bringing me intelligence of the arrival at Monterey of the United States storeship *Southampton*, with important letters from Commodore Shubrick and Lieutenant-Colonel Burton. I returned at once to Monterey, and dispatched what business was most important, and on the 17th resumed my journey.

We reached San Francisco on the 20th, and found that all, or nearly all, its male inhabitants had gone to the mines. The town, which a few months before was so busy and thriving, was then almost deserted.

On the evening of the 24th the horses of the escort were crossed to Sausolito [Sausalito] in a launch, and on the following day we resumed the journey, by way of Bodega and Sonoma, to Sutter's Fort, where we arrived on the morning of the 2d of July.

Along the whole route mills were lying idle, fields of wheat were open to cattle and horses, houses vacant, and farms going to waste. At Sutter's there was more life and business. Launches were discharging their cargoes at the river and carts were hauling goods to the fort, where already were established several stores, a hotel, etc. Captain Sutter had only two mechanics in the employ—wagon-maker and a blacksmith, whom he was then paying $10 per day. Merchants pay him a monthly rent of $100 per room, and while I was there a two-story house in the fort was rented as a hotel for $500 a month.

At the urgent solicitation of many gentlemen, I delayed there to participate in the first public celebration of our national anniversary at that fort, but on the 5th resumed the journey, and proceeded twenty-five miles up the American fork, to a point on it now known as the lower mines, or Mormon diggings. The hill sides were thickly strewn with canvas tents and bush-arbors; a store was erected, and several boarding shanties in operation. The day was intensely hot, yet about 200 men were at work in the full glare of the sun, washing for gold—some with tin pans, some with close woven Indian baskets, but the greater part had a rude machine known as the cradle. This is on rockers, six or eight feet long, open at the foot, and its head had a coarse grate, or sieve; the bottom is rounded, with small cleets nailed across. Four men are required to work this machine; one digs the ground in the bank close by the stream; another carries it to the cradle, and empties it on the grate; a third gives a violent rocking motion to the machine, whilst a fourth dashes on water from the stream itself. The sieve keeps the coarse stones from entering the cradle, the current of water washes off the earthy matter, and the gravel is gradually carried out at the foot of the machine, leaving the gold mixed with a heavy fine black sand above the first cleets. The sand and gold mixed together are then drawn off through auger holes into a pan below, are dried in the sun, and afterwards separated by blowing off the sand.

A party of four men, thus employed at the lower mines, average $100 a day. The Indians, and those who have nothing but pans or willow baskets, gradually wash out the earth, and separate the gravel by hand, leaving nothing but the gold mixed with sand, which is separated in the manner before described. The gold in the lower mines is in fine bright scales, of which I send several specimens.

The Place of Discovery

As we ascended the south branch of the American Fork, the country became more broken and mountainous, and twenty-five miles below the lower washings the hills rise to about 1,000 feet above the level of the Sacramento plain. Here a species of pine occurs, which led to the discovery of the gold. Captain Sutter, feeling the great want of lumber, contracted in September last with a Mr. Marshall to build a saw-mill at that place. It was erected in the course of the past winter and spring—a dam and race constructed; but when the water was let on the wheel, the tail race was found to be too narrow to permit the water to escape with sufficient rapidity. Mr. Marshall, to save labor, let the water directly into the race with a strong current, so as to wash it wider and deeper. He affected his purpose, and a large bed of mud and gravel was carried to the foot of the race.

One day Mr. Marshall, when walking down the race to this deposit of mud, observed some glittering particles at its upper edge; he gathered a few, examined them, and became satisfied of their value. He then went

A painting of Sutter's Mill by Arthur Nahl (1851)

to the fort, told Captain Sutter of his discovery, and they agreed to keep it secret until a certain grist-mill of Sutter's was finished. It, however, got out and spread like magic.

Remarkable success attended the labors of the first explorers, and, in a few weeks, hundreds of men were drawn thither. At the time of my visit, but little more than three months after its first discovery, it was estimated that upwards of four thousand people were employed.

At the mill there is a fine deposit or bank of gravel, which the people respect as the property of Captain Sutter, though he pretends to no right to it, and would be perfectly satisfied with the simple promise of a pre-emption on account of the mill which he has built there at a considerable cost. Mr. Marshall was living near the mill, and informed me that many persons were employed above and below him; that they used the same machines as at the lower washings, and that their success was about the same—ranging from one to three ounces of gold per man daily. This gold, too, is in scales a little coarser than those of the lower mines.

From the mill Mr. Marshall guided me up the mountain on the opposite or north bank of the south fork, where in the bed of small streams or ravines, now dry, a great deal of coarse gold has been found. I there saw several parties at work, all of whom were doing very well; a great many specimens were shown me, some as heavy as four or five ounces in weight; and I send three pieces, labeled No. 5, presented by a Mr. Spence.

You will perceive that some of the specimens accompanying this report hold mechanically pieces of quartz—that the surface is rough, and evidently moulded in the crevice of a rock. This gold cannot have been carried far by water, but must have remained near where it was first deposited from the rock that once bound it. I inquired of many if they had encountered the metal in its matrix, but in every instance they said they had not; but that the gold was invariably mixed with wash-gravel, or lodged in the crevices of other rocks. All bore testimony that they had found gold in greater or less quantities in the numerous small gullies or ravines that occur in that mountainous region.

AMAZING RICHES

On the 7th of July I left the mill and crossed to a small stream emptying into the American Fork, three or four miles below the saw-mill. I struck the stream (now known as Weber's Creek) at the washings of Suñal & Co. They had about thirty Indians employed, whom they pay in merchandise. They were getting gold of a character similar to that found in the main fork, and doubtless in sufficient quantities to satisfy them. I send you a small specimen, presented by this company, of their gold.

From this point we proceeded up the stream about eight miles, where we found a great many people and Indians, some engaged in the bed of the stream, and others in the small side valleys that put into it. These latter are exceedingly rich, two ounces being considered an ordinary yield for a day's work. A small gutter, not more than 100 yards long by four feet wide, and two or three deep, was pointed out to me as the one where two men, William Daly and Percy M'Coon, had a short time before obtained in seven days $17,000 worth of gold. Captain Weber informed me, that he knew that these two men had employed four white men and about 100 Indians, and that, at the end of one week's work, they paid off their party, and had left $10,000 worth of this gold.

Another small ravine was shown me, from which had been taken upwards of $12,000 worth of gold. Hundreds of similar ravines, to all appearances, are as yet untouched. I could not have credited these reports had I not seen, in the abundance of the precious metal, evidence of their truth. Mr. Neligh, an agent of Commodore Stockton, had been at work about three weeks in the neighborhood, and showed me, in bags and bottles, over $2,000 worth of gold; and Mr. Lyman, a gentleman of education, and worthy of every credit, said he had been engaged with four others, with a machine, on the American Fork, just below Sutter's saw-mill, that they worked eight days, and that his share was at the rate of $50 a day, but hearing that others were doing better at Weber's Place, they had removed there, and were then on the point of resuming operations.

I might tell of hundreds of similar instances; but, to illustrate how plentiful the gold was in the pockets of common laborers, I will mention a simple occurrence which took place in my presence when I was at Weber's

A group consisting mainly of Nisenan Maidu, c. 1858. The Nisenan were, at that time, a collection of affiliated Central California tribes, which in turn were one of three groups of Maidu—as they still are today. By the 1850s, the Nisenan had been reduced to about eight hundred individuals who lived in several villages in the Grass Valley area. The man standing between the kneeling man on the left and the tree was one of the Nisenan chiefs. Named Weimer—also spelled Wema or Wemah—he was often referred to as Captain Weimer or King Weimer.

store. This store was nothing but an arbor of bushes, under which he had exposed for sale goods and groceries suited to his customers. A man came in, picked up a box of Seidlitz powders [which produces intestinal gases that are supposed to regulate digestion and have laxative effects], and asked its price. Captain Weber told him it was not for sale. The man offered an ounce of gold, but Captain Weber told him it only cost 50 cents, and he did not wish to sell it. The man then offered an ounce and a half, when Captain Weber *had* to take it. The prices of all things are high; and yet Indians, who before hardly knew what a breechcloth was, can now afford to buy the most gaudy dresses.

The country on either side of Weber's creek is much broken up by hills, and is intersected in every direction by small streams or ravines which contain more or less gold. Those that have been worked are barely scratched, and, although thousands of ounces have been carried away, I do not consider that a serious impression has been made upon the whole. Every day was developing new and richer deposits; and the only impression seemed to be, that the metal would be found in such abundance as seriously to depreciate in value.

On the 8th July I returned to the lower mines, and on the following day to Sutter's, where, on the 10th, I was making preparations for a visit to the Feather, Yubah [Yuba], and Bear Rivers, when I received a letter from Commodore A. R. Long, United States navy, who had just arrived at San Francisco from Mazatlan, with a crew for the sloop-of-war *Warren*, and with orders to take that vessel to the squadron at La Paz. Captain Long wrote to me that the Mexican Congress had adjourned without ratifying the treaty of peace, that he had letters for me from Commodore Jones, and that his orders were to sail with the *Warren* on or before the 30th of July. In consequence of these, I determined to return to Monterey, and accordingly arrived here on the 17th of July.

ALSO FOUND ALONG OTHER RIVERS

Before leaving Sutter's, I satisfied myself that gold existed in the bed of the Feather River, in the Yubah and Bear, and in many of the small streams that lie between the latter and the American Fork; also, that it had been found in the Cosumnes, to the south of the American Fork. In each of these streams the gold is found in small scales, whereas in the intervening mountains it occurs in coarser lumps.

Mr. Sinclair, whose rancho is three miles above Sutter's on the north side of the American, employs about fifty Indians on the North Fork, not far from its junction with the main stream. He had been engaged about five weeks when I saw him, and up to that time his Indians had used simply closely-woven willow baskets. His net proceeds (which I saw) were about $16,000 worth of gold. He showed me the proceeds of his last week's work—fourteen pounds avoirdupois [a system of weight based on 16 ounces to a pound] of clean-washed gold.

The principal store at Sutter's Fort, that of Brannant & Co., had received in payment for goods $36,000 worth of this gold from the 1st of May to the 10th of July. Other merchants had also made extensive sales. Large quantities of goods were daily sent forward to the mines, as the Indians, heretofore so poor and degraded, have suddenly become con-sumers of the luxuries of life. I before mentioned that the greater part of the farmers and rancheros had abandoned their fields to go to the mines. This is not the case with Captain Sutter, who was carefully gathering his

The interior of a store at Sutter's Fort

wheat, estimated at 40,000 bushels. Flour is already worth, at Sutter's, $36 a barrel, and will soon be $50. Unless large quantities of breadstuffs reach the country much suffering will occur; but as each man is now able to pay a large price, it is believed the merchants will bring from Chile and the Oregon a plentiful supply for the coming winter.

The most moderate estimate I could obtain from men acquainted with the subject was, that upwards of 4,000 men were working in the gold district, of whom more than one-half were Indians, and that from $30,000 to $50,000 worth of gold, if not more, were daily obtained.

The entire gold district, with very few exceptions of grants made some years ago by the Mexican authorities, is on land belonging to the United States. It was a matter of serious reflection to me, how I could secure to the Government certain rents or fees for the privilege of securing this gold; but upon considering the large extent of country, the character of the people engaged, and the small scattered force at my command, I resolved not to interfere, but permit all to work freely, unless broils and crimes should call for interference.

I was surprised to learn that crime of any kind was very infrequent, and that no thefts or robberies had been committed in the gold district. All live in tents, in bush houses, or in the open air, and men have frequently about their persons thousands of dollars' worth of this gold; and it was to me a matter of surprise that so peaceful and quiet a state of things should continue to exist. Conflicting claims to particular spots of ground may cause collisions, but they will be rare, as the extent of country is so great, and the gold so abundant, that for the present there is room and enough for all; still the Government is entitled to rents for this land, and immediate steps should be devised to collect them, for the longer it is delayed the more difficult it will become.

One plan I would suggest is to send out from the United States surveyors, with high salaries, bound to serve specified periods; a superintendent to be appointed at Sutter's Fort, with power to grant licenses to work a spot of ground, say 100 yards square, for one year at a rent of from $100 to $1,000, at his discretion; the surveyors to measure the grounds and place the renter in possession. A better plan, however, will be to have the district surveyed and sold at public auction to the highest bidder, in small parcels, say from 20 to 40 acres. In either case there will be many intruders, whom for years it will be almost impossible to exclude.

A NEW CALIFORNIA

The discovery of these vast deposits of gold has entirely changed the character of Upper California. Its people, before engaged in cultivating their small patches of ground, and guarding their herds of cattle and horses, have all gone to the mines, or are on their way thither; laborers of every trade have left their work-benches, and tradesmen their shops; sailors desert their ships as fast as they arrive on the coast; and several vessels have gone to sea with hardly enough hands to spread a sail. Two or three are now at anchor in San Francisco, with no crews on board.

Many desertions, too, have taken place from the garrisons within the influence of these mines; 26 soldiers have deserted from the post of Sonoma, 24 from that of San Francisco, and 24 from Monterey. For a few days the evil appeared so threatening that great danger existed that the garrisons would leave in a body; and I refer you to my orders of the 25th of July to show the steps adopted to meet this contingency. I shall spare no exertions to apprehend and punish deserters; but I believe no time in the history of our country has presented such temptations to desert as now exist in California. The danger of apprehension is small, and the prospect of higher wages certain; pay and bounties are trifles, as laboring men at the mines can now earn in *one day* more than double a soldier's pay and allowances for a month, and even the pay of a lieutenant or captain cannot hire a servant. A carpenter or mechanic would not listen to an offer of less than $15 or $20 a day. Could any combination of affairs try a man's fidelity more than this? And I really think some extraordinary mark of favor should be given to those soldiers who remain faithful to their flag throughout this tempting crisis.

No officer can now live in California on his pay. Money has so little value, the prices of necessary articles of clothing and subsistence are so exorbitant, and labor so high, that to hire a cook or servant has become an impossibility, save to those who are earning from $30 to $50 a day.

This state of things cannot last forever; yet, from the geographical position of California, and the new character it has assumed as a mining country, prices of labor will always be high, and will hold out temptations to desert. I therefore have to report, if the Government wish to prevent desertions here on the part of men, and to secure zeal on the part of officers, their pay must be increased very materially. Soldiers both of the volunteer and regular service discharged in this country should be permitted at once to locate their land warrants in the gold district.

Many private letters have gone to the United States giving accounts of the vast quantity of gold recently discovered, and it may be a matter of surprise why I have made no report on this subject at an earlier date. The reason is, that I could not bring myself to believe the reports that I heard of the wealth of the gold district until I visited it myself. I have no hesitation now in saying, that there is more gold in the country drained by the Sacramento and San Joaquin Rivers than will pay the cost of the present war with Mexico a hundred times over.

This photograph of a Chinese miner was taken by the famous photographer Eadweard Muybridge. It's thought this was shot near Jacksonville in Tuolumne County or at Mongolian Flat on the American River.

No capital is required to obtain this gold, as the laboring man wants nothing but his pick and shovel and tin pan, with which to dig and wash the gravel, and many frequently pick gold out of the crevices of rocks with their knives, in pieces of from one to six ounces.

Mr. Dye, a gentleman residing in Monterey, and worthy of every credit, has just returned from Feather River. He tells me that the company to which he belonged worked seven weeks and two days, with an average of 50 Indians (washers), and that their gross product was 273 pounds of gold. His share, one-seventh, after paying all expenses, is about 37 pounds, which he brought with him and exhibits in Monterey. I see no laboring man from the mines who does not show his two, three, and four pounds of gold.

A soldier of the artillery company returned here a few days ago from the mines, having been absent on furlough 20 days; he made by trading and working during that time $1,500. During these 20 days he was traveling 10 or 11 days, leaving but a week, in which he made a sum of money greater than he receives in pay, clothes, and rations during a whole enlistment of five years. These statements appear incredible, but they are true.

Gold Is Practically Everywhere

Gold is believed also to exist on the eastern slopes of the Sierra Nevada, and when at the mines, I was informed by an intelligent Mormon that it had been found near the Great Salt Lake by some of his fraternity. Nearly all the Mormons are leaving California to go to the Salt Lake, and this they surely would not do unless they were sure of finding gold there in the same abundance as they now do on the Sacramento.

The gold "placer" near the mission of San Fernando [just north of Los Angeles] has long been known, but has been but little wrought for want of water. This is a spur that puts off from the Sierra Nevada (see Fremont's map), the same in which the present mines occur. There is, therefore, every reason to believe that in the intervening space of 500 miles (entirely unexplored) there must be many hidden and rich deposits.

The placer gold is now substituted as currency of this country; in trade it passes freely at $16 per ounce; as an article of commerce its value is not yet fixed. The only purchase I made was of the specimen No. 7, which I got of Mr. Neligh at $12 the ounce. That is about the present cash value in the country, although it has been sold for less. The great demand for goods and provisions made by this sudden development of wealth has increased the amount of commerce at San Francisco very much, and it will continue to increase.

I would recommend that a mint be established at some eligible point on the bay of San Francisco, and that machinery, and all the apparatus and workmen, be sent by sea. These workmen must be bound by high wages, and even bonds, to secure their faithful services; else the whole plan may be frustrated by their going to the mines as soon as they arrive in California. If this course be not adopted, gold to the amount of many millions of dollars will pass yearly to other countries, to enrich their merchants and capitalists. [. . .]

I have the honor to be your most obedient servant,

R. B. Mason
Colonel 1st Dragoons, commanding.
[To:] Brigadier-General R. Jones,
Adjutant-General, USA, Washington, DC

Trading for Dust

Franklin Buck

Franklin Buck was twenty-two years old when he caught gold fever. Originally from Bucksport, Maine, he was living in New York City when credible reports of gold discoveries began flowing in. He set off for California in January 1849, intending to make his fortune as a storekeeper rather than as a prospector. He wrote about his experiences in personal letters to his sister back in Maine.

UNBELIEVABLE NEWS
[New York; December 2, 1848]

I had heard from R. P. B. that Father was going to Lynn but did not believe it. On some accounts I am sorry that he has sold his house. We have a great many pleasant associations connected with it and no other place that he can go to will ever seem like home. But if he can do better to emigrate, I say go, but while he is about it he had better go to California. Have you read the account from there about the Gold? There is no *humbug* about it. I have seen letters from Captains whom I know, who write that their men have all run away and are digging up $20 a day, PURE GOLD, for some of it has been sent home.

It has created a real fever here. Two steamships sailed yesterday and there are five vessels advertised for California. Several young men of my acquaintance are going out and you need not be at all surprised to hear of my going. I shall not go unless I can get some chance in trade to fall back on, but if I only had about $1,000 to invest in goods, wouldn't I sail! (Oh, Poverty, thou art a crime!) But I shall wait my time.

~ • ~

"I Have Seen Some of It Myself"
[New York; December 17, 1848]

When I took your letter out of the Post Office this morning I said to myself, "Now here comes a blast from Mary!" for from what Father wrote, I thought I had thrown you all into fits, but I am rejoiced to see from your letter that you think in some measure as I do.

When I heard the accounts from the gold region I thought, at first, it was all *humbug*, gotten up to induce people to emigrate. But now I am fully convinced and the most slow to believe are also. I have seen letters from the son of Secretary Macey to a friend in the city. A. G. has received letters from his agent. Uncle Richard has had letters from Captains he sent out and also from two young men who took out goods last spring. These young men have made $40,000 and one of them is coming home with it. A. G.'s agent, Bob Parker, (you know him) writes that he has sold out his goods at an enormous profit. He kept one man constantly weighing gold dust and he has $100,000 on hand and was going down to Mazatlan to exchange it for coin.

Young Macey writes that he did not believe it at San Francisco and went up to the mines to see for himself. He saw them washing out the gold in tin pans and digging it up with sheath knives. One man got $4,000 in one day, but the most of them about $50 to $100 per day. This is hard to believe but all the letters and accounts go to prove that the half has not been told us. Great quantities have been sent here to the banks and Mint. I have *seen* some of it *myself*, in little scales and grains, pure as our gold coin.

But there is another proof, yet. Look out on the docks and you will see from twenty to thirty ships loading with all kinds of merchandise and filling up with passengers, and when I see business firms—rich men—going into it, men who know how to make money too, and young men of my acquaintance leaving good situations and fitting themselves out with arms and ammunition, tents, provisions, and mining implements, there is something about it—the excitement, the crossing the Isthmus, seeing new countries, and the prospect of making a fortune in a few years—that takes hold of my imagination, that tells me "Now is your chance. Strike while the iron is hot!"

You know that I am in the prime of life—a good constitution, know how to shovel, can live in a log house or a tent, and build one too. You know that I always had a desire to travel, to see something of the world. Now, when shall I ever have a better chance? I can hardly make a living here. We have no capital to carry on business with and it will be a long time before we can get a start. Labor is *capital* out there. I am assured by persons that have lived there that it is a fine country, perfectly healthy and room enough for us all.

I have looked at the subject in all its bearings. I have looked at my chance here and I have made up my mind to go and I am going if I have to go out as a common sailor. It has taken nearly every cent I have made here to pay my expenses as I go along so I have but very little money on hand. Uncle Richard has very kindly given me one hundred dollars and intends to send us a consignment of goods. There are five of us going out together. John Benson goes on Saturday to look after their business. We have paid our passage in the Steam Ship *Panama*, which sails from Panama on the Pacific, the 15th of February, for San Francisco. We go from here to Chagres in a sailing vessel and cross the land to Panama.

Now, my dear sister, much as I regret leaving you and my parents for so long a time, still I think it is the best thing I can do. I thought you would approve of it and believe me I feel greatly obliged to you for your good intentions. I wish I could see and embrace you once more but there is not time for me to come home. Don't look on the dark side—that's my philosophy—but think of those $4,000 *lumps* that I am going to pick up and remit to you.

Harriett Pond is full of it. Her brother is one of our party and she thinks about going herself.

Captain Cole is in the office now. Says, "Tell Mary I am going with my vessel."

It is time for me to go to supper and I must stop. The weather is beautiful and warm. The cholera is still killing them off at Staten Island and there has been one case in the city but, as you suppose, we think nothing of it. The California fever has actually frightened it off.

Preparing for the Voyage
New York; January 3, 1849

Saturday night Captain Cole and myself rode out to Harlem, and Monday evening after I got through making calls, we got in with a merry set and rode out to Bloomingdale and sung ourselves hoarse. New York, "with all thy faults I love thee still." After all there is no place that I feel so much at home in, as this vast city. I know every street and alley in it, and every corner and building. From the Battery to Union Park is as familiar to me as the front street in Bucksport. [...]

You probably know by Father's letter that I am going around the Horn with Captain Cole. *The plot thickens!* We shall take the Brig down town this afternoon. She has been put in complete order, caulked, coppered and painted. We are going to have a fine cabin, have torn the old one all to pieces, and shall have it fitted up in good style for ten passengers. Our list of stores is made out and we are going to live high. I shall purchase 100 volumes of books, at least, and exchange my French for Spanish and learn that on the voyage.

It is a long time to be at sea—four months and a half at least. We shall stop at the Isthmus of Panama and at Valparaiso. I should much prefer going across, but Uncle Richard made me such a good offer that I could not refuse it. It will be much better, after I get there, to go in this way, for I have a place to live and something to eat. If we have a pleasant set of passengers we shall enjoy ourselves, no doubt.

❧

The California Fever
[New York; January 17, 1849]

Ho for California and the Gold Regions!

Westward the Star of Empire takes its Way!

So does the *George Emery* tomorrow! No doubt you thought us off before this but we have been getting ready for the last week and are not ready yet.

We have our cargo all on board and to-night the chickens and pigs come down. We have our cabin fitted up in splendid style. The curtains cost 56¢ per yard. We shall take them out and put them up in our house in California. Cole and I have bought everything we can think of for our comfort. We have raced all over New York and made some of the greatest bargains this side of Connecticut. We bought 58 volumes of books for $9.44 and a B.G. board and one dozen packs of cards. We have 24 rifles, powder and shot, harpoons, fishing tackle and a sail boat, and all the little etceteras you can think of, to amuse ourselves on our long voyage. I can't realize that I am going yet, but suppose I shall in about two days.

Our passengers I like the appearance of very well. There are seven of us altogether, all young men but one. [. . .]

The docks are crowded with fathers and mothers, brothers and sisters and sweethearts, and such embracing and waving of handkerchiefs and "I say Bill! If you send me a barrel of Gold Dust, don't forget to pay the freight on it!"

One fellow who went in the *Brooklyn,* threw his last five dollar piece ashore. Says he: "I'm going where there is plenty more!"

"Now boys, give 'em the cheers," and the boys from the ship give us nine back with a will. All those that have friends bid them farewell and those who have none shake hands with themselves and cut their individual sticks. It beats all!, I declare, this California fever.

Every minister is preaching on the subject. Geologists are lecturing on it. It is dramatised at the theatres and it is the subject of conversation everywhere. Even clerks' salaries have gone up, so many have left.

Tell Father that the best thing he can do is to follow me, if he has his business closed up. We will have a house put up all ready soon after we arrive, as we have four, all framed windows, doors and everything. We ought to have a good carpenter go out with us, though I think I can put one up myself.

The worst feature of the business is: There are no females going out. Everything else that you can think of is going, but the ladies hang back. What are we going to do? Society is bad, you know, composed all together of either sex. The women must follow the men shortly, or they will be too thick on this side—and to think what rich husbands they could get! I should think this would be an inducement for the old maids of Bucksport to start!

PLENTY OF GOLD
[San Francisco; August 22, 1849]

There is plenty of gold here, no doubt of that. It is legal tender and worth $16 the oz. There is no spurious either. That is all humbug. You can't counterfeit it. When we landed our goods at the foot of Sacramento Street, a little ways from the water, our men washed out several grains of gold. It is found in little scales in the sand. This was right in the street. One man stuck to it all day and got five dollars.

The mines are on the forks of the Sacramento and San Joaquin rivers. The miners average about $16 per day but it is hard and just now hot and sickly. The cost of transportation is so great that it cost them four dollars a day to live. I have seen several of my friends who have returned from the mines, some of them with a thousand dollars, others with a great deal less. From what they have told me, I have no desire to go to the diggings. I am satisfied I can make in trade. Land speculation is all the rage and men who bought lots here last winter find themselves rich. We have arrived too late to go into this.

New towns are being laid out every day. There is a large place at the head of navigation, Sacramento City [now just Sacramento]. Another town at the mouth is called Benicia, the government is building a navy yard here. It is impossible to keep sailors here. They get perfectly crazy and are all off for the diggins. Sunday a boat's crew escaped from the *Ohio*. They fired on them but without effect. We have kept three of our men by promising to pay them off when the vessel is discharged. The Captain and myself had to take hold and work to land cargo but it's no disgrace here. The steamer got in Monday but I received no letters from her. She will sail on the first.

Friday we go up the river to try the market at S.C. We can't sell here at wholesale at all. At Sacramento City we can tie the brig to the bank and retail out of here, and goods are higher there. If we can rent a lot reasonably we shall put up our house and trade in that. If not, we can sell it for a great price. I think we shall come out whole with the cargo, but no more. We have to pay a pilot from here up, a distance of 150 miles, $400!

Captain Cole and I are living on board. We have the cabin all to ourselves. The cook stayed by. They are all going to leave the moment she is made fast at S.C. I don't blame them. Sailors are getting $200 per month to ship on the coast. The ship *Greyhound* is lying here offering $800 for men to take her home but can't get a man.

I wish I could send you a lump. I have seen some big pieces. The largest we have weighs 1½ oz., and that's nothing. I don't regret coming out at all and just as long as the gold mines last, business will be good.

The country is as quiet and peaceable as you can expect where there is no government, no police, no society and where every man does what is right in his own eyes. Sunday is respected but there is no church and no parson. There are more females here than I expected to see. A great many brought their wives but none whom I know.

Write me every steamer. You don't know how I prize a letter in this far-off country. [. . .]

PEOPLE OF ALL NATIONS
[San Francisco; August 23, 1849]

The two passengers that we took at Callao proved to be fine gentlemenly fellows, Peruvians, although one of them came on board so drunk that we immediately put him to bed, where he lay for three days and then came to himself and was all right until the glorious fourth, when he got rather patriotic. We celebrated the day with all the honors, fired the regular salutes, displayed the bunting and had, as far as we could see, the whole world to ourselves. And then, such a dinner: roast turkey and plum pudding! But perhaps one day you will have the pleasure of reading my journal. I made a full entry of the doings.

Neither of these fellows could speak a word of English and one of them brought out his grammar and began to study. I thought it would be a capital chance to learn Spanish. I got my grammar and began. We taught each other, and while I found it rather hard work to study at first,

I persevered and learned a lesson every day. I had a good chance to practice, too, and by the time we arrived I could "*habla Espanola mucho.*" I can translate it from a book with ease and converse quite fluently.

There is plenty of it spoken here, although most of the people are Yankees, yet you meet in the streets people of all nations. Most of the foreigners are Chilenos, Peruvians, and Mexicans, and quite a sprinkling of the native Californians are seen wrapped in their gay-colored ponchos, with pants split open all the way down the side of the leg and buttoned up gaiter fashion. They make a great display, dashing through the streets on horseback. They are excellent riders and their saddles and stirrups would be a curiosity with you. I have ridden on one myself and it is like sitting in an arm chair compared to our hard things that we call saddles. [. . .]

You speak of looking at my picture. . . . It will give you a faint idea of me now. I have not put a razor to my face since leaving N.Y. It is not the fashion here, for it would cost a dollar. Dirty shirts are all the fashion as it would cost $12 per dozen to have them washed. Dust is very fashionable

Four prospectors pose with their mining tools.

and common for the wind blows tremendously every day and kicks it up at a great rate. This is a great annoyance here and it is next to impossible to keep clean. The climate is cool and thick clothes are worn. The nights are foggy but I think it is healthy here. Up on the river people say it is sickly, very hot and plenty of mosquitoes. I have been at work hard since I arrived but enjoy good health.

CALIFORNIA STYLE

[Sacramento City; October 25, 1849]

We have arrived, sold most of our cargo, put it ashore ourselves, put up our store, and the place has grown one half in size. You have no idea how this country is going ahead. Last spring there was nobody here and now the people are as thick as in the city of New York.

Stages run regularly to the mines; steamboats run on the river; a theatre, church, and several large handsome hotels with billiard saloons and bowling alleys and all the fixings, have been put up. Even a couple of girls are around with a hand organ and tambourine. Civilization is making rapid strides. You may consider me squatted, settled, regularly enrolled as a citizen of this city. I like the climate situation and the people here first rate and I believe it is bound to *blaze*. This and San Francisco will be *the places* in California. [...]

A great many women came across the country with their husbands and it is no uncommon sight to see one in the streets. I believe Mrs. Lindley is the first American woman I have spoken with since I left Rio [de Janeiro].

I am getting to be perfectly savage and at the same time quite domestic, for until within a week we cooked on board and I washed up the dishes. Have washed my own clothes ever since I left N.Y. I don't use much starch. White shirts I have discarded. They get dirty too quickly and don't wash half as easily as red flannel or calico. Shaving is all humbug. Nobody shaves here and you can't find a better looking set of men. I am going to have my daguerreotype taken and sent home to show you how I have improved.

Full dress here is a pair of buckskin pants, fringed, with a red silk sash, fancy shirt and frock of buckskin trimmed with bell buttons and broad brimmed felt hat and revolver slung on one side and a Bowie knife on the other, with a pair of skins about a foot long. The horses are fine looking animals. The saddle I can't describe and here you have a picture of most of the miners.

Although most everyone goes around with a revolver I have never seen one used but once. In the crowd at the horse auction one man struck another over the head with the butt of a rifle. What for I never learnt. The man drew himself out of the crowd, took out his six shooter and commenced blazing away, right into the crowd of fifty men. One man was shot in the breast but not mortally. He fired three shots and stopped. Then, says he: "I'll let you know I am a man of honor! By God!" Nobody took any notice of it. There is no police here and the man went off.

THEY HAVE NOT YET BEGUN TO DIG
[San Francisco; October 31, 1849]

I had to get down to the office before twelve o'clock with my bills of lading. There is an immense quantity of gold going in this steamer. Her yawl boat was loaded with boxes. I heard in Messrs. Symmons and Hutchinson's office that it would come up to $2,000,000. Don't stare! This country raises gold and they have not begun to dig it up yet. If you had seen the heavy valises that came down the river when I came, you would think there was some here, if not more. I know of three men who are going "home" with $150,000.

There are some rich men here. Samuel Brannan, one of the proprietors of Sac. City and who owns the city hotel there, has an income from his rents alone of $160,000 a year, besides a store here and at the place. He is a young man who came out here three years ago. When mine amount to that I shall come home.

I have sent you a small specimen of the native gold, also some to Father and Mother. You can have it manufactured into some article of jewelry (take it to some one who will not cheat you) and wear it in remembrance of the *gold fever* . . . that has brought me and so many thousands from home. Those are small pieces. I have seen one lump that weighed a pound and two ounces but the large ones are all bought up to send home and are getting scarce. Most of the gold is like the dust that I sent Father.

LIKE GRAINS OF SAND
[Sacramento City; November 25, 1849]

Trade has fallen off some since the rainy weather but week before last we sold out of our little store $1,500 worth of goods. All cash trade in one day. Tell Joseph to beat that. We make a percentage here, too. The flour that I bought in San Francisco for $18 per sack (200 lbs) we sold for $44 and are all out. Flour is a little cheaper now. We sold at the top of the market and for once were lucky, for great quantities are arriving from Chile. It is now worth $35 here and $2 a lb. in the mines. It costs 75¢ a pound to transport goods from here to the mines and our merchant from

Sacramento City, as it appeared in January 1850 during what they called "the great inundation." The tents in the foreground were set up on something of an island, although it too was underwater. A levee was completed in 1852, but three weeks later another deluge broke through it and portions of the city were once again underwater. It flooded once more in 1853; following this better levees were built, which held until the great flood of 1862.

Weaver Creek, 50 miles from here, whose team we loaded, paid $1,000 for having one load hauled. This is on account of the muddy roads.

So much for California. It has gotten to be an old story to me. The first dust that I received, $2,800, on our selling two houses in San Francisco, made my eyes sparkle and my heart beat rather quickly as I spooned it into a two quart pail. But now, I receive it and weigh it out with as little feeling as I would so much sand.

SACRAMENTO CITY IS UNDER WATER
[Sacramento City; February 12, 1850]

I have learned a great deal about the country—one thing in particular—that the valley of the Sacramento was originally and is now during the greater part of the rainy season, a part of the Pacific Ocean.

You have probably heard ere this of the flood at this place—almost equal to the one in which Noah figured. It only shows that the people of the States know no more about this country than they do about the interior of Japan. [*Note:* Japan was a closed country at this time, allowing no one in or out.]

I have ceased to wonder and am open to conviction. We were told by some of the old residents that the site of this city was liable to be overflowed, but as the Sacramento was then fifteen feet below the top of the bank and the country dry, we laughed at the idea every one. But we have had to acknowledge the corn.

About the 10th of January we had warm weather that melted the snow on the mountains, followed by a heavy south east rain storm. The water in the river was nearly to the top of the bank at the time. At 12 o'clock (noon) it boiled over the bank of the American Fork and came down on the city. The bank of the Sacramento is higher than the country back. That night the Sacramento flowed over also, and about dark the water was up to the floor of our store. We piled the dry barrels upon the wet ones and on the counter and took part of our stock up stairs. At 9 o'clock the water was over the counter.

Boats were taking people out of one story buildings. A large adobe bakery close to us fell in with a tremendous crash. The water kept rising and things began to look serious. We had no boat and began to calculate

Sacramento on January 10, 1862, facing east from 4th Street, looking down K Street

how long it would be before we should float. Mrs. Lindley began to be alarmed and we took a strong brandy sling all around and sat down.

About 12 o'clock it stopped rising. The next morning there were three feet ten inches in our store and five feet in the street in front. We got into a whale boat and went down to the shipping. There were about 25 vessels lying at the bank. They were crowded with sick people and women and children.

The scene in the city was curious. It was a second Venice. A great quantity of merchandise floated off and was either stolen or lost. We lost over $500 worth of rice, besides dried fruits and other things damaged, though most of our goods we had taken upstairs.

We lived just as comfortably as before. Rigged a side ladder out of the chamber window, built a flat boat and paddled over the country extensively. Instead of the people wearing long faces as you would suppose, the city never was more lively. The streets were filled with boats and everybody was for having a frolic.

Captain Cole and myself took a whaleboat and took our lady and five young ladies from the Brig *Toronto* and took them out to the [Sutter's] Fort to call on the McClellan girls who reside there. The fort is on high land and was dry, but from there to the shipping was all plain sailing.

The prairie where I used to ride last summer, as far as you see, was covered with water. All the cattle on the plains were drowned. It was a hard sight to see them swimming about or lying dead in heaps on some little hill. There must be an immense quantity of them lost. [. . .]

The flood of early 1850 was unusual for the area, although much worse occurred in December 1861 and January 1862. In the 1861–62 flood, much of the Central Valley, which is approximately 450 miles long and around 50 miles wide, was underwater. Houses floated off their foundations and blocked streets. Furniture, goods, and parts of collapsed houses bobbed among debris from the many mudslides that had washed down from the foothills. An estimated 200,000 cattle drowned, along with domestic and wild horses, elk, deer, and other wildlife, giving off a terrible stench. Many people also died, reportedly including an entire Chinese settlement on the Yuba River.

In some places the water was thirty feet deep, with newly installed telegraph poles completely underwater. In a letter, Yale-educated botanist William Brewer wrote, "Thousands of farms are entirely under water—cattle starving and drowning. [. . .] Steamers ran back over the ranches fourteen miles from the river, carrying stock, etc., to the hills. Nearly every house and farm over this immense region is gone."

Sacramento City was under about ten feet of muddy water and was in the middle of a giant lake. The new governor was forced to take a boat to the capitol building to be sworn in. On his return to the governor's mansion, he had to climb in through a second story window. The new state government was forced to move to San Francisco. It took about six months for Sacramento to dry out enough so the government could return to the capital. The flood bankrupted the state. The 1850 flood was almost as bad, with most of the city underwater as well.

As you ascend Feather River, the banks grow higher and twenty miles from the mouth at Captain Sutter's town, it is really a fine country. Captain Sutter has here a fine house and out buildings, and a large farm under cultivation. He resides here having sold his Fort at Sac. City.

Forty five miles from the mouth of Feather River the Yuba comes in. Here is a new city started on the site of an old Indian Rancheria, called Yuba City. I went on shore and liked the situation very much. There are about twenty stores and houses built and more going up.

Marysville

Shakespeare says "What's in a name?", but I concluded partly on account of the name to go on up the Yuba to the head of steamboat navigation to [Charles] Covillaud's new city, which he has called after his young wife, "Marysville." [*Note:* Mary Murphy Covillaud was a Donner Party survivor.] I found it going ahead of its rival, Yuba City, and a better place for trade and nearer to the mines on both rivers. Here I put up my store, bought a lot of land for $250, and went to trading. There is no overflow here and it is beautifully situated on the banks of the Yuba. It was formerly Nye's Ranch and was purchased by Covillaud and Foster for $52,000. They have laid out a city one mile square and here is where you will see the go-aheaditiveness of the Yankee nation. In one fortnight's time they sold $25,000 worth of lots at $250 each. In ten days, while I was there, 17 houses and stores were put up, and what was before this a ranch, viz: a collection of Indian huts and a corral for cattle, became a right smart little city.

Marysville (I like the name) is 80 miles above Sacramento City and eight miles from the mountains. It is colder here, the mountains being covered with snow, but it never froze while I was there. [*Note:* Marysville is actually about 45 miles from Sacramento and is directly across the Feather River from Yuba City.]

Although the name is feminine and would imply a quiet sort of a place, yet I regret to say that it contains the hardest set of "hombres" it has been my fortune to live among in this country. Every night gambling, drinking, fighting, and shooting are carried on to a great extent.

I saw two fellows who had come down from the mines with some dust spend, in one evening, all their money and then get into a row. One got knocked into a ditch and had his leg broken. The other had his head broken. They rather thought that they got their money's worth.

A POSSE TO CAPTURE RUSTLERS

There was a gang of men on the ranch who had been killing cattle and sending the beef down to Sacramento City by the boat load. They told Covillaud that all the cattle running at large belonged to the public and they should shoot all they pleased, and if he (as he threatened to do) tried to take them he must send one hundred men, armed with rifles, and Yankees not Indians. Judge Wilson of Sacramento City, being in the place, appointed a Sheriff and made out the necessary documents to take them. Covillaud then offered to furnish with a horse and arms any man who would volunteer to go out with him and the Sheriff to take them.

You know my love of adventure too well to think I let this chance slip. I buckled on my armor and vaulted into the saddle. He [Covillaud] soon raised fifteen able-bodied men, all armed with rifles and revolvers, and we set out.

We rode over the ranch all day in search of them. This farm contains 15,000 acres, lying between the Feather and Yuba Rivers, and has 1,000 head of horses, and mules and cattle without number. They are all branded with a hot iron, every ranch having its private mark. We saw some splendid droves of horses, never broken, so perfectly wild. It's a beautiful country to ride in—open prairie and the banks of the streams timbered with oak and cotton wood. Covillaud offered me a farm of 640 acres and I could pick it where I chose, for $1,000. I think I shall take him up.

We rode 20 miles from home and on the banks of a small stream we came upon a collection of tents and found one of the gang, "Armstrong." The Sheriff told him he was our prisoner but he said he would not go except by force, and started for his tent. On looking around and seeing several rifles pointed at him he concluded to cave in and come along. In his wagon was found a quarter of beef with Covillaud's brand on it.

We rode to another ranch about three miles and got there at dark. Here Covillaud put the whole party through, at his expense. We had a fine supper—were *some hungry,* I reckon. It was a fine moonlight evening and with our prisoner on a led horse we rode home in triumph. It was romantic and I could imagine myself back in the times of [Sir Walter] Scott's novels.

We got home about nine o'clock, after riding 40 miles. I shall never tire of riding on horseback. There is a charm in it for me and these California horses are so different from ours. They either walk or run and the motion is like that of a cradle. How many of our horses do you suppose would stand it to run ten miles and keep their wind, as ours did that day?

The next day a Grand Jury was formed to indite them according to law and your humble servant had the honour of being one of the twelve wise men summoned to deliberate on this momentous question: whether law and order or anarchy and confusion shall exist in this country.

Working in the Mines
[Hermitage Rancho; January 1, 1852]

Since I wrote you on the 15th of May last, I have been in Downieville, 80 miles above Marysville, at the forks of the Yuba. I have been at work in the mines. My health has been excellent; my food: beef steaks and bread; but my success? That is the question. Had I made some thousands I should take great pleasure in describing to you the operation of mining, the mode of life, etc., but as it is, I will refer you to Father's letter and to the *lament* I send you enclosed. It hits my case exactly. For some reason I am not permitted to accumulate any of that substance called: GOLD. Further than enough to live comfortably, I have never

A sketch of Downieville in 1850, with the North Yuba River on the right

been dead broke and owe nothing in this country, on the contrary I have a great deal of money and favours due me and have always fed well and dressed to suit my taste, but these *big stakes* that some make are denied me.

Now, I am particularly anxious to make $2,000 to pay all my debts. I thought this past summer I could do it and I have tried hard from early morn till dewy eve for five months. I have laboured hunting after gold and when I got through I had $100. Less than when I began. Now, is not this rather hard luck? What have I done? What sins have I committed to be visited with such luck? But I am as light hearted as ever and do not despair of being able to come out all right in the end. The gold is not all dug out yet.

Downieville is one of the richest mining towns in the State. Upwards of $2,000,000 has been dug there this season by some three or four thousand men. The last 50 miles of the way to Downieville is only a mule trail, no wagons are seen in the streets, everything is packed, and yet in this "hole in the ground" as it is called, you will find two hundred buildings, two saw mills, a theatre and all the necessaries of life and cheap, too, for this country. Downieville is only 20 miles from the summit of the Sierra Nevada, which is covered with snow the year round.

The climate was truly delightful last summer, but the winter is very much like Maine.

By June 1852, Buck had moved by steamboat and stagecoach to Weaverville in the Shasta area—about 175 miles northwest of Sacramento City. Here he set up a store because of the successful gold mines in the area. While his business did well, at one point he noted that after three years in California he was worse off than when he arrived; in another he said he and his partner had doubled their initial $2,000, then later he noted they were $3,000 in debt, but whether he had money or not, he seemed happy with his new life.

Still, Weaverville could be a bit dangerous at times. In one letter he wrote, "As to the society—it is decidedly bad, gambling, drinking, and fighting being the amusements of the miners in their leisure hours. Saturday night is usually celebrated by such hideous yells and occasionally a volley from their revolvers which makes it rather dangerous to be standing around. At least a poor inoffensive jackass found it so the other night. [. . .] According to the California Code if one man strikes another without provocation he has a perfect right to shoot him down. Everyone goes armed and at the least quarrel at a gambling saloon out come the revolvers. Someone sings out, 'Don't shoot,' the crowd surge back, and they blaze away. A man's life is but little thought of. Sunday these two persons were killed; yesterday buried; and today almost forgotten."

In another letter he adds, "Nothing fatal has taken place since my last letter but there have been some awfully close shaves. One man has been shot through the cravat, one through the hat and one in the arm. The Weaverville Hotel has been sacked and fist fights without number have come off, but as nobody has been killed nothing has been done."

COLONEL HARPER, STAGE ROBBER
[Weaverville, June 5, 1853]

I forget the date of my last letter but believe that it is time to say something and keep you posted up in our affairs. We are a great and growing people here and I am proud to be able to state to you that Weaverville is going ahead, also the firm known as Buck & Cole. Their affairs are in a healthy condition. County scrip has gone up for one and the other had a store full of goods and good credit.

All traces of the fire have vanished and the old log cabins have been replaced by elegant buildings. We have now been here one year and during this time the town has doubled in size. We now have fourteen stores, four hotels and four gambling saloons in full blast.

Last Sunday we had a cock-fight; today, three horse-races for three hundred dollars a side. I am sorry to have to record these last but you ought to know it all and to brighten the picture I will state that fighting has diminished and our efficient officers arrest the offenders at once and make them come down to the tune of twenty dollars and costs. Our jail is in a fair way, also, to open on the 20th.

Speaking of jails, Col. Harper, who left here a short time since, ostensibly to go after his wife, robbed a woman in the stage going down, of $1,800, and is at present in jail at Hamilton awaiting his trial. This rather took us aback although we all believed him to be a scoundrel. His wife is said to be with him. There must be some kind of a compact between such persons that I can't understand. He knows she has "the act of shame a thousand times committed" and as to his guilt there is proof positive, and yet they stick to each other and theirs is not the only instance of the kind that I know of.

Sarah has made and received a number of calls on the ladies here. She will probably give you an account of them better than I can. We are living *en famille*. The Metropolitan has closed. Two of the old Mess board with us. Sarah does very well in housekeeping, but what is the use of having a woman unless she can cook? [***Note:*** This is probably a joke. From Buck's letters it's difficult to tell who Sarah was. Obviously his sister, who he was writing to, knew her. He mentions her arrival from the East Coast and had been expecting her, so it's likely she's the Sarah he talks of visiting in his New York letters, and it's possible she was from Bucksport, Maine. In a letter from 1864 he refers to her as Sarah Cole, so she may have been the wife or a relative of his partner, Captain Cole.]

You spoke of the Chinese in your last letter. We have lots of them about and they are among our best customers and certainly the best foreigners we have. They buy lots of provisions, chiefly rice, flour, lard, codfish, tea, etc; drink whisky and smoke like other people. I rode down to the river yesterday. There are three hundred of them on one bar that has been worked out by our people and they are perfectly satisfied if they make two or three dollars per day. [...]

A Chinese man in about 1851. According to the 1848 census, there were only three Chinese residents in California. Just seven years later there were around 20,000.

You who live under the Maine Liquor law can have no idea of the immense quantity of liquor consumed in one of these mining towns. There are fourteen bar rooms in this little town and I only wonder that there is not more drunkenness than there is. Although we all drink, the "getting drunk" is done by very few and no man of any standing in the town ever thinks of doing such a thing.

The Rush Begins

Elisha Oscar Crosby

Elisha Oscar Crosby was born and raised in rural New York. At the age of twenty-five he became a lawyer, taking a job at a law office on Wall Street. When Colonel Mason's report to President Polk was published on December 5, 1848, and wild tales of golden riches suddenly gripped the nation's imagination, Crosby, as he put it, "took the California fever bad." His boss and primary client were also extremely interested and encouraged him to go in order to verify the amazing stories they were hearing. So at the age of thirty he left behind his reliable and respectable job of five years and leapt into the unknown by catching a ship for Panama on Christmas Day. He recorded what happened next in his memoirs, which were published almost a hundred years after he set sail to begin his new life.

A Ship More Populous than the City

We arrived here in San Francisco on the 28th day of Feby 1849. The Pacific Squadron was then lying at Sausalito, and not another vessel or mast of any thing lying off the present city of San Francisco. With 450 people on board, and no way of getting ashore except with the steamer's small boats; and with a great mud flat lying between the ships channel and Montgomery Street, and a few low buildings on shore, mostly constructed by the Russian Fur Company; the prospect did not look very inviting. That golden halo that seemed to pervade the Eastern skies of the Eastern world before we left had faded out very much, and the sterner realities of our new life and home presented themselves. The ardor and glow of most of the passengers was pretty well dampened: and a good many expressed the opinion that they had been made the victims of false reports and their own rash credulity in regard to what looked to them then, as very mythical gold prospects. However we commenced getting ashore as fast as possible. It was pretty well understood that every fellow must look out for himself as best he could.

There was nothing to be seen on the bay; it was just a desolation. The crew began to desert the steamer the first night. The passengers commenced discharging their baggage, and pulling off with the ship's boats, and camping about on the side of Telegraph Hill. Our landing was all made on the rocks at Clarks Point, near the foot of Broadway, the rocks projecting there into the water. [. . .]

We found at San Francisco a population estimated at about 300. If the 450 who came off the steamer had remained there, they would have considerably more than doubled the population. Those who were there when we arrived were mostly women and children and old men. They were some of them remnants of Col. Stevenson's Regiment, that had been sent out here before and during the Mexican war, also early emigrants who had drifted in, and some Kanakas [Hawaiians]. Some few had been to the mines and returned. There were two or three mercantile houses. Ross Bros. (C. L. Ross), Howard F. Meller, Green, Clark of Clark's Point, and some others.

CRUDE ACCOMMODATIONS

Dr. [Thaddeus M.] Leavenworth was then acting alcalde [mayor and justice of the peace] of San Francisco, and had his office in a room in a little one story building at the S.W. corner of Clay and Kearney Streets opposite the Plaza. He came out to California as Chaplain and Surgeon on board one of the vessels that brought Stevenson's Regiment. I knew Dr. Leavenworth in New York, a rather eccentric man in many respects, but on the whole a good man. He received me in a friendly way certainly, and extended the hospitality of his office, which was all he could do. He had built with his own hands a little bunk in one corner of his office where he slept himself, and told me I was welcome to lay my blankets in another corner on the floor, which was a great privilege at that time, and about equal to extending the hospitalities of the Palace Hotel at the present time.

I slept there the first night I passed on shore in San Francisco and we arranged a temporary bunk next day for my future occupation. A great many of the passengers sought boxes or large casks, or crates or sheds, or any thing that would shelter them from the night dampness and cold. It is said some even paid a dollar a night for the privilege of sleeping in some crates and boxes that had straw in them, and arranged for that purpose along a shed adjoining a building called the City Hotel, corner of Clay and Kearney Streets.

At this famous Hotel we got our meals in those first days of California life, consisting of boiled beef, rather indifferent bread, a decoction called coffee, and sea biscuit sometimes, but they were rather a luxury and seldom provided at the public table; but those who were fortunate enough to secure them outside, would bring their dessert in their pockets, in the shape of sea biscuit or sometimes a bottle of pickles. The bread, beef, coffee, and very indifferent sugar were all we were entitled to, and for these we paid a dollar a meal, and they paid a dollar for the privilege of going into the garret, and putting their blankets on the floor to sleep. It was very difficult to get any thing like supplies.

The *California* discharged considerable stuff that afforded more or less supplies for the people here. There was a general disposition to get away from the city, to the gold mines, some men putting three boards together to make a skiff, that looked more like a coffin, to cross the bay to Oakland Point, and thence to make their way over land to the mines the best way they could.

The First Gold

Crosby eventually made his way to Sutter's Mill, where the first gold was discovered, and talked with James Marshall about the discovery.

It was the merest accident in the world, one of those occurrences which was not premeditated, as gold was the last thing they were looking for. Marshall went down to the Fort, and submitted these specimens for examination and test to Capt. Sutter.

The Fort was a place of general rendezvous for all the northern part of California, and there were more people there than anywhere else. I think he said the specimens were tested there by some one else who professed to know something about chemistry besides Capt. Sutter.

But to satisfy themselves more fully, they sent down pieces to San Francisco, where they were tested and pronounced to contain gold, and from that on, the thing kept developing itself until it became a settled fact that the metal was gold. People then began to settle along the American River, and when I arrived, there were parties who had collected very considerable amounts. There was a man named Daley living on the Consumnes River [Cosumnes River] who had a cattle ranch and quite a band of cattle, and had quite a band of Indians under his control, and by their aid he had collected a considerable amount of gold when I arrived in that part of the country. Petit the trader at Sutter's Fort had also collected quite an amount, in fact a little fortune.

The favorite receptacle for it seemed to be pickle jars, for the reason there were more of them to be had than of any other kind of vessel; canned fruits were not known much then and these bottles were common.

A forty-niner pans for gold on the American River in 1850.

A man named Grimes on the north side of the American River above Sacramento had obtained some considerable quantity. Sam Brannan had secured quite a large amount. When I went there I found parties prospecting the different rivers and ravines along the foot hills of the Sierra Nevada, sometimes a single man, and sometimes two or three in company. Generally they would dig in and get the dirt where they could see the color, and put it in a tin pan, and carry it to the water, fill the pan, and agitate it by a circular rotating motion, by which the dirt would loosen and dissolve and flow out, the gold settling to the bottom. They would pick out the stones and work it out until they got it clean, and then collect the black sand and gold in the bottom of the pan and dry it, and then blow the sand off, the heavy gold remaining. Most of the gold washing up to that time had been done in that way. These miners had found a good many pieces of gold in the beds of streams and crevices of the rocks. I saw a piece weighing seven ounces, from a gulch on one of the forks of the American River. Gold dust was rated at $12 an ounce at that time, about the middle of March "49."

EXPENSIVE MINING EQUIPMENT

About that time a small trading vessel of five or six hundred tons burden, sent out from New Bedford I think to carry articles for sale on this

Using a rocker in Columbia sometime before 1866

coast, and carry back hides and tallow, arrived in San Francisco, and was with much difficulty warped up to Sutter's landing. They had on board some sheet iron, tin cups, pans, and tin ware of various kinds, nails, and articles of that kind, to trade for hides and tallow. These proved to be just the things wanted in the mines. Capt. Simmons was part owner of the cargo, and I think master of the vessel. These articles sold at most fabulous prices. A little tin cup would sell for half an ounce of gold, a piece of sheet iron, perhaps two feet square, would sell for an ounce of gold, and used to cover the bottom of a small hand rocker. Common tin pans sold for an ounce of gold apiece, and all the cargo went in much the same proportion, realising a fortune for the owners. Hundreds of dollars of this kind of goods would swell into tens of thousands of dollars in money or gold dust.

Miners in the Sierras, by Charles Christian Nahl and August Wenderoth, painted in 1851–52. It's possible this picture features Wenderoth, Nahl, and Nahl's two brothers at their claim on Deer Creek, just outside of the Rough & Ready mining camp. Nahl's wife did laundry to make extra money and you can see laundry drying near the cabin. The miners are using a long tom to separate the gold from the dirt, sand, and rocks.

When these supplies of sheet iron and nails began to arrive the miners commenced to make small rockers. They put a small quantity of dirt into the rocker, let a stream of water run through, at the same time rocking it back and forth, and while the dirt washed away, the gold would find its way down through the perforated sheet iron, and lodge in the crevices in the bottom of the rocker. This was considered quite an invention, and proved a great improvement, upon the washing of gold with a tin pan.

Along in April and May, they began to make these rockers much longer. They would take a tree cut off a log the required length, and hollow it out, forming a long trough, and put strips acrost the bottom an inch high, the upper part of the trough would be covered by perforated sheet iron, and on this they threw the dirt. Below the iron, and covering part or the whole of the remaining part of the trough, on an incline below the iron, a wooden grating. The stream of water was carried by a spout on to the dirt at the upper end, and by constantly rocking the trough, the dirt and stones were washed out, the gold and black sand finding its way down through the perforated sheet iron, and lodging in the cleats on the bottom. The supply of dirt was kept up by one or more men, the rocking done by another, and this was called the Long Tom washing, and proved a very successful way of getting gold during the early days of Placer mining. This finally led to sluicing.

Hollowed-out logs were quickly abandoned, and long toms were then made from wood planks forming a trough. These were not rocked, relying instead on the motion of the water and a man with a shovel agitating the dirt and removing the large rocks to enable the gold to drop through the holes in the iron plate. The gold fell into the bottom trough where, because of its superior weight, it was caught in the cleats or riffles, while the dirt was washed away.

After leaving the American River I came back to Sutter's Fort a short time and then made a trip to the Yuba Mines. Foster's Bar was one of the first known localities on the Yuba River when they discovered gold. That was above the present city of Marysville. Foster, for whom the bar was named, was one of the men who established Marysville, which was named in honor of his wife. [*Note:* Foster was actually Mary's brother-in-law.] I visited Foster's bar and several other small camps where parties, or perhaps a solitary man, were at work. All the little streams along the foot hills were being prospected for gold, and more or less of it was found everywhere.

It was a rough rude life and scanty food and of the plainest simplest kind, and prepared by the miners themselves. But all seemed happy and contented, and the safety to life and property, was never more perfect and complete than at this time, all through the then known mining regions. [. . .]

Mailing Gold Home

[In early May 1849] I sent home to New York a package of gold dust, secured in a small tin box that had formerly done service as a pepper box. This gold I had collected in trade, mostly with things I had in my two trunks, worthless to me for use in the rough life we then led in California, consisting of surplus white shirts, white vests, kid gloves, one or two pair of fine calf skin boots, and things of that class, which were proper for New York life, but not very useful in California. These things were bought up at fabulous prices, by young men who had been in the mines, and who were anxious to have a refit in "biled shirts," as they were termed there. [**Note:** Boiled shirts were those that were heavily starched.]

I had attended one or two law suits in Frank Bates's court at Sutter's Fort—Daley had some trouble there and I was his counsel, and as the result was satisfactory to him he gave me a purse of gold dust. I objected to taking it, as it seemed out of all proportion to the services I had rendered him. Frank said I had better take it, as he had plenty more and it would be thought discourteous by my client to refuse. I asked Frank how much it was worth, he said about a thousand dollars [roughly $200,000 in today's dollars].

The case occupied two or three days longer, and finally resulted in a compromise, Daley getting all or nearly all he wanted. I drew up the papers for a settlement, and they both made up another purse of $2,000 and gave me for a final settlement. That was the first fee I rec'd in California. A few days afterwards Daley sent me over to Sutter's Fort a very fine saddle horse, all nicely equipped with a complete "California" outfit. He was a fine large horse, well broken to the saddle. That was a little present, he said, that he wanted me to take, and have a horse of my own to ride over to his Ranch sometimes to see him. He lived on the Cosumnes River and had a large cattle ranch, well stocked with cattle and horses. These cattle he sold off gradually to the miners afterwards at enormous prices. I did some other business for parties litigating, and my clients were always disposed to pay liberally.

Some of the gold dust I sent to New York by the [steamship] *Oregon* was the result of these services, and the sales of things I had no use for. I had this on hand, and some besides, and as it was of not much use to me then, I thought I would send it to show my friends at home what there really was here. That gold dust was kept on exhibition some little time in New York, and then sent to the Mint at Philadelphia and coined, turning out near $3,000—and the coin was also on exhibition in New York. That did not help to allay the gold fever among my friends in that quarter.

HOW I CAME TO CALIFORNIA

In regard to my coming to California, at that early day, I will explain a little how it happened. Mr. Benedict was an elderly man, an old practitioner, who was disposed to live rather easily, after he had made his fortune. He had taken me in to his office really to do the work of the concern. There was a great deal of business, and I worked very hard, and my health began to fail, my lungs not being very strong, and I had arranged to go to Cuba to spend the winter of "48–49."

When this intelligence of the discovery of gold was received on the first of Decr. "48," Mr. Benedict, as well as Messrs. Howland & Aspinwall, said to me: "Go on to California. You can just as well go there, and let us know about this; see whether those fellows out there are humbugging us." The opportunity seemed favorable, and I thought I might go to California and pass the winter; and the next summer make my way back home. Upon arriving here and finding things as I did, and receiving such liberal compensation as I did from Daley, and others, I concluded it was a good place to stop in. The climate agreed with me, and it was wonderful how rapidly I recuperated. Things were so attractive I could not resist the temptation to stay on, and finally did not think of returning home.

FOUNDING THE TOWN OF VERNON

After the *Oregon* sailed I went back to the Fort and I there met Sam Norris, who had been an old Californian. He and Frank Bates proposed to me that we purchase some land of Sutter, and lay out a town at the mouth of Feather River. We did so, buying some 1,800 acres on the east bank of the Sacramento right opposite the junction of the Sacramento and Feather Rivers. I went up there and superintended the laying out of the little town.

On my first arrival at Sutter's embarcadero, they conceived the idea of laying out a town on the banks of the Sacramento, and perhaps as early as the first of April, they commenced making their survey of the site of Sacramento City, and laid out the town, and commenced establishing trading points there, as people arrived from abroad.

Our town was called Vernon. That was thought to be the head of navigation on the Sacramento. It assumed quite a little importance as a trading point for the Feather River Mines, and later began to be in demand, and I sold quite a number for joint account. To run out the history of Vernon briefly. That summer it grew considerably, and in the fall of "49," it had a population of some six or seven hundred people. When the winter rains came on, that whole country was flooded, and one vast sea of water surrounded the little elevation where the town was situated, stretching in every direction, and boats could navigate almost anywhere acrost the plains. That put a quietus to the town of Vernon.

Foster commenced laying out the town of Marysville that winter, on the highlands on the north side of Yuba River, and that superseded "Vernon," and in three or four years there was nothing left. The buildings were taken down and carried to Marysville or Sacramento.

THE USELESS AND ABANDONED

During my stay at Vernon in the summer of "49" I made frequent visits to all the new mining camps along the Yuba River and thence south on Bear Creek and the north fork of the American River, and was pretty well acquainted with their rapidly increasing development, and population. The ocean fleet began to arrive in San Francisco in June, and the constant stream of newly arrived emigrants kept increasing these camps and spreading over the territory of country along the foot hills, where no mining had been attempted before.

The roads leading out towards the mountains, from Sacramento, Vernon, and other points on the Sacramento River, where the water emigration landed, were strewed with every conceivable variety of gold-washing machines, and useless articles they had brought along to facilitate the operation of gold washing. So far as I know, not one of these many contrivances and inventions proved to be of service, but were utterly valueless, and abandoned along the roads. The way to the mines from these points were well defined by these abandoned wrecks, pickle jars, ale bottles, debris of camps, and bones of dead animals, and sometimes the melancholy sight of a lonely grave, where the last remains of some hopeful miner had sunk to rest, before reaching the golden goal for which he had struggled.

Elisha Crosby went on to become a California state senator and helped write the California Constitution of 1849. During the Civil War he was the US minister to Guatemala. While the job he abandoned as a Wall Street lawyer was a good one, he was so overworked that his health was failing. In California his health was restored and his life became much more interesting and profitable.

A Flood of Pioneers

Alonzo Delano

Alonzo Delano was a well-respected merchant and community leader in Ottawa, Illinois, when gold was found at Sutter's Mill. On discovering he had tuberculosis (then called consumption) his doctor recommended a change of climate, fresh air, and lots of exercise, so he took off overland for California. Delano left St. Joseph, Missouri, on April 27, 1849. He finally arrived in Sacramento City on or about September 27, 1849.

The following letter was written by Delano to Henry Hurlbut, the sheriff of La Salle County, and was published in the

Alonzo Delano

Ottawa Free Trader of Ottawa, Illinois. This was probably written at Dawlytown, where Delano had just opened a store with F. C. Pomeroy.

GOING TO CALIFORNIA
Upper Diggings, Feather River; October 12, 1849

Dear Sir—I have tried a long time to write you, but, since crossing the Missouri River, either sickness, extreme fatigue, or constant labor have totally prevented me. I have scarcely been able to write to my own family; and I have been compelled to make my journal, hastily written, subserve the place of correspondence to my most intimate friends, to whom I hoped and intended to have written frequently.

You can form no idea of the labor, fatigue, trials, and patience of an overland journey to this country. While traveling along the Platte [River] for hundreds of miles, cold and rainy weather benumb your fingers while pitching tents, guarding cattle, preparing meals, gathering fuel so scantily distributed, and a thousand etceteras blunt your faculties; and when the hour of quiet arrives at dark, you sink on your hard couch exhausted. It is the same when you reach the burning sand after passing the Platte; and, in addition to this, while traveling down the Humboldt (or Mary's River) the utmost vigilance is required to keep marauding bands of Indians from stealing or maiming your cattle; and you become wearied and worn out, so that if you lay over a day, you cannot collect sufficient energy scarcely to wash a shirt or mend your ragged and dilapidated garments. Any man who makes a trip by land to California deserves to find a fortune.

The most of my writing has been done at our noon halts, often in the burning sun, for the little shade afforded by the wagon would be occupied by the wearied men. But we have got safely through without losing or laming any of our cattle, a somewhat unusual circumstance, and no serious mishap occurred except running short of provisions and living about three weeks on hard, dry bread and coffee.

My journal, published in the *Free Trader*, will give you a general outline of our daily marches and adventures by the way; so I will not speak of them here. We made two grand errors: first, in taking the Nemaha Cut-off, which put us back eight or ten days; and next, leaving the Mary's River and taking the Oregon and California Trail, by which we lost three weeks' time in getting in, and on account of which we ran short of provisions and had to pass four hundred miles through hostile Indians that kept us on the lookout day and night.

The Valley of the Sacramento, instead of being such a delightful region with its perennial spring, its blooming flowers, and clear sky, we found to be parched with drought, the grass dried to a crisp, the earth filled with wide cracks from the effects of a scorching sun and months without rain; indeed I have seen no rain from the 1st day of July to the

9th day of October, and there was nothing green for over a hundred miles that I have traveled except the oak and willow that line the banks of the streams. The atmosphere has been so smoky that I could rarely see the high mountains on either side of the Valley from the road, though only a few miles distant; while the nights have been uncomfortably cold (without frost), the days often burning hot. [. . .]

To those who wish to come I would recommend the route by the Isthmus or around the Cape, for, disagreeable as it may be, they will suffer less than by an overland trip; but whoever comes, let him not think of returning in less than two years, for it will take that time to bring matters around right. I have made something and am getting matters in a train to make more, I hope.

As a newspaper correspondent, Delano wrote many letters that appeared as articles in the *Ottawa Free Trader* and the *New Orleans True Delta*. He then collected his articles and published them as *Life on the Plains and Among the Diggings* in 1857. What follows is from this book.

DIFFICULTIES CROSSING THE PLAINS

It will be as well to speak here of the emigration in the latter part of the fall of 1849. Those who started from the Missouri late in the season, or who, by the vicissitudes of the plains, could not arrive till November, experienced almost incredible hardships. The previous trains had consumed all the grass, and thousands of cattle perished by the way. The roads were lined with deserted wagons, and a vast amount of other property; the Indians grew still more bold and troublesome by success; and many families were reduced to the utmost distress, with no means of getting forward but to walk.

Provisions, which had been abundant at the commencement of the journey, had been thrown away, or abandoned with the wagons, and the last part of the emigration resembled the route of an army, with its distressed multitudes of helpless sufferers, rather than the voluntary movement of a free people. Worn out with fatigue, and weak for want of nourishment, they arrived late in the season in the mountainous region of the Sierra Nevada, where still greater struggles stared them in the face.

SNOWSTORMS

The rains and snow commenced much earlier than usual, and fell to an unprecedented depth, and it seemed utterly impossible for them to get through. In addition to other calamities, many suffered from scurvy and fevers—the consequence of using so much salt or impure provisions; and while many died, others were made cripples for life.

Reports of these sufferings reached the settlements, when the government, and individuals, who contributed largely, sent out a detachment to afford all the relief they could, and to bring the suffering emigrants in. The last of the emigrants had reached Feather River, on the Lawson route [Lassen Trail?], when the government train reached them with mules. Some had been without food for two or three days, and with others a heavy body of snow lay on the ground.

Three men made a desperate effort to get through. For some days they had been on an allowance of but one meal a day, when, packing up all the bread they had left, which was only a supply for two days, they started for Lawson's, a distance of seventy miles. The snow was between two and three feet deep, yet they waded through it for a few miles, when they came to a wagon containing two women and two or three children, who had eaten nothing for two or three days. With a generosity which was rare, under such circumstances, they gave all they had left to these helpless ones, and went on without. They succeeded in reaching Lawson's.

Many knocked their exhausted cattle in the head, and lived upon them until the government train reached them. Women were seen wading through the deep snow, carrying their helpless children; and strong men dropped down from utter exhaustion. The only food they had was their animals, and men became so famished that they cut meat from the mules and horses which had perished from hunger and thirst by the road side.

When the government train arrived, the women and children were placed upon the mules, exposed to a furious snow storm, in which many of the animals perished; but the emigrants finally succeeded in getting through, when the government furnished boats to carry them to Sacramento, as the roads along the valley had become impassable.

FATAL ERRORS

In the succeeding year, the emigration was quite as large as in 1849. The reports of the error of the immigrants of the preceding year, in loading their wagons too heavily with provisions, had reached the States, and very many took the opposite extreme. This was a most unfortunate mistake, which led to horrible results, in addition to other calamities. On reaching Fort Laramie, the provisions of many were consumed; but with a headlong determination to persevere, they went forward, depending on chance for supplies—a step which the reader can now well understand was entirely desperate, in the country through which they were compelled to pass.

Many others were well supplied until they reached the Humboldt, when their stores became exhausted. Another difficulty was, that many started with horses, and in their anxiety to get forward, drove too fast, so that when they arrived at the barren wastes beyond the Platte, their animals were worn down with fatigue, and gave out by the time they reached Green River, and they were thus obliged to leave both wagons and supplies, with a long, doubtful, and dangerous journey still before them.

Added to these causes of suffering, another existed, which did not the previous year. In 1849 there was more grass than had ever been known before. Traders who had been in the country fifteen or twenty years assured us that they had never known such a plentiful season, and that grass was then growing in abundance where they never saw any before, and they universally said that had not such been the case it would have been utterly impossible for such an emigration to get through.

There was an unprecedented fall of snow and rain the following winter, but the weather was dry and hot in the spring; and when the second emigration came on, the grass was dried up in many places where we had found it good, and the melting snows rendered the streams so high, that they were crossed with much difficulty. The lower valley of the Humboldt, where we found a smooth, level road the previous seasons, was now (in 1850) overflowed, presenting one vast lake, and the emigrants were compelled frequently to keep to the hills or uplands, either in deep sands, or among rocks and ravines, with their worn-out animals, while the overflowed valley afforded no grass. Long and laborious detours were necessary, to avoid lateral valleys, now under water; and on the Humboldt there

Although the California Trail was heavily traveled, portions of the trail had no road. Occasionally wagons had to be unloaded and taken apart so they could be hauled over obstacles. Ascending Carson Pass into the Sierra Nevada was one of the most difficult portions of the trail.

was one point where they had to go thirty miles over difficult mountains, where we made the distance in six.

In traveling down that river, grass was obtained frequently only by wading or swimming to islands, and cutting it with a knife. In one instance, which came to my knowledge, a man paid an Indian fifteen dollars to swim to a little island and get enough to feed his mule.

In addition to all these unfortunate circumstances, the cholera broke out among the emigrants, and reached from Fort Kearney to Fort Laramie. It raged with dreadful violence, marking the road with the graves of the unfortunate victims.

Although many came through well and safely, is it to be wondered at that horses, mules and cattle broke down, that provisions were exhausted, hundreds of miles from the settlements and far from human aid, and that men, women, and children were left destitute, without a mouthful to eat, and without the means of getting forward, exposed to a burning sun by day, and the chilling cold of night? Perhaps an exhausted, worn-out horse, or mule, might be left to carry a remnant of supplies; yet even without this slender aid, mothers might be seen wading through the deep dust or heavy sand of the desert, or climbing mountain steeps, leading their poor children by the hand; or the once strong man, pale, emaciated by hunger and fatigue, carrying upon his back his feeble infant, crying for water and nourishment, and appeasing a ravenous appetite from the carcass of a dead horse or mule; and when they sank exhausted on the ground at night, overcome with weariness and want of food, it was with the certainty that the morning sun would only be the prelude to another day of suffering and torture.

Is it strange, then, that under such destitution and trial, when for weeks a draught of good water could not be had, some should become desperate, and commit suicide, rather than continue a living death? In one day, on the Humboldt, three men and two women drowned themselves, having become frantic from suffering. The men were observed, and [at] once rescued; but they persisted in declaring that death was preferable, and finally succeeded in committing the desperate deed. The women had families, and unable longer to witness the suffering of their children, with no prospect of relief, chose the dreadful alternative.

It can scarcely be realized by those who have not been placed in such situations, to what desperation the human mind may be excited; yet, from what I have witnessed myself, I can readily understand their perfect despair under the circumstances.

RESCUE EFFORTS

By the earliest arrivals, in June and July, of those emigrants who reached the valley, the sufferings and destitution of those behind were made known, and the government and individuals once more extended the hand of relief. San Francisco, Sacramento City, and Marysville made large contributions, and trains loaded with provisions were dispatched to meet them.

In addition to this, traders pushed their way over the snows to Carson's Creek, and Truckee River, and even to the Sink of the Humboldt [a generally dry lake bed in what is now Nevada], with supplies; and although much good was done, and many lives saved, yet aid could not be rendered to all. Indeed, it seemed as if this aid was scarcely felt. Five pounds of flour was doled out to a man from the free supplies, which was afterwards reduced to two and half, and with this they had to travel over the mountains two hundred miles before they reached the settlements.

The traders asked and obtained two dollars and a half per pound, for flour and pork. Hundreds had no money, and if they had, a large amount would have been required to sustain a family. Some parted with their horses and cattle for a few pounds of flour; while others lived upon the dead carcasses of animals by the road side.

When at length the emigrants arrived at the end of their journey, destitute and exhausted, they were attacked with fevers and bloody flux, and many perished miserably, after having endured all but death in crossing the plains. Were the personal adventures of a moiety [a portion] of the emigration of 1850 to be written, they would furnish a volume of absorbing interest, forming a sad commentary on the California gold-seeking mania, which produced more wide-spread misery than any similar occurrence in the annals of mankind.

A BAD ROUTE

But a small portion of the emigration this year, came this northern or Lawson [Lassen?] route. The character of this route was now generally understood, and but few attempted it, fortunately. Those who did, almost without exception, suffered severely. The Indians on Pitt River were very hostile. In one night they stole twenty-seven mules from one train, which so completely broke it up that the emigrants were compelled to leave their wagons, and on the few mules that were left they packed what things they could, leaving their wagons and goods to be plundered by the savages.

One gentleman told me that he walked three days without a mouthful of food, leaving three companions, who fell exhausted in the road, one day's journey from Lawson's ranch. Supplies were sent back, and they were rescued. Another company of seven men were surrounded by a band of two hundred Indians, stripped of their clothing, and driven into the river, when they were assaulted by a murderous discharge of arrows. The whites had but a single gun, with which they dared not commence any defence, hoping that after being robbed the Indians would spare their lives.

Six of them were killed, and the seventh badly wounded, when providentially two men, who were hunting along the river, unconscious of the horrid butchery going on near them, discharged their pieces at some ducks. This alarmed the Indians, who thought a force was at hand, and they fled precipitately. The wounded man crawled out of the river, and being discovered, was taken to their train, and eventually recovered from his wounds.

These are only among the many incidents of that eventful year. From the Sink of the Humboldt, across the desert to Truckee River, like that of the previous year, the road was covered with the putrefied carcasses of dead animals, and the effluvia arising from them poisoned the atmosphere, and produced disease among the emigrants, and on their arrival in Hangtown [now Placerville], one of the lower mining districts, the cholera broke out, and raged with violence, thus adding pestilence to their other misfortunes.

AMAZING CHANGES

A large portion of the emigration of 1849 explored and occupied the northern mines, while those of 1850 either stopped in the central, or proceeded to the southern diggings, and the two emigrations wrought a change in California, wonderful as the magic influence of Aladdin's lamp.

Sarah Anne MacDougal, with Elizabeth in January 1850, shortly after arriving in California. She appears to show the effects of exposure to the elements from traveling by covered wagon to the gold fields.

The difficulties of prospecting for gold, with the consequent exposure attending it, and the difficulty of obtaining food and shelter, in a great measure vanished. As soon as placers were discovered on the mountains, roads were opened; ranches and trading posts were established, and public houses opened at convenient distances on the road; so that in twelve months it was no longer necessary to carry blankets, even into the lower mines. Still, at this moment, no new discoveries are made in isolated regions without exposure and privation. These things will appear in the course of my narrative in their proper places, and although my own adventures are more particularly described, they are only a single instance of what thousands passed through.

The emigrants of 1850 were not exposed to the same difficulties after their arrival, as those of the previous year. Provisions the first year could scarcely be had in many places, and were enormously high; but competition and the means of access scattered them through the mines, so that the second year there was no danger of starving.

THE NEED FOR MONEY

It was a common error which emigrants generally fell into on leaving home, that little or no money would be needed on the route, and that in the land of gold it would be more an encumbrance than otherwise; and many who might have provided themselves sufficiently neglected this important consideration. They found, however, that money was necessary to pay ferryage across streams, to buy provisions on the road, when accident or circumstances reduced their own supplies, and often to replace their worn-out and dying animals, which could occasionally be done.

And when at length they had successfully passed desert and mountain, and reached the grand haven of wealth, weeks, and sometimes even months, elapsed before they were successful in digging enough to pay their daily expenses, while many were taken sick immediately on their arrival, and for a long time were unable to help themselves. The consequence was that starvation and misery stared them in the face, after all the trials they had encountered on the plains; for, notwithstanding public and private charity [that] was extended for their relief to a great degree, their numbers were too great for all to be relieved, and many suffered and died for the want of the care and proper nourishment which their way-worn and debilitated frames required.

A REVERSAL OF FORTUNES

Many were happy at first in getting employment to pay their board; even those who never had been accustomed to labor at home, and who had been surrounded by the luxuries of life, were glad to get any servile employment adapted to their constitution and abilities. It was found, too, that talent for business, literary and scientific acquirements, availed little or nothing in a country where strength of muscle was required to raise heavy rocks and dig deep pits. It was strength, absolute brute force, which was required to win the gold of the placers, and many a poor fellow, unable to endure the severe labor under a scorching sun, was finally compelled to give it up in despair, and seek employment more congenial to his former habits of life.

California proved to be a leveler of pride, and everything like aristocracy of employment; indeed, the tables seemed to be turned, for those who labored hard in a business that compared with digging wells and canals at home, and fared worse than the Irish laborer, were those who made the most money in mining. It was a common thing to see a statesman, a lawyer, a physician, a merchant, or clergyman, engaged in driving oxen and mules, cooking for his mess, at work for wages by the day, making hay, hauling wood, or filling menial offices. Yet false pride had evaporated, and if they were making money at such avocations, they had little care for appearances.

I have often seen the scholar and the scientific man, the ex-judge, the ex-member of Congress, or the would-be exquisite at home, bending over the wash-tub, practicing the homely art of the washerwoman; or, sitting on the ground with a needle, awkwardly enough repairing the huge rents in his pantaloons; or sewing on buttons *a la tailor,* and good-humoredly responding to a jest, indicative of his present employment—thus:

"Well, Judge, what is on the docket to-day!"

"Humph! a trial on an action for *rents*—the parties prick anew."

"Any rebutting testimony in the case?"

"Yes, a great deal of re-*button* evidence is to be brought in, and a *strong thread* will uphold the suit."

—Or, to the ex-Congressman at the wash-tub—"What bill is before the house now!"

"A purifying amendment, sir: one that will make a *clean* sweep of the vermin which infest the precincts of our constituents."

"Will not the bill be laid on the table?"

"At all events, a thorough *renovation* will take place; for the state of things requires a *soap*-orific modification of existing evils."

Almost Broke in Sacramento City

[*Note:* This excerpt follows Delano's arrival in California.] We had driven half of the previous night to reach our resting place; and we now learned that we were within three miles of Sacramento City and Sutter's Fort.

After a frugal dinner of hard bread and water, Doctor Hall, Mr. Rood, and myself doffed our soiled garments, and after assuming habiliments more in accordance with civilized life, we set out for town, leaving our cattle and wagon in the care of Mr. Pope.

Taking off our clothes on reaching the ford, we waded across the American, a clear and beautiful stream, about four hundred feet wide, and reached the city of tents about four o'clock in the afternoon. And here I found myself more than two thousand miles from home, in a city which had risen as if by enchantment since I had crossed the Missouri, a stranger, way-worn and jaded by a long journey, half famished for want of even the necessaries of life, practicing domestic economy to the fullest extent, with every prospect before me of continuing in the practice of that useful science; for, on examining the state of my treasury, I found myself the wealthy owner of the full sum of four dollars!—enough to board me one day at a low-priced hotel. And I had come in the pleasant anticipation of raising a full supply of provisions, which would cost not less than two hundred dollars. This afforded me an opportunity of enlarging my views of political economy, by studying "ways and means." How the thing was to be done, I could not conceive. Dear reader, could you, under these circumstances?

While I was cogitating on the strange course of human events, as exhibited in my own particular case, and wishfully eying a piece of fat pork, which was temptingly exhibited for sale on a barrel head in a provision store, I met my old Captain, Jesse Greene, who, by keeping the old route and avoiding Greenhorn Cut-off, had got in four weeks before, and made something in the mines. A short time after, I met Doctor M. B. Angel, who had been equally successful, and they, understanding by intuition the state of an emigrant's treasury, generously offered to supply me with the *quid pro quo*, verifying the old proverb that "friends in need are friends indeed," and I think that under the circumstances, I was more rejoiced to see them than they possibly could have been to see me.

Thus, through their kindness, an arrangement was made by which I could obtain a load of provisions, and which I designed to take to the mines, either to sell, or live upon, till McNeil and myself could make something by mining. It was with reluctance, however, that I accepted

their proffered kindness, from the very uncertainty of California operations; but necessity compelled me to do so, or die, and I did not relish the
idea of dying there, so far from home.

While strolling through the streets during the evening, I chanced to
go into a hotel, where I met an old acquaintance, F. C. Pomeroy, who had
been unsuccessful in the mines, and was looking for business. As it was
necessary for me to have assistance, I immediately made an arrangement
with him to go with me to the mines. Fortune seemed to be smiling on
me, from a small corner of her vacillating mouth.

During the two days that I remained in town, Pomeroy and myself
took up our quarters under a large oak tree near J street, where we luxuri-
ated on the fat things of a bacon cask, with a bountiful supply of bread
and butter; in short, we fared sumptuously, by cooking for ourselves. One
night, feeling a little aristocratic, we spread our blankets on the ground in
an unoccupied tent, but the owner came in the morning before we were
up, and charged us fifty cents for sleeping under the canvass roof! We
thought it smacked of inhospitality, but we got used to it in time, and
discovered that in California it was custom and not extortion.

A Tent City

Sacramento City, at the period of which I write, contained a floating
population of about five thousand people. It was first laid out in the
spring of 1849, on the east bank of the Sacramento River, here less
than one-eighth of a mile wide, and is about a mile and a half west of
Sutter's Fort. Lots were originally sold for $200 each, but within a year
sales were made as high as $30,000. There were not a dozen wood or
frame buildings in the whole city, but they were chiefly made of canvass,
stretched over light supporters; or were simply tents, arranged along the
streets. The stores, like the dwellings, were of cloth, and property and
merchandise of all kinds lay exposed, night and day, by the wayside, and
such a thing as a robbery was scarcely known. This in fact was the case
throughout the country, and is worthy of notice on account of the great
and extraordinary change which occurred. There were a vast number of
taverns and eating houses, and the only public building was a theatre.
All these were made of canvas.

At all of the hotels and groceries, gambling was carried on to a remarkable extent, and men seemed to be perfectly reckless of money. Indeed, it seemed to have lost its value, and piles of coin and dust covered every table, and were constantly changing hands at the turn of a card.

At high water the river overflows its banks, and a notice of a dreadful disaster of this kind will appear hereafter. For a mile along the river lay ships, barges, and various water craft, laden with merchandise and provisions. Trade was brisk, and prices exorbitantly high.

On the north side of the city is a large and deep slough, in which cattle frequently mire and perish, and at this time the effluvia arising from their putrid carcasses was almost insufferable. A little beyond the slough the American River empties into the Sacramento. This river is not navigable for vessels. The Sacramento River, though affected by the tide, is pure and sweet, and generally is better to drink than the water of the wells, some of which are slightly brackish.

COYOTES, COUGARS, AND BEARS

On the first day of October, all things being in readiness, Pomeroy and myself, taking Mr. Pope, with McNeil's cattle, set out for *somewhere,* but with no definite location in view. Arrived at Bear River, we encamped under the trees on the bottom, and after turning out our cattle, and cooking our suppers, we placed our provision chest at our heads, and spreading our blankets, were soon asleep, despite the howling of the cayotes all around us. On awakening in the morning, we discovered that the thievish animals had been at our bedside in the night, and had actually taken the cloth which covered our provisions, and dragged it across the road, without awaking us.

These animals are of the dog species, and appear to be a connecting link between the fox and wolf. They frequently go in packs, but rarely attack a man, unless pressed by hunger, which is not often, for the number of horses and carcasses of wild cattle in the valley furnish them food, and they are not looked upon as dangerous. I have seen them stop and play with dogs, which had been set upon them, returning their caresses, and showing no disposition to fight. They would even playfully follow the dogs, which had been set upon them, to within a short distance of the wagons.

On searching for the cattle in the morning, it was discovered that one of my best oxen was missing. This was a serious loss, and although we searched two days and a half, we finally had to give it up without finding him. Nearly a mile below our encampment, there was a swampy morass, which extended a mile or more to Feather River, into which the Bear flowed. On the last day, while searching for my stray ox, I got lost in the tangled grape and pea vines, which covered the trees and bushes in an almost impenetrable maze. At every turn I found the tracks and beds of the grizzly bear, the cougar, and black wolf, and momentarily expected to meet some of these interesting natives of California; but Providence directed otherwise.

After wandering about half a day, completely bewildered, breaking my way through the thick maze with difficulty, I finally came to a stand, and commenced firing my gun, to attract the attention of my companions. I fired away all but one charge of my ammunition, without effect, and then sat down to wait until the declining sun should indicate the direction to my camp. At length this occurred, when I could take the true bearings, and I finally succeeded, with infinite toil, in getting out of the swamp.

I soon met Mr. Pope, who, alarmed at my long absence, had started after me. Further search appearing useless, the following morning we went on, and in the course of the day I was enabled to purchase an ox of an emigrant, which, though not near as good as the one lost, answered the purpose.

At night we halted near a muddy slough, where there was a little water, and set about preparing our evening meal. While we were thus engaged, a fine, rollicking, young fellow drove up, and requested to mess with us till morning, to which we assented cheerfully. In the course of the conversation, with some exultation, he told us that he had made fifteen hundred dollars in a short time, and taking out his purse, exhibited the money in gold coin. As it was heavy in his pocket, he arose, and going to my bed, which was spread under a tree nearby, he turned a corner of the blanket down, and then put the purse under it, leaving it there till morning, without going near it again, apparently with as much unconcern as if it had been so many chips, although we were entire strangers.

In the morning, after breakfast, and when he had harnessed his mules, he went to the bed, and taking his gold, jumped into his wagon and drove off as carelessly as if he had run no more risk than in depositing his money in the vault of a bank. Such was the security felt at the time from robberies.

Delano remained in the mining camps during the boom, selling supplies to the miners.

Rich Diggings

James Ayers

These excerpts from the personal account of Colonel James Ayers were written in 1896. Ayers took a steamship for California, leaving St. Louis, Missouri, in early February 1849. After arriving in Honduras, he hiked for seventeen days across the isthmus to the Pacific, but found it difficult to get a ship as the Pacific side was packed with people trying to find transportation to San Francisco. After a couple of months, his party was finally taken aboard an old ship, where they were packed like sardines with a hundred other passengers. Enduring many hardships, Ayers finally reached San Francisco in October 1849—just over eight months after leaving the States.

CALIFORNIA BEFORE THE RUSH

The history of California, before the influx of gold-seekers brought it prominently before the eyes of the world, may be told in a few words.

Until April, 1769, Upper California was to the white man a *terra incognita*. It was known to exist, for its coast had been navigated at intervals by hardy explorers for over two hundred years. Cabrillo had skirted it some forty odd years after the discovery of the continent by Columbus. Francis Drake had brought his ships to anchor in a bay a few miles north of San Francisco in the reign of Queen Elizabeth, and the Spanish galleons, making their yearly voyages to the Philippine Islands, had, on their return trips, regularly, for nearly two hundred years, raised the headlands at Cape Mendocino, and then, taking advantage of the northwest trade winds, had pursued their voyage to Acapulco; and it raises a grave doubt in the minds of geographers whether the Golden Gate could have existed at that time and escaped the accident of discovery by the explorer Drake, who anchored for weeks within fifteen miles of it, and eluded the research of the annual arrival within a few leagues of it of the Spanish galleons making the coast at Cape Mendocino for a long series of years. But during all this time absolutely nothing was known about the matchless country we now occupy.

In April 1769, the *San Antonio* sailed into the splendid harbor of San Diego. She had been sent out from Mexico and had a few friars on board, a detachment of soldiers, and a handful of colonists. Juan Crespi, an intrepid friar, marched overland until in October he reached San Francisco Bay, which had before been unknown to civilized man. Then followed the expedition of Father Junipero Serra, who founded Missions from San Diego to Monterey. The domination of the Missions, of which there were twenty-one, lasted till 1822, when Mexico declared her independence from Spain. The Missions were in their most flourishing condition in 1814, when they had 24,611 Indians attached to them as neophytes; possessed 215,000 head of horned cattle, 135,000 sheep, and 16,000 horses. They harvested that year 75,000 bushels of grain. After the Mexican flag had taken the place of the broad ensign of Spain in California, the Missions entered upon a career of rapid decadence. The rancheros and pobladores [ranchers and townspeople] envied their wealth and coveted their lands, and in 1835 the Missions were secularized.

From that time down to the 7th of July, 1846, the political power of California was in the hands of the leading families of the province, and although Mexico exercised the right of sovereignty by sending out Governors to rule over her, yet the turbulence of her people resulted in a number of bloodless revolutions, pulling down unpopular Governors and exacting changes in that office from Mexico. There was a constant struggle going on between Monterey and Los Angeles to be recognized as the seat of government. When Commodore [John D.] Sloat took possession of Monterey the power of the native Californians was virtually at an end, and the era of American authority over Upper California commenced. The discovery of gold by Marshall, on the 24th of January, 1848, opened to California a new era. One of the most wonderful migrations ever known set in from all parts of the Atlantic states when the news of the discovery slowly reached the populations east of the Mississippi. By sea and land they flocked in untold numbers to the new El Dorado, and all parts of the civilized world sent contributions of their people to California to seek for gold.

At this point my story commences [...]

Obtaining Supplies

We found Stockton quite a busy place. It was the commercial entrepôt [port of entry] for all the southern mines, reaching from the Mariposa to the Mokelumne rivers. Like San Francisco, it was a canvas town, but had not, like that city, the relief here and there of a red-tiled adobe building. After considerable trouble we chartered an ox-team and large wagon to take us and our belongings to the mines.

A wagon train pauses on the Placerville Route in the early 1860s.

We required more supplies than we had bought in San Francisco to carry us through the winter. We therefore drove to the store of Douglass & Thorne, which we were told had the largest assortment of any place in town. We selected a bill of goods and as we were about to drive away Mr. Thorne came out and took a careful look at the stuff we had in our wagon.

"Why," said he, "you haven't got half enough supplies there to carry you through the winter." We admitted the truth of his observation, but told him that we had got to the end of our purse, and must do with what we had. I shall never forget his rejoinder.

"You boys just fill up your wagon. Take what you want, and as soon as you are able to send me the money do so."

We were perfect strangers to him, and you may well imagine that the hearty and off-hand manner in which he offered us unlimited credit was as surprising as it was agreeable. We filled the wagon with such supplies as we thought we should need, and on casting up accounts we found that we had incurred an indebtedness to his house of several hundred dollars. I had no doubt from the way he had dealt with us that it was a business custom, and I venture to say that the percentage of loss made in this way was far less than is incurred now by merchants who do a credit business with customers they know all about. A credit of that kind became a debt of honor, and unless the parties who assumed it were absolute rogues, it would be scrupulously paid.

ROCKERS AND PANS

Our first experience in mining was not as encouraging as we had anticipated. The paying claims were on the bars, and as far as we could learn, they had all been located. However, we took the best we could find and worked the best we knew how. All mining at that time was done in the simplest way. A rocker, consisting of three smooth boards, four or five feet long, nailed closely together at the lower edges, with a square hopper at the upper end, into which a screen, made of sheet iron with holes in it, fitted. The frame was set upon rockers, such as are used for babies' cradles. The rocker was provided with two or three riffles to catch the gold as it was separated from the dirt by the action of the water which the operator poured constantly from a dipper upon the auriferous earth placed in the screen. One man was engaged in stripping the top dirt from the claim, whilst another filled a bucket with the gold-carrying material found near the bed rock, and carried it to the rocker which was kept in constant motion. After running through a certain number of buckets, the black sand and gold which, on account of their greater gravity, remained behind the riffles, were placed in a pan, or "wash-bowl," taken to the river, and carefully manipulated in the water until the sand was washed out and only the gold remained in the pan. We could make all the way from five to eight dollars a day to the hand, but that seemed so small compared with the wages the claims on the bars were yielding to our neighbors, that we were not at all satisfied. But as the rainy season was rapidly approaching, and the river was beginning to rise, we determined to send two of our party into the gulches to prospect for winter diggings, and in the meantime to work our river claim as long as we could.

To show the crude ideas which then obtained about mining I will mention one notable circumstance. In prospecting for winter diggings we opened a claim in a gulch some four or five miles from our camp. It paid moderately well until we came to a stratum of blue clay. We reasoned that the gold could not sink below this formation, and that there would be no more use in working below it than there would be to go deeper than the bed rock in a river claim. Therefore we only washed the earth above the blue clay, but as the pay was not inviting we soon abandoned the place, and located our camp near the Iowa Cabins, in a locality where there were a number of unworked gulches. The value of our conclusion, that it was impossible for the gold to sink below the blue-clay stratum, was exemplified two years afterwards. At that very point the Marlette series of mines were opened. They were immensely rich, and the flourishing town of San Andreas owes its origin and prosperity to them. Had we gone through the blue-clay stratum we would have struck a vein of rotten quartz, which carried gold with it to great depths and in wonderful profusion.

Chasing the Next Big Strike

One reason why so large a percentage of the miners failed to "make their pile," as it was then called, was the spirit of unrest that pervaded them. They were constantly on the go, prospecting for new diggings. If they had a moderately good claim and heard of better ones somewhere else, they would pack up and start for them, to find either that the stories they had heard were untrue, or that the choice claims had all been taken up before their arrival. Everyone wanted to make a big strike, and there was a prevailing conviction that the farther they went up into the heart of the Sierra Nevada, the surer they would be to get at the source from which the gold had been washed down into the rivers and gulches near the base of the range. To trace the gold to its great mother source would, in their crude opinion, be to discover an exhaustless deposit of auriferous wealth. The gold-seekers who kept constantly following this will-'o-the-wisp were filled with the popular delusion that "far-off fields are ever green." Those miners were the wisest, and accomplished the best results, who were satisfied with moderate-paying claims and stuck to them.

Another reason for the many failures was that nearly everybody had a theory about the logical distribution from natural causes of the precious metal. But the fact is that the distribution observed no law or regularity, and theories based upon the tenets of geological science were found to be practically barren of results. Rich deposits were found in the most illogical places, hill diggings of immense auriferous value would unfold themselves to the prospector by the merest chance, and even the law of gravity was often defied by the curious ways in which the gold would be distributed. The men who had a theory based upon geological principles would be baffled at every turn, whilst often the ignorant sailor or vaquero, who knew nothing about primary formations or secondary assimilations, would blindly sink a hole in a place where no reasoning man would look for gold, and make an immensely rich discovery.

I recollect an instance of this kind which occurred near Mokelumne Hill. A man named Clarke, who was famous for finding rich diggings, came into the camp, and, as usual, went upon a protracted spree. After he had spent all his money and could get no more liquor, he started out "to make a rich find," as he said. It was winter, and he was overcome with fatigue and inebriation, for he had induced some considerate friend to provide him with a flask, and lay down on the top of a steep hill. During his restless sleep he rolled down the side of the hill and landed in a gulch. When he came to his senses he turned over, drew his case knife and commenced to dig up the earth. After a while he uncovered a lump of gold. Then, as he went deeper into the ground with his case knife, he brought out more nuggets, some of them very large. To make our story short, he had discovered a ravine that was afterwards known as Rich Gulch, and from which many millions were taken. The secret of Clarke's success in finding rich diggings was that he had no theory, but that he would go around prospecting in the most inconceivable places, untrammeled by the laws of science or even by the likelihood of auriferous distribution. His knowledge of cause and effect began and stopped at the proposition that if he drank too much whisky he would get drunk, and he was very assiduous in demonstrating the truth of his proposition.

FOUNDING A NEWSPAPER

In the fall of 1851, H. A. De Courcey, Henry Hamilton, and myself bought a printing outfit and started with it for Mokelumne Hill, which, through the discovery of rich mines in its vicinity, had grown to be a large and nourishing camp. When we reached the Hill with our press I marveled at the change that had taken place in a little over a year. There was evidence of prosperity on every hand. On Sundays the miners flocked to the Hill, and the streets were almost impassable with the crowds that blockaded them. Business was booming, and at night the gambling saloons and fandangos [outdoor dance, ball, or shindig] were the centers of attraction. Adams Express Office was buying gold from the miners in prodigious quantities. The output from the deep diggings in the adjoining hills was tremendous. The gold was coarse, and nuggets, or chispas, as they were called, weighing from one ounce to one hundred and twenty ounces—the latter, of horseshoe shape, was the largest ever brought into camp—gave proof of the richness of the diggings.

Lumber for building purposes was scarce and very dear. We found at one of the stores a large lot of sheet iron which the merchant had bought to supply the miners with screens for their Long Toms. The demand for it had fallen away, as other methods of separating the gold had been found more suited to the mines of this vicinity; so we bought all the sheet iron he had, and covered the frame of our office building with it. On the 18th of October, 1851, we issued the first number of the *Calaveras Chronicle,* and that paper still lives [in 1896], having been consecutively published under its original name for a longer period than any other newspaper in the state.

NATIVE AMERICAN PROSPECTORS

A feature of the camp, and one that was common to all the camps in the Southern mines, was the great number of Sonoranians who dwelt in and around it. They were really Indians of the Yaqui tribe, those stalwart aborigines who occupy the fairest part of Sonora, and who have successfully resisted all attempts of the Mexican government to invade their territory and bring them under subjugation to Mexican rule. Their mode of mining was peculiar. They used neither shovel, pick, nor machine. Their whole outfit consisted of a short bar, a wooden bowl, or *batea*, and a horn spoon. With these they would prospect around until they found a place to suit them. With their crowbar they would sink a shaft just wide enough for their bodies to enter, and when they got to the bed rock they would drift until they found a lead or a rich crevice.

It made little difference to them whether they were convenient to water or not. If they were, they would at long intervals come to the surface with their wooden bowl filled with auriferous dirt, which they had carefully assorted, and wash it till only the gold remained in their *batea;* if there were no water handy they would dry-wash, as it was called, the contents of their vessel. This was done by a curious method of manipulation. They would agitate the earth in their bowl until the gold had settled at the bottom, then they would blow off as much of the lighter earth at the top as they could and repeat this process until they had blown off all the dirt and only the gold was left in the bowl. Sometimes they would deftly pour from a height the contents of one bowl into another, blowing upon the descending column, and thus eliminate the lighter material from the heavier, until after many repetitions of this curious process, the gold would be separated from the dirt. A high wind would help them out in this kind of work.

Instinctively these people seemed to know where rich crevices and leads were to be found, and in their solitary and quiet way they were supposed to take out a great deal of gold from the mines. At any rate, they were the pioneers of many rich discoveries. Wherever one would go their coyote holes would show that they had been there before.

Of Miners and Gold

Carl Meyer

In 1849, Carl Meyer sailed from New Orleans to San Francisco. Originally from Basel, Switzerland, he was one of many Europeans to join the rush for California's gold. He published an account of his experiences in Switzerland in 1855, titled *Nach dem Sacramento.* The following excerpts are from his book.

A MINER'S LONELY LIFE

Working for a better future or for his family, the miner is seen alone, away from everything that might distract him from his work. A small tent, pitched under a shade tree, contains all his possessions and willingly yielding to his fate, he enjoys his quiet life and fills his mind with noble thoughts. Having become practiced in finding Nature's hidden treasures, he also becomes accustomed to commune with her. His mind is occupied not only with Nature's materials, but also with her forms. He finds pleasure in the various creations about him, with which he must become familiar as they are his daily companions. They become more and more animated for him, speaking stimulatingly to his senses and soothing his desires. Soon Nature gives him not only material but also ideal satisfaction. [. . .]

Here fate plays tricks; cares, dangers, and tortures of the wild life are present in sufficient numbers to mediate resignation and exuberance. Accidents, of which there are many in the mines, throw men down from the heights of fortune or determine their ascent; accidents either lead men to calm and privacy or disturb them. Everything in the mines is accidental but a man with a strong will can still find elbow-room, and though he be unable to move mountains he can avoid them.

CHASING RUMORS OF GOLD

A miner's life is hard enough. He has heard that far away in the mountains new gold mines have been discovered. The rumors of their riches are like fairy tales. Determined to go there he packs his belongings with accustomed ease and hurries off. He encounters the steepest mountains, the deepest valleys, rocky, rushing rivers, and insufficient feed for his pack or riding animals; but he soon surmounts all obstacles. Frequently courage and perseverance seem about to desert him, when he meets with some great mishap, but usually he climbs out unaided from the deepest traps.

He cannot go to rest at nightfall if he has not found a suitable camp with feed and water for his animals. He travels on until he has found the camp where he sinks down exhausted and weak. He must use his provisions sparingly as his goal is uncertain; his destination being the place where he finds the most gold. If he loses the trail in the dense forests or on the bare rocks, the sun or his instincts guide him. If he falls from a cliff and lies crushed in the depths, no one looks for his bones; all that is known of him is that he has left and not returned.

But he finally does arrive at his destination. This is the place where rumor has it there is much gold, and other miners are here already. The rumors are often true, the gold is being ladled from the depths; but frequently all is false, not even the color of gold or a trace of gold can be found. The gold seeker pushes on deeper into the mountains or, deceived, he undergoes the same exertions to return to his old mining place. But here he finds newcomers and the ground which he has left recently and in which he thought he would dig again is now in the possession of another who had the right to take possession just twenty-four hours after the departure of the former owner. The miner is again disappointed.[1]

DAM COMPANIES RUINED

The companies seeking gold also experience many mishaps. A river is forced into an artificial bed so that the gold in the old bed may be removed. This

---

1 [Meyer's footnote:] Every miner has the right to "claim" twenty square feet of earth, which remains his property as long as he works in it. No other person can set foot in his mine if tools are in it and the Claimer has not stopped work in it for more than twenty-four hours. According to state law every miner who is not an American citizen is supposed to pay a small tax, but it is to the credit of the state that this law has never been enforced.

work takes years, but the results are wonderful. Wonderful? Yes! If the work is not as far advanced as had been planned, at the beginning of winter a single rainy night can destroy the work of several hundred human hands and of a whole year and in a moment wipe out visions of fortune. This has happened to many a "Dam Company."

The individual in such enterprises pays dearly for his share; he works; he feeds himself; by his words and deeds he encourages others to work; daily he stands in water, exposed to the sun's blaze, bathed in sweat. His health ruined, he hopes and prays, and when the work is almost completed the swollen river overflows the dam so that the work must either begin again or be "damned" by the afflicted company.[2]

In spite of these bitter experiences, such a method of gold seeking is becoming more and more common. The gold thirst forces man to a Danaïd labor [endless and pointless labor], which enables him to forget himself while he helps both himself and others. As a rule, self-control is attained only by harsh experience.

FAILING QUARTZ MILLS

The quartz mills' companies have also suffered similar misfortunes. When a quartz vein is found to be rich it is dug out with much effort and expense and the stone is crushed. The expensive machine is meanwhile brought to the place. However, not infrequently, one of its cast-iron parts is broken during the difficult transport over the mountains. Months pass until it can be replaced.

Experience has taught that the deeper one digs in the vein, the richer it becomes. Yet when the machine is finally set up and in order, the discovery is probably made that the quartz vein, not having been sufficiently prospected, contains no more gold in its depths. Hopes are disappointed and time and money expenditures are great. [...]

During my stay in the Mariposa Valley, an English company operated such a quartz mill near the tent town where a great quartz vein existed in the diluvium [areas scoured by glaciers]. The business was very profitable.

---

2 [Meyer's footnote:] Damning is most customary in America. The American damns everything that causes him the slightest annoyance. Among these Goddams-sons, one could learn to curse like Gresset's traveling parrot.

During the following year the greater portion of the mining population departed. The Indians returned to their native heath and destroyed and butchered all that seemed foreign or unaccustomed. The "fiery mountain eater," the quartz mill, was naturally not spared. Military intervention again freed the valley of its wild inhabitants and the discovery of new quartz veins and of the first California diamonds drew new adventurers to this rich mining valley.

SUDDEN DESOLATE QUIET

At the time of the rapid decrease in population, I also left Mariposa Valley. The clanking of many gold cradles was suddenly followed by desolate quiet. Only in hidden places was the oft repeated cry, "Sant' Antonio!" heard at sunrise and sunset from the lips of a superstitious Mexican who hoped by entreaty to obtain his fortune from this patron. And occasionally the shrill sound of the quartz mill was heard in the lonely valley and awakened the echoes of the mountains. The valley looked like a cemetery. Everywhere deep scars marked the place where this one or that had found or buried his fortune. On all sides piles of earth, like burial mounds, were visible on which broken or discarded tools formed crosses or monuments. The wild animals of the mountains approached and made night even more terrible in the deserted valley.

FLOWERS, BUTTERFLIES, AND MINERS

We visited several mining regions along the Towalumne [Tuolumne], Stanislaus, and Calaveras rivers. The scenery here is more idyllic than wild. The rapidly growing towns give a pleasant aspect to the valleys which, very dry in summer, are enclosed by low mountains. Regular alpen flower beds of flowers and ferns decorate the craggy mountain peaks over which the colorful butterfly flits, giving evidence of the wild climate in which it spends its joyous sweet days. The industrious miner crawls in and out of the dark shafts of his *cajote* mine [coyote mines were the traditional shaft mines] at the foot of these mountains, bringing his golden treasures to light. When seen from a distance these *cajote* mines, typical of only the southern mines, resemble animated bee hives.

CRYSTAL CAVES

These mountains on the Calaveras are famous for several enormous natural caves which can be entered through a narrow opening at the top. They contain many bones, some fossilized, of four-footed animals and are richly decorated with stalactites and crystals giving an appearance of a fairy crystal palace. The music made by the tapping of an iron hammer on these crystals, one to two feet long, also makes a magical impression on the visitor. At first it sounds like the jingle of bells, and then like the soft melancholy tones of an Aeolian harp. The miners have bestowed peculiar names on such caves and the ingenious Americans are quick to fit them with fables of mystery and stories of adventure. Names like Imperial Chamber, Devil's Cave, Witches' Den, and Baker's Oven have already been bestowed.[3]

The Imperial Chamber, not far from the Valcano Bar, resembles the German Kiefhäuser in which Barbarossa sleeps hidden, as the poet says "for as long as the old ravens will fly there." In the middle of the crystal room is a stalactite marble table on a grotesque pedestal and the enchanted Emperor, made of the same material, bends over it with his head propped on his hands and his beard grown through the table-top. Thus Nature furnishes the material for legends and not infrequently for later historical researches.

INDIANS PACIFIED

Before the discovery of the mines these valleys were inhabited by many bands of Indians who stubbornly opposed the entrance of the white people. Without military interference the Indians could hardly have been forced to relinquish their lovely territory. Later, the government of California, through her "Indian Commissioners," made treaties with the Indians of several of the mining regions. They were given lands, better habitations were built for them, and at regular intervals were provided with clothing, tools, and provisions. Thus most of the Indian

---

3 [Meyer's footnote:] The hellish adversary and assailer is supposed to have been in the Baker's Oven and a ridiculous anecdote is circulated about this retired hero. The Devil's Cave, so named because at times warm vapors and mephitic gases gather there, is supposed to resemble a baker's oven because at first its heat is bearable and then it gradually becomes hot. In the Baker's Oven overpowering vapors also frequently rise.

tribes became reconciled with the whites and gradually came to discard their more crude customs.

Even in the most wild and distant regions, like that of the *Scotsh* Valley in northern California, they are peaceful now and carry on agriculture and cattle raising in the territory apportioned them. The most effective work in the converting of the California Indians was that of first giving them some conception of civilization. That is the way by which the twenty-seven missions were able to exact obedience from 22,000 Indian proselytes and use them for agriculture. The Indians still remember those times of conversion, which must have been effective in spite of their return to a savage state, otherwise the present work of reconciliation in California would surely be more difficult.

ATTACKS ON EARLY MINERS

The first miners on the Towalumne [Tuolumne River] in late 1849 were Mr. Rippstein, a Swiss gentleman; Don Luis, a Frenchman; and Robinson, an American. The first told me the following:

> Driven by adverse fate, a desire to make new discoveries, and the restlessness of the first gold fever days, I went with my two friends, Don Luis and Robinson, to prospect the Stanislaus and the Towalumne. We were within several hours' travel of our destination when nightfall forced us to make camp in a thicket on a high plateau. This we did, not however without taking precautions as we had just discovered signs of Indians. The place which I thought suitable was a small grassy plot in the midst of the thicket over which towered a powerful oak at whose foot we spread our blankets to camp for the night.
>
> To our left, several paces distant, burnt the watch fire and opposite us grazed our only mule, bound with a lasso to a stake. Our mining type of supper was soon consumed and we drew straws to determine who should be guard for the first half of the night; this duty fell to Don Luis. Smoking his pipe the fearless Frenchman sat down cheerfully by the fire, stirring it energetically. He remained all ear while Robinson and I, wrapped in our blankets, talked softly for quite a while. Robinson finally fell asleep and I turned away from him. I longed to sleep also but that night it was impossible.

About an hour later, I had been lying tired, awake, and watchful, with my face turned toward the fire, I heard a soft sigh soon followed by devilish laughter. A band of ghosts seemed to float above me in the air and branches and mock at my astonishment. A shove woke Robinson and brought him to his knees. He was annoyed and accused me of dreaming. At the same moment our mule brayed anxiously and ran the full length of the lasso into the bushes. I rose and looked at Don Luis only to see him fall backwards with two arrows in his breast.

Another wild yell sounded on all sides, whizzing arrows flew past us and grinning Indian faces were visible everywhere in the bushes.—Never in my life have I seen such a terrible sight as those wildly grimacing faces in which the pale beams of firelight made visible fiendish smiles which showed only too plainly the bloody murder lust of the redskin band.—I took up my gun immediately and aimed at one of the wild beasts, but an arrow struck the finger with which I pressed the trigger and my shot went amiss. A scar remained as a life-long souvenir.

I looked around for my companions. Don Luis had disappeared. Robinson was on his knees, holding up in his left hand the woolen blanket as a shield and fighting desperately with the most daring of the enemy. He had thrust his hunting knife deep into the breast of his wild adversary. With a raging death cry the latter sank down and the other Indians—I could never understand whether because of fear or cowardice—retired from the place of battle for few minutes.

"Flee! Flee!" shouted Robinson to me, while he disappeared sideways into the thicket. With one jump I gained a protecting boulder behind which I cowered. The Warwhoop was repeated several times. Then the Indians saw that we had fled, and singing a song of victory they passed single file in a long row close by my hiding place. As soon as the last of the line passed me I jumped up and zig-zagged through the little wood until I reached its edge, no, until I fell down exhausted.

A cloudburst brought me back to consciousness. With renewed strength I hurried through the night and at sunrise arrived in a small valley in which I recognized several tents where I had been with

friends the day before. In one of these I woke three hours later from
violent delirium and learned from several miners who were standing
around me that they had picked me up in an unconscious condition.

My clothes were torn and hands and face were covered with
scratches and blood. Robinson arrived in the afternoon in a similar
pitiful condition. Not far from the mining valley we found Don
Luis drawing his last breath. He had crawled there on his hands
and knees and died in terrible pain from the arrow wounds. This
event was revenged. Eight days later the united miners fell upon
two Indian settlements on the Towalumne and burnt them. From
this time on no Towalumne Indian was seen again in the vicinity of
a white miner's dwelling.

HANGTOWN

Most of the American mining towns have been built on the sites of the
burnt-off Indian settlements. Sonora, James-Town, Mokolumne Hill
[Mokelumne Hill] and Hangtown [later renamed Placerville] are the
best known of those in the southern mines. They were built and named by

Placerville in 1849, which at that time was called Dry Diggins. It was in that
year that it also earned the name Hangtown.

chance, Hangtown being one of the most significant examples of this. It was named from a deed which was as horrible as the name is barbarous. *Nomen et omen.* [The name predicts its future.] The oak still stands in the center of the town which served as a gallows for several criminals who fell into the hands of the excited mob. This is Uncle Sam's fashion; wherever he goes he leaves pasted in his footsteps the names of his adventurous deeds.[4] The names Syracus or Bethlehem may be frequently found in the United States right next to a town with a barbarous name.

Approaching Stockton

Crossing a wide plain covered with oak forests one approaches the land town, Stockton. These forests resemble artificially planted avenues as there is no underbrush and the trees are placed at fairly regular intervals. No young trees grow because the acorns seem to be the favorite food of the prairie animals and are immediately devoured by them. The age of these forests must be greater than that of the animals and the enormous size of the trees and their thick branches show how ancient they must be. This is the resort of the coyotes or prairie wolves and of the owls (*Stryx cunicularia*), the colonists of the prairie, who live with them. These cave dwelling animals of the marmot class disturb the traveler and the farmer more by their horrible howling than by their rapacity. These wolves are not dangerous, but they are as sly as the wolves in sheep's clothing of my native land, who snap up every opportunity to attack the peaceful humans—a trait held in common with dogs.

We had bidden farewell to the southern mines and finally arrived in Stockton, my companion's destination. Stockton is the third largest city of the country and is the main center of communication between San Francisco and the southern mines.

The city was founded in 1849 by a German named [Captain Charles M.] Weber and grew rapidly in spite of its unhealthy marshy site. To the north it is connected with Sacramento City by a road and to the south with San Jose, which is famous for its rich quicksilver mines. These are

---

4 [Meyer's footnote:] Uncle Sam, used more frequently than "brother John" as a nickname for the United States and taken from the initial letters, US.

in the coast range and are probably the richest in the world. The metal is found under layers of red and yellow cinnabar. The richest Spanish cinnabar contains ten per cent; cinnabar of one per cent can be used effectively. The California red cinnabar contains thirty-eight to forty per cent quicksilver and the yellow fifteen to twenty per cent.

The mines of San Jose and the newer ones of Santa Barbara are mostly in the hands of English companies who reduce great masses of mineral every year in a simple, but not in a very economical way. In the first year of the gold discovery a pound of quicksilver cost six dollars, today it costs half a dollar. This price reduction made it much easier to obtain gold from the quartz rocks.

Nature has been very generous in California in furnishing the means with which man with only a little art can obtain more of her treasures. In the coast range enormous deposits of lead, asphalt, and sulphur are found near the lagoon, fifty to sixty miles long, north of Sacramento and about sixty miles distant from *San Bai*.

They have not been exploited but the value which they have for the country is evident. California, whose coat of arms should be the horn of plenty, has been destined by Nature to become a great land of industry. [. . .]

THE STREETS OF SAN FRANCISCO

The streets of San Francisco, like those of all modern American cities, are laid out at right angles. The long streets are laid out parallel with the meridian and form with the broad streets which lead to the harbor a 360-foot square which is crossed by a communicating street. Montgomery is the oldest and in every way the most important street. The prettiest brick and iron buildings and the most magnificent shops lie between it and Kearney Street. A single space of ground floor, twenty by thirty square feet, costs $100 to $300 rent a month. Thus, the cost of a building can be paid in five years from its rent.

It is also generally the same in other sections of the city. Building enterprises have become the most alluring and profitable speculations, especially since fire insurance has been inaugurated in the country. That is why San Francisco will rapidly increase in size and become indestructible.

It is needless to say that business must be tremendous when such an enormous rent has to be paid.

The year in California has only thirty days and each hour is worth a day for the capitalist as well as for the merchant. If you do not know how to make both clever and diligent use of your time, do not dare to come to the California emporium.

THEIR HEARTS ARE WHERE THEIR GOLD IS

The main seat of the gold exchange is in this Montgomery quarter; also the new California State mint is here. Most of the California gold may therefore be said to have its depot in this quarter before it leaves the country. This quarter thus forms the heart sacks (pericardium) of American trading companies whose shareholders, like all members of the business world, frequently do not have their hearts in their heart sacks but in their money sacks, and as in the mollusks, this seems to be in the rectum.

To leave San Francisco without visiting this place is like visiting Rome without seeing the Pope. Here Mammon is really exhibited in all his power, greatness, and glory. Piles of gold coins and gold dust lie here and there like grain in the granary and the smirking gold-changer stirs it up like the ant-eater burrowing in his food.

GETTING PROCESSED

The gold changer's busiest time is the last three hours of forenoon. The bees of the gold region, the busy miners, arrive then and bring their honey to the hive, which, like the Danaïdes' barrel, can never be filled and about which has been written: "Diamonds are not to decorate those who find them and gold is not for the gold washer."

The assayer works in the afternoon melting the gold like wax. When it reaches this state it serves as a sign that he should pour the fluid metal from the melting pot into the iron form. After he has refreshed himself to his heart's content at the sight of the glittering gold bar, he assays it, or tries it. Thus taken from his cleaning process he stamps it and sends it forth from his gold hearth into the world, never to see it again, as it will be broken up into coins which must roll because they are round like this odd world, in which after all golden folly plays the greatest role!

GOLD NEVER SLEEPS

The gold scales, which never rest, are very sensitive if they are not rusted at the balancing point, or if a magnet has not been placed at a well-calculated distance. The gold dust is constantly sieved and separated; the last grain of quartz or magnetic iron sand is blown from it or cleaned out, during which process not even color of the gold can disappear from the office. This seems an impossibility when one sees the extract in the shop bin which the gold melter or assayer in every banker's service must weekly reduce.[5]

BACK IN THE DAYS OF GOLD DUST

California gold was formerly put on the market as gold dust or in its natural form. Now, however, it rarely leaves its home unmelted and without having its value chemically analyzed and calculated. Formerly the value was determined by weighing. Although these are still fat times for the gold buyer they are different from what they were.

"Then and now!" he sighs, and scolds about the newcomers in the gold country who brought all kinds of chemical apparatus and sensitive physical instruments to serve as aids to justice. At first the ignorant miner made his scales himself out of wood and used gold coins for weights, or like the Mexican, determined the sum of gold in a measured quill and used this for paying. Then, when he came to the shopkeeper, he actually had to

---

5 [Meyer's footnote:] It is well known that the main parts of California gold—silver and gold—are to each other as the parts of water—oxygen and hydrogen—namely 11.1:88.9. In the different kinds of gold there are several variations of this ratio, which the practiced assayer or banker can practically recognize in the shade of color of the gold. This approximate calculation of carats is the customary procedure in gold buying of all California bankers and not a little profit is added to the business in which only assayed gold is put up for sale.

In a similar manner additional percentages are obtained in the purchase of larger quartz or stone pieces, in which the seller is content to have the gold content hastily calculated according to the formula:

$$x = a(c-b)/c(a-b)\ w$$
whereby a the specific weight of the gold (=19)
b the specific weight of the stone (=2.6)
c the specific weight of the entire mass, and
w the absolute weight of it.
the absolute weight of the stone controls this or:
$$y = .b(a-c)/c(a-b)\ w$$

Workers in the basement of the San Francisco Mint with gold ingots in 1873

find the weight of his purchases in gold or pay for them with spoonfuls of gold dust. Sometimes, to satisfy his needs, he would be handed a gold measure, scaled in ounces, and occasionally, especially when it was a lovely hand that had served him, he was supposed to fill the measure with as much gold as there had been liquid in it.

The Chinese displaced this primitive gold barter, bringing the first metal scales, which still prove the most useful.

PRIVATE COINS

Some gold merchants then melted gold into *pipedas* [a piece or chunk] weighing an ounce and introduced these in trade. They were followed by the manufacturer of the first private coins. These will be remembered forever. Two years after this coin factory was started the proprietors were called to justice and sentenced for the crime of mixing metals in the coin. It was rumored that they knew how to make gold, an ancient art which the chemist, Tifferau, had recently brought from the gold country and laid before the French Academy of Science. The names Balduin and Moffat

Washing blanks before sending them to the Adjusting Room at the San Francisco Mint in 1873

are still written in black ink in the Great California ledger of Crimes and Criminals, which Nemesis will take to hand at the end of the world.

In the summer of 1851 the people of California first found power and means to make a State coin and to pass laws for its use, and from this time on there was order in the gold quarter of the young harbor city.

PERSONALITIES OF MINING REGIONS

Every mining region has its own peculiar population and activity, which is determined by the kind and arrangement of the mines. This difference is shown between places located on the upper and lower parts of the rivers. The southern fork of the American river now resembles the valley of a productive region of Old England, but only a few miles from here, turning away into the mountains, one recognizes at first glance the uncertain life of adventure. A systematic, technical procedure will spread only gradually to this region.

Where Weber Creek flows into the South Fork there are several regular gold fields which look as if they had been watered and plowed. The water of the brook has been turned into many small ditches across the floor of the valley and several hundred miners work on it with the Long-Tom. The town of Salmon Fall here will have a wonderful future. Two bridges, very well built and in good taste, already span the river, and a good road leads to the abandoned mining town, Pilot Hill, in the northern part of the Eldorado region.

THE DEATH OF PILOT HILL

Pilot Hill presents one of the most characteristic pictures of feverish mining life. In the summer of 1850 several sailors first discovered gold there, in the dark ravines, and at the bends of the main valley. Platinum was found in pieces as large as an ounce but ignorant miners, thinking it to be another metal of no value, threw it away. Thus one of these men once presented me with a pretty specimen of it. Soon a town of about thirty houses was built and it was thought that by the end of the year it would double in size. Three months later the region was again wilderness. Not a soul was to be found in the little town built on earth which contains gold. Its single street had been transformed into a bubbling brook and every house was undermined and almost caving in. It looked as if the Angel of Death had taken up his abode there.

Riding through this place in the twilight with a friend, I involuntarily pressed my spurs into my horse's loins and was unable to rid myself of its depressing influence until we arrived at cheerful Salmon Fall.

BULL AND BEAR FIGHTS

Although all efforts and attention in Sacramento City are directed towards earning and profit, after working hours the people devote themselves in every possible way to pleasure and recreation. The inhabitants of the city seem more inclined to pleasures which take them out of doors than to home entertainment. Horse racing, and bull and bear fights seem the most popular amusements.

Bull fighting is a Spanish entertainment; a Spanish celebration with which man stimulates animal lust and animal rage to its highest degree until a bloody victim falls to the battle ground amidst the barbarous jubilation of the crowd. Among these people, however, are some in whom sympathetic feeling, common to all humans, is intensified to complete exhaustion at sight of the suffering and horror. The Spanish-American occupation of the gold country is not solely responsible for the waking of this passionate desire for bull fighting, but an attempt is made to satisfy this in fights which not only have their original Spanish character but also combine an American feature. The rage of the bull is not stimulated here by deception, spear, or fireworks, but by a bear who, whether he likes it or not, has been honored with the position of Matador and chained to the front foot of the bull.

The first of these bull fights took place in the summer of 1851 in Sacramento City. At this time I was an eyewitness of one, the preparations of which foretold something extraordinary. A long grandstand was built at the mile-long race track in Brighton, six miles from the city. The entrance price was $2.50 and enormous placards on every street corner announced for weeks ahead the glorious fight between the American gray bear "General Scott" and the Mexican bull "Sant' Anna." [*Note:* The animals were named after General Winfield Scott and General Antonio Lopez de Santa Anna—the great US and Mexican generals of the Mexican-American War.]

On the night before the celebration the managers went out to rivet an iron chain on to the right rear paw of the bear, who was locked in a huge wagon cage made of oak and iron bars. First, several lassos were thrown through the iron bars and bound around his limbs and neck. With these he was pulled to the bottom of the cage by horse power and held fast there. This was accomplished in a short time. But the grizzly's jaws opened raging and resembling a fiery abyss into which the clever tamers sunk pieces of boards and wood from time to time, an excellent measure, for while the grizzly sharpened his teeth on the wood and vented his wrath on it he had no time to remember the strange things occurring to his feet, where an iron band with ring and chain was being fastened to his ankle joint.

"Give him lumber!" cried those engaged in this when the tortured creature rebelled or interfered with the work, and a new supply of boards reached his jaws with the desired results. The gray bear revenged himself on them with the same rage as the American general, General Scott, is supposed to have been revenged on his Mexican enemies. General Scott tore them all into splinters, the boards I mean, and could hardly be subdued.

By the time the work was finished the bear's jaws were sore, filled with wood splinters and bloody foam. After this terrifying, torturous ordeal he received an ox, weighing fifteen pounds, for his supper. Scott devoured it in a moment and would have gladly let them rivet on another chain for a second ration but he received no more as his hunger for meat was to be satisfied by his opponent, Sant' Anna. To the strains of pompous Yankee music and accompanied by a crowd of spectators Scott finally proceeded to the battle field.

A Fierce Contest

It was a burning hot afternoon and the arena was shaded only by some oak trees under which the mounted spectators had gathered, while most of the crowd was in the grandstand or pushing against the balustrade of the battle field. The wild bull was a large stately brown animal, young and fat, broad-browed and with sharp horns. Several bold Americans rode close by the bull and as if he were really the hated Mexican enemy Sant' Anna himself, they struck him with their hide lassos with such force that we could hear the slap. Sant' Anna, however, had soon pushed a rider from his saddle and then with his horns ripped open the belly of a beautiful horse.

Several trumpets blew a signal and quiet and order reigned in the arena. The bull was lassoed and laid on his back in front of the trap-door of the bear cage, the chains of the two opposing, hostile elements were soon connected and the trap-door raised. The bull, freed of his lassos, lay quietly for about a second, until the bear, bellowing terribly, fell on his enemy with all his fourteen cwt. [centum weight, or 100 pounds]. Sant' Anna did not waste much time in surprise but, snorting and horning, suddenly swung himself up from under his living burden. A thick cloud of dust and the peculiar voices of the animals, which sounded like thunder breaking through a cloud, gave evidence of the great struggle. Above this noise could be heard the "Carajo el Torre!" of several Mexicans who looked from the top of a tree into the midst of the cloud of dust and who feared the superiority of the American fighter. The bull stood paralyzed and the bear hung to his head like a living padlock. The bear squeezed the bull in his arms with all his strength, sunk his claws deep behind his ears and buried the bull's nose in his bloodthirsty jaws while he braced his rear legs on the ground, clawing into it with them. It seemed as if he either wanted to blow out the breath of his opponent or suck his life out. That was a bear kiss!

The bull emitted such a moan of pain at this that I gritted my teeth and joined him with a sigh. He shook his head several times, waved his tail high above his hips and fell as he was unable to carry out his plan of throwing the bear on his back by turning a somersault over him. That was clever; by this manoeuver the bear failed to obtain the fresh bull tongue for which he probably had slyly aimed and with which he could have devoured his enemy's life. The crowd paid him the tribute of ringing applause.

Now, however, Sant' Anna became aggressive. At the full length of the chain, a distance of about twelve feet, he stood facing the bear, foaming with rage and waving his tail about in eagerness for battle. The bear sat down comfortably as if he wished to revel in the anger of his enemy or mockingly say to him "No fair trying to frighten me."

The bull lowered his dangerous head and as if driven by steam threw himself on the bear's breast. The latter turned completely over twice and just when about to take his revenge, he flew up again like a rubber ball and fell to the ground like a full sack of flour. That was a bad fall. But uninjured, the grizzly rose to his full height and swung his paw to strike the bull a rough blow. The bull deftly side-stepped and now thrust his horns into the bear's fur. No blood flowed but the bear, overcome by a panic of fear, took to flight. The chain broke and in the wink of an eye old Bruin was sitting up in the nearest oak tree.

How amusing! You should have seen the speed with which those jackanapes spectators left their reserved seats. Some of them simply let themselves fall straight down while others slid down from the outer branches. It looked as if old Bruin had jumped into a pond and driven out all the frogs.

Up to now the struggle had been entertaining and not at all revolting even for the greatest enemy of cruelty to animals but, alas, its finish was not less painful and disgusting than the animal torture of bull fights in Spain and South America in which, one after the other, a selected group of the most beautiful bulls must bleed to death before the eyes of the crowd.

The bear was skillfully lassoed by a young vaquero and soon thereafter the fugitive fell from the tree, eighteen feet high, to the ground. It seemed as if only a cat had fallen because he immediately rushed after the vaquero's horse to destroy it. But before he had gone far a second lasso fell around his hind legs and several others were about his fat body, holding him in a net like a powerful spider. In a short time and with little trouble the bull and bear were again chained together.

Again several attacks were made by each whereby, however, the bull gained the advantage every time. Again he threw the grizzly high into the air, threatening to crush him against an oak trunk, but the bear remained uninjured.

I never thought that a Mexican bull possessed so much strength; I knew that a well-developed bull can carry five cwt. and can pull about eighteen but no vaquero had ever told me that he could throw fourteen cwt. high in the air with his horns. Probably the living elasticity of the bear and the stormy onrush of the bull were essential aids to this.

The bear soon showed signs of fatigue and became cowardly. The crowd, however, clamored for a decision and two mounted vaqueros forced him to fight by dragging him towards the bull on a lasso which they had thrown over him from behind and then held between their horses. The bull welcomed him with a hard head butt so that the feared General Scott soon lost all his power of sight and sound.

It was pathetic to see the poor animal, completely exhausted, forced by men to fight while dying just to decide their bets. The sight became unbearable. I withdrew and mounting my horse disappeared towards the city in the growing darkness of nightfall.

DEGRADATION OF THE FIGHTS

Several such bull fights were staged in Sacramento City. Rarely, however, was the bear the victor. The bull was soon thought to be a too powerful opponent for the king of the California forests and he was supplanted by a . . . donkey. A California longear, or several of these, were brought into the arena with the bear, and it was horrible to see the bear quench his bloodthirstiness on these weak creatures. Of course some rough kicks were directed at the bear's head but sometimes the angry bear bit the donkey's leg off or bit his head off.

Frequently the enraged bear was then put in a well-closed arena in which were loosed many of the gray rats[6] which infest California cities, who crawling under his fur, enraged him the more. The affair passed through all stages, from the heroic to the lowest, and the Yankees mocked the dignity of the bear as they do that of a king.

When the American desire for novelty and interest could find no more satisfaction in bear fights they were completely discontinued. "Tiempe passate!" now sighs the Mexican when he remembers the first California bull fights.

------

6 [Meyer's footnote:] Sacramento City gives a most excellent example of the quick increase of these rats when circumstances favorable to their multiplication are not lacking as: wooden houses, piled up badly preserved victuals, and dirty courtyards and streets. In 1847 no inhabitants of Sacramento had seen a single rat in the city. A year later the first were brought by ship and seen in Sutter's Fort. In the summer of 1851, after Sacramento City was built, I tried to calculate the approximate number of rats in the city. Every night at the same hour I strode through the three main streets, each about one-third of a mile long, and the ten other streets, and counted the rats fleeing before my footsteps. There were about 400 in each of the first three and 180 in each of the last ten. Assuming, which is not an exaggeration, that six times as many rats were in the thirty houses, or blocks of houses, enclosed by these streets, and that there were seventy per cent young in the nests, we obtain the sum of 30,600 rats, that is, a ratio of 1:1 to the inhabitants of Sacramento City. Calculating from another angle, these rats would have furnished two days' nourishment for the 3,000 Chinese inhabitants of Sacramento as they really did more to destroy the creatures than did poison and cats. Cats do not seem to get along very well where there is a superfluity of food—a fact which is also often true in human society. The ratio of rats to citizens in other California cities is the same and this repulsive, bestial creature can be said to be the most faithful companion of a starting civilization.

Living Dead in Califor-nee

Alonzo Delano

Alonzo Delano's narrative in this book began with his experiences crossing plains on the overland route to California. In the following selections, from his book *Life on the Plains and Among the Diggings,* he describes life at the diggings.

TO THE GOLD FIELDS

On reaching the Yuba [River], we could learn nothing of McNeil. We had thought, when parting, of taking our load to Redding's diggings, above Lawson's [Lassen's?], but that would be to depend on his report from the Yuba; in our course up to Bear River, we received from miners very favorable accounts from the Feather River mines, not only of the diggings, but for the sale of provisions, and we decided to go there, hoping that McNeil would overtake us, or follow us there.

As Mr. Pope did not feel at liberty to take his cattle further, he concluded to leave them with a Mr. Barham, (who crossed the plains with us, and who was temporarily stopping on the Yuba,) and then go himself in search of McNeil, up the Yuba. On finding him, he would follow us to Bidwell's bar. But we never met again; and it gives me pleasure to attest to his real worth and honesty, and kindness of heart.

Proceeding the next day to Charlie's Ranch, (familiarly known as "Old Charlie,") the route here led off the road which we had previously traveled, and the next morning we started for the mountains, after leaving a note for McNeil, which we subsequently learned he never received. It was fifteen miles across the plain to the first water, within the first gorge of the mountains. A portion of the distance we found broken by dry sloughs, which were impassable in the rainy season, but were now narrow and deep sluices, somewhat troublesome to cross.

We halted for the night at a hole where there was a little water, which was surrounded by weary travelers, and which strongly reminded me of the plains. As we proceeded in the morning, the hills became higher and more abrupt, yet not difficult, and in the afternoon we reached the hill immediately above Bidwell's bar, and descended a mile by a steep and sometimes sideling path to the lower end of the bar, known as Dawly-town, named after a young merchant who first opened a store on that point about two months before.

DIGGING AND SICKNESS

It was on the 10th of October when we reached this place of our destination, and, pitching our tent, opened a store, after sending our cattle back to a small valley where there was a little grass, trusting to luck for finding them again when we should need them.

The river was a rapid, mountain stream, flowing through deep cañons and gorges more than a thousand feet high on each side sparsely covered with oaks and pines. In this vicinity more than a thousand men were at work, with pans and cradles, who were making, variously, from five to fifty dollars per day. The bed and banks of the stream were composed of slate rock, and the gold was found in the dirt and crevices.

On the bar the gravel was removed to the depth of from three to six feet, and the dirt in the immediate proximity to the bed rock was washed, and generally yielded well. The labor was quite equal to that of digging canals and wells, and the quantity of gold looked small for the large amount of dirt required to be handled. It had been our original intention that one of us should work at mining while the other attended the store, but I was soon visited by my old companions, chill and fever, and had scarcely recovered when Pomeroy was taken with fever. Thus instead of digging, it became necessary for one to take care of the other. There was much sickness among the miners, especially those who had recently arrived in the country, and many lay ill with scurvy, fevers and flux [diarrhea or dysentery], without the shelter of a tent, and our first advent in the mines presented no agreeable aspect.

We had scarcely arrived an hour before an application was made for my buffalo skin and blanket, from two poor fellows who lay ill of fever under a tree, in a rain without covering, exposed to the cold night air, destitute of the comforts of life, which their debilitated condition so much required. I cheerfully complied with their request, but it availed little, for in a few days they both expired. In Dawly's store, nearly adjoining ours, lay a poor fellow in the last stages of consumption and flux, which he had contracted in the mines—delirious with disease, raving and tossing in his agony—who, after a few days of suffering, expired. He had accumulated five thousand dollars, the result of a year's hard labor and privation, which he had buried, and never disclosed its place of concealment, so that it neither benefitted him or anyone else. He had no family.

At the end of two weeks we found our profits to be about $600, with about two hundred dollars remaining on hand, and I made preparations for going to the city to replenish our stock.

We spent three days in hunting our cattle, which I fortunately found just as we had given up all hope of seeing them again; and after many little vexatious delays, I finally started on the 25th for Sacramento, with a very different feeling from that with which I had entered it a short time before, for now I had a capital of my own to commence on. With no adventure worth relating, I reached the city in four days and a half, and commenced laying in my stock.

Cattle Thieves

When the high water in the spring of 1850 arrested the progress of our works, and our two companies temporarily separated, I learned that cattle stealing had become common in the valley. During the rainy season, the miners who owned teams were obliged to drive their cattle to the valley, where there was grass; for none grew on the mountains. They were left there from necessity, without care, till spring. I frequently met many who had lost all their cattle—unprincipled men having seized and driven off whole teams, and either sold them, or used them to haul loads to the mines after the roads became passable.

One day a teamster drove a wagon into our settlement at Dawlytown, when Mr. Billinghurst recognized one of his own oxen in the team. As he had an abundance of proof at hand, the fellow was glad to compromise the matter by paying him a hundred dollars and taking the ox. Scarcely had the thief gone twenty yards before another yoke was claimed by a miner; and before he left the diggings his cattle were all claimed and taken by their owners. The fellow had made an unfortunate mistake, and had driven his load into the very settlement where his cattle belonged.

This wholesale stealing excited much surprise among us, for the almost unheard-of honesty of Californians, as it had been the previous fall, was a subject of general remark. But a change seemed coming "o'er the spirit of *their* dream," for soon we began to receive accounts of robberies beyond anything we had ever heard. In this state of things I deemed it advisable to look after my own cattle; and taking my blankets and provisions on my back, I set out for the valley.

NEW TOWN MANIA

Twenty-five miles brought me to the meadow land, and I was fortunate enough to find three out of four; but the fourth was lost. Being unable to continue mining and have a care over my cattle at the same time, I drove them to Marysville and sold them. And here I met with a surprise.

When I forded the Yuba, in September previous, there stood then but two low adobe houses, known as Nye's Ranch, but early in the following winter a town had been laid out, which, in this short space of time, had grown to over a thousand inhabitants, with a large number of hotels, stores, groceries, bakeries, and (what soon became a marked feature in California) gambling-houses. Steamboats were daily arriving and departing, which seemed strange, for it had been a matter of doubt the previous fall as to Feather River being navigable for craft larger than whale boats.

On this river, a mile from Marysville, Yuba City had sprung into existence, with a population of five hundred inhabitants; and two miles below, the town of Eliza had been laid out, and buildings were rapidly going up. The two latter places, however, were eventually swallowed up by the rapid growth of Marysville, which has become a beautiful city, while the others, at the moment of writing this, have dwindled into nothing, and are nearly deserted. Speculation in towns and lots was rife; and on every hand was heard "Lots for sale"—"New towns laid out"—which looked as well on paper as if they were already peopled.

There seemed to be a speculative mania spreading over the land, and scores of new towns were heard of which were never known, only through the puffs of newspapers, the stakes which marked the size of lots, and the nicely drawn plat of the surveyor. Not a single town was laid out on land where the title was indisputable; and as might be expected, litigations were frequent. Squatting followed, which resulted, in many cases, in riot and bloodshed. And to this moment, when the State contains probably over three hundred thousand souls, three years from the first emigration, claims are contested, and there is a vagueness and uncertainty in the possession of lands in the great valley, and in San Francisco, which renders the purchase of landed property uncertain, and the risk so great that prudent men hesitate to invest large sums.

Before the conquest, many of the old Californians had either taken possession of lands without authority, or held grants under revolutionary governors, which were not acknowledged by the supreme government of Mexico; and in some cases, where these grants were given by an acknowledged Mexican Governor, the proprietor had neglected to have them confirmed by the parent government; and in others, if this was done, they had neglected to comply with the requisitions of the grant—so that, where there were so many loop-holes, some shots of contention would enter.

Still, some of the claims were undoubtedly good, and will be acknowledged by the government of the United States, while squatters, in many cases, will very likely be able to hold the land they have taken up, after it has been decided that such lands belong to our government by the Commission instituted to examine the merits of claims, and we may look forward to the time when litigation and uncertainty on the subject shall cease, and consequent happiness and thrifty progress of the people of California ensue.

THE RAPID EXPANSION OF SACRAMENTO CITY

Before returning to the mines, I visited Sacramento, and the improvements not only in the city, but in the country around, which a few months had produced, astonished me. Along the road hotels and dwellings had been erected at convenient distances; and where we had traveled the previous fall without seeing a human habitation, was now the abode of civilized man.

At Nichols' Ranch, near the mouth of Bear River, where then but a single adobe house stood, a town had been laid out, and buildings were going rapidly up, (but this, however, eventually declined) and under the bank, in the river, a large brig was moored, which had doubled Cape Horn. Vernon and Frémont, at the mouth of Feather River, appeared flourishing, but subsequently shared the uncertain fate of new towns in a new country.

All these may revive, as the country advances in population, and its agricultural resources are properly developed. Sacramento City had become a city indeed. Substantial wooden buildings had taken the place of the cloth tents and frail tenements of the previous November, and, although it had been recently submerged by an unprecedented flood, which occasioned a

Sacramento's El Dorado Saloon in 1852, with intense attention paid to the monte table. Simply put, in monte, two cards are laid face up on the table and the player bets on them, or four cards are laid out and the player chooses two of them. The dealer then lays out a third card, called the "gate." If either of the two cards are the same suit as the gate, the player wins. If not, then the player loses.

great destruction of property, and which ruined hundreds of its citizens, it exhibited a scene of busy life and enterprise, peculiarly characteristic of the Anglo-Saxon race by whom it was peopled.

An immense business was doing with miners in furnishing supplies; the river was lined with ships, the streets were thronged with drays, teams, and busy pedestrians; the stores were large, and well filled with merchandise; and even Aladdin could not have been more surprised at the power of his wonderful lamp than I was at the mighty change which less than twelve months had wrought, since the first cloth tent had now grown into a large and flourishing city.

I regret to say that gambling formed a prominent part in the business of the city; and there appeared an infatuation, if not unprecedented, certainly not excelled in the annals of mankind. Long halls had been erected, which were splendidly lighted, and beautifully decorated with rich pictures, having magnificent bars where liquors and various refreshments were exhibited, to tempt a depraved appetite; and along the centre and sides of the room tables were arranged, where piles of money were seductively laid out to tempt the cupidity of the unexperienced. And to crown all, on raised forms, or finely-wrought galleries, bands of music "discoursed harmonious sounds" to attract a crowd. These places of resort were daily and nightly thronged with men of all ages and conditions in life, eager to tempt the fickle goddess of Fortune, too often to their own rum. Large sums were freely staked, and often changed hands, and the hard earnings of the infatuated miner, which he had been months in accumulating by incessant toll and wearying hardships, frequently passed from his well-filled purse to swell the gambler's bank that was spread seductively before him.

A day or two previous to my arrival, I was told that a young man, having started for home, came to the city from the mines with nineteen thousand dollars. On his arrival he deposited sixteen thousand with a friend, and with the rest went into one of these splendid hells, and commenced betting at monte. He soon lost this, and under the excitement which it occasioned, he drew the sixteen thousand from his friend, notwithstanding all remonstrance, and determined to retrieve his luck. He returned to the table, and continued playing till he had lost every farthing, when, instead of making his friends happy, by returning to their embrace with a competence, he was compelled to return to toil and privation in the mines.

Another, with fifteen hundred dollars, began playing, with the avowed attention of breaking the bank; but the result was, as might have been anticipated, the gambler won every dollar in a short time. With the utmost coolness the poor fool observed to the banker, "You have won all my money—give me an ounce to get back to the mines with." Without saying a word, the gambler handed him back sixteen dollars, and the victim returned to his toil again.

Even boys of twelve and sixteen years of age were sometimes seen betting. But little else could be expected, from the extent of the demoralizing influences thus set before them.

In passing down to Sacramento through some of the mining settlements, I could not but observe the march of refinement which was going on, or, more properly speaking, the comforts which were introduced. Crockery and table-cloths appeared on the tables of the hotels along the road; glass tumblers, and even wine glasses, were used; berths, similar to those on steamboats, were made around the rooms, and occasionally spare blankets could be found, so that on the principal thoroughfares it was no longer necessary to sleep on the ground, nor carry one's own plate, knife, and tin cup; and as early as July 1850, a line of stages commenced running from Sacramento to Marysville, which the following year became a very important and well-regulated route, from which, in 1851, lines diverged to various points in the mines.

THE GREAT FLOOD

During the winter of 1849 and '50, one of the greatest floods occurred which had ever been known in the valley of the Sacramento. From the top of a high hill on the left bank of Feather River, not far from the Table Mountain, where I could command an extensive view of the valley, I estimated that one-third of the land was overflowed. Hundreds of cattle, horses, and mules were drowned, being carried down by the rapidity of the current in their attempt to reach higher ground; and Sacramento City, then being without its levee, was almost entirely submerged. A small steamboat actually [ran] up its principal streets, and discharged its freight on the steps of one of the principal stores (Starr, Bensley & Co.'s). But at that time the limits of the city were not more than a third equal to its present size [in 1852]. A vast amount of property was destroyed, and many of its lighter buildings washed away.

The number of dead carcasses of animals, which floated down and lodged as the waters retired, produced a most loathsome effluvia, and it was the work of several days to rid the city of their putrid remains. All intercourse with the mines was suspended, and although it was predicted that the prosperity of the city was ruined, the substantial improvements which followed soon showed that the ardor and energy of its people could not be checked, even by an extraordinary catastrophe.

From Drawing to Town Speculation

By the 29th of March [1850] I was once more at Dawlytown, but as the water still continued too high for mining operations, I resolved to go to Marysville, and endeavor to get into some business which would at least afford me the means of living.

Of all the money I had received, but thirty-two dollars remained— enough to sustain me one week, as the price of board then ranged. A man may be placed in circumstances where all the ingenuity he is possessed of may be called forth, and this was emphatically my case. In vulgar parlance, I was *strapped,* and it was necessary that I should do something to raise the *quid pro quo.*

Having a little skill in drawing, I took some crayons and drawing paper, and a few days saw me installed in town as a miniature painter, doing a thriving business. For three weeks I plied my pencil in copying the outre phiz [the unconventional faces] and forms of the long-bearded miners, at an ounce a head, when I found myself the wealthy recipient of four hundred dollars; but wishing to make money a little faster, I played the speculator, purchased paper town lots, and lost nearly half of my earnings in the operation! It was, however, at this period that one of the most interesting events of my California life began.

The rage for town speculations was still rife, when a friend proposed that we should make a claim twenty miles above Marysville, on Feather

River, lay out a town, and get rich by selling the lots. We proceeded accordingly, made our claim, laid off the lots, and in a few days I was installed the patroon of our new village, with a fine stock of goods, cheap enough, if customers could only be coaxed to that really beautiful, but isolated spot. But that was a difficulty not easily overcome. My friend, by adverse circumstances, was finally compelled to give up the speculation, and I called my town an addition to one which my nearest and only neighbor, Captain Yates, had laid out.

INDEPENDENCE BAR

Nelson's Creek rises about fifteen miles above Independence, near the base of the main ridge of the Sierra Nevada, and like nearly all the streams in that high region, flows through a deep gorge till it disembogues into the Middle Fork of the Feather river, about sixty miles in a direct line from where the latter unites with the main or North Fork. Independence Bar was first located in June 1850. Enormous hills rise on each side, exhibiting a highly volcanic appearance, based upon a talcous slate formation, and the country is highly auriferous. In the deep dell of the bar, the sun does not make his appearance above the mountains till eight o'clock in the morning, and disappeared behind the western hills a little after four in the afternoon.

Although the nights are cold—the ice frequently forming in our buckets—the days are hot, and oppressive. Scarcely a night passed in which we did not hear rocks rolling from the hills into the gulf, which were loosened from their beds by the action of frost, rain, and sun; and egress and ingress was over steep hills by means of zigzag paths, difficult, and often dangerous.

As a description of mountain life may not be wholly uninteresting, and as it possesses a general character in these isolated wilds, I shall give a brief description of some of the occurrences which transpired there. And again I beg the reader to remember that my object is to exhibit the struggles that all miners first undergo, at new points, through the whole length and breadth of California, though frequently diversified in their character.

From the mouth of Nelson's Creek to its source, men were at work in digging. Sometimes the stream was turned from its bed, and the channel worked; in other places, wing dams were thrown out, and the bed partially worked; while in some, the banks only were dug. Some of these, as is the case everywhere in the mines, paid well, some, fair wages, while many were failures.

SKIN AND BONES

One evening, while waiting for my second supply of goods, I strolled by a deserted camp. I was attracted to the ruins of a shanty by observing the effigy of a man standing upright in an old, torn shirt, a pair of ragged pantaloons, and boots which looked as if they had been clambering over rocks since they were made—in short, the image represented a lean, meagre, worn-out, and woe-begone miner, such as might daily be seen at almost every point in the upper mines. On the shirt was inscribed, in a good business hand, "My claim failed—will you pay the taxes?" (an allusion to the tax on foreigners). Appended to the figure was a paper, bearing the following words: "Californians—Oh, Californians, look at me! once fat and saucy as a privateersman, but now—look ye—a miserable skeleton. In a word, I am a used up man. Never mind, I can sing, notwithstanding,

> *O California! this is the land for me;*
> *A pick and shovel, and lots of bones!*
> *Who would not come the sight to see,—*
> *The golden land of dross and stones.*
> *O Susannah, don't you cry for me,*
> *I'm living dead in Califor-nee."*

Ludicrous as it may appear, it was a truthful commentary on the efforts of hundreds of poor fellows in the "golden land." This company had penetrated the mountain snows with infinite labor, in the early part of the season, enduring hardships of no ordinary character—had patiently toiled for weeks, living on the coarsest fare; had spent time and money in building a dam and digging a race through rocks to drain off the water; endured wet and cold, in the chilling atmosphere of the country, and when the last stone was turned, at the very close of all this labor, they did not find a single cent to reward them for their toil and privations, and what was still more aggravating, a small, wing dam, on the very claim below them, yielded several thousand dollars. Having paid out their money, and lost their labor, they were compelled to abandon the claim, and search for other diggings, where the result might be precisely the same. The only wonder is that the poor fellows could have courage enough to sing at all.

GAMBLING IT ALL AWAY

The population of Independence represented almost every State in the Union, while France, England, Ireland, Germany, and even Bohemia, had their delegates. As soon as breakfast was dispatched, all hands were engaged in digging and washing gold in the banks, or in the bed of the stream. When evening came, large fires were built, around which the miners congregated, some engrossed with thoughts of home and friends, some to talk of new discoveries and richer diggings somewhere else; or, sometimes a subject of debate was started, and the evening was whiled away in pleasant, and often instructive, discussion, while many, for whom this kind of recreation had not excitement enough, resorted to dealing monte, on a small scale, thus either exciting or keeping up a passion for play. Some weeks were passed in this way under the clear blue sky of the mountains, and many had made respectable piles.

I highly enjoyed the wild scenery, and, quite as well, the wild life we were leading, for there were many accomplished and intelligent men; and a subject for amusement or debate was rarely wanting. As for ceremony or dress, it gave us no trouble: we were all alike. Shaving was voted a bore; the air holes in our pants were *not* "few and far between," and our toes were as often out "prospecting" from the ends of our boots as any way, and two weeks before my last supplies arrived I was barefoot, having completely worn out my shoes. At length a monte dealer arrived, with a respectable bank.

A change had been gradually coming over many of our people, and for three or four days several industrious men had commenced drinking, and after the monte bank was set up, it seemed as if the long smothered fire burst forth into a flame. Labor, with few exceptions, seemed suspended, and a great many miners spent their time in riot and debauchery. Some scarcely ate their meals, some would not go to their cabins, but building large fires, would lay down, exposed to the frost; and one night, in the rain. Even after the monte dealer had cleared nearly all out who would play, the game was kept up by the miners themselves in a small way, till the fragments of their purses were exhausted.

There were two companies at work near me, who, when I first went there, were taking out daily in each company from one hundred to one hundred and fifty dollars. This they continued to do for more than two weeks, when it seemed as if the gold blistered their fingers, and they began a career of drinking and gambling until it was gone. Instead of going to work on their claims again, they were seized with the prospecting mania, so common at that time among miners, and after spending some days in looking for other diggings, in snow and rain, finally went to the valley— many not having money enough to pay small bills against them.

Among the miners was one who lost nine hundred dollars, another, eight hundred—their whole summer's work—and went oft poor and penniless. The monte dealer, who, in his way was a gentleman, and honorable according to the notions of that class of men, won in two nights three thousand dollars! When he had collected his taxes on our bar, he went to Onion Valley, six miles distant, and lost in one night four thousand, exemplifying the fact that a gambler may be rich to-day, and a beggar to-morrow.

Gambling at that period was more prevalent in the mines than it is now; and it is but justice to say that very many men did not play at all, nor incline to dissipation; and that at this time (1852), a great reformation has taken place throughout the mines, although gambling is carried on to some extent.

ROBBERY AND MURDERS

We were startled one morning with the report that two men had been murdered a short distance above us. On repairing to the spot, a ghastly spectacle presented itself: Two men, having their heads cut open with a hatchet, lay in the creek, perfectly dead. The circumstances were these: Three men from near Vergennes, Vermont, named Ward, Lawrence, and Luther, lay in a tent on the bank of the creek, at the foot of a high, steep hill. Their bed was a flat rock, and their feet reached within a few inches of the water. As they all lay asleep, about ten o'clock at night, Ward was suddenly awakened by a noise; when looking up, he saw a man standing over him with a hatchet, in the act of striking. Instantly he sprang to his feet, and encountered another man, who made at him, but he turned and ran out at the lower end of the tent, and clambering over a pile of rocks, escaped, and continued his flight in the dark towards a cabin about forty rods distant, shouting "murder!"

Reaching the cabin the inmates turned out as soon as Ward was able to give a distinct relation of the affair; and on reaching the scene of slaughter, they found that the assassins, after completing their work of death, had robbed their victims of about four hundred dollars each, and then had thrown their bodies into the creek and escaped. As the parties were going down, they heard the sound of somebody scrambling on the hill-side, overhead, but in the gloom of night, and from the nature of the country, pursuit was impossible. Suspicion naturally enough fell on poor Ward, but an investigation being held, all circumstances were in his favor, and he was fully acquitted. Indeed, his terror, and his almost miraculous escape, scarcely allowed him to sleep for many nights. They were industrious, prudent men, and esteemed by all who knew them.

Robberies, too, occasionally occurred. One poor fellow's cabin was robbed of fifteen hundred dollars while he was at work. Thus in a moment he was stripped of the result of months of hard labor. He could scarcely suspect the author of his misfortune.

At a gambling house near the mouth of the creek, a man who had started for home was induced to try his luck at the monte table. When under the influence of liquor, and in the excitement of having lost his money, he attempted to seize it again, drawing his pistol on the gambler, when the latter shot him dead! He had previously written to his family that he was about starting for home, but this one thoughtless and imprudent act cost him his life, and his family would look long and in vain for the return of the husband and father, and probably without ever learning his sad and discreditable end.

Climbing a Volcano
About four miles below Nelson's Creek, on the Middle Fork of Feather River, arose to a great height an old extinct volcano, which curiosity

impelled me to visit. Crossing the river at the mouth of the creek, I commenced a toilsome ascent of the steep mountain, and after half a day of hard climbing, I gained the summit of what had once been its crater.

Vast quantities of lava had been ejected, which, mixed with quartz and volcanic debris, formed a mass of flint-like hardness, and it was heaped up and piled around the apex of the mountain, in rough, columnar shapes, resembling in some measure rude pillars and cones, while in cavities the action of the flames seemed to be as fresh as if it had been recently done. In one place was a deep, narrow chasm, which the eye could not fathom, and on throwing down a stone, a sound was heard as though it was striking against rough points, till gradually it was lost to the ear, without apparently reaching the bottom.

It appeared as if the flames had burst forth, throwing out the rock in a melted state, which had cooled without forming a regular crater, leaving the lava in a cemented mass, with chasms which reached to a vast depth in the bowels of the earth. On the side next the river, projections had been thrown out, and a little farther east, on the southern slope, the sides were smooth and shining, and a miss step would have precipitated the unfortunate traveler a quarter of a mile down its sides, before any jutting would have caught his mangled and bleeding form.

The panorama around was beautiful and sublime, and I counted in the view no less than five volcanic peaks in the wild, broken range of the wonderful Sierra. My thirst prevented the full indulgence of my curiosity. I gladly would have spent the night in this elevated and inspiring situation, but I was reluctantly obliged to descend.

Taking a circuitous route—indeed the only practicable one in that direction—I commenced a descent towards Rich Bar, which lay at its base. It required nearly two hours to accomplish the descent. Indeed, the labor was quite equal to the ascent.

The bar at its base proved to be one of the richest which had been discovered, and a large amount of gold was taken from it. One man took out of a pocket fifteen hundred dollars at one panful of dirt. This, of course, was only a single instance, for as at every other bar through the mines, while some were richly rewarded, others scarcely got enough to pay expenses.

Seeking Richer Diggings

John S. Hittell

John S. Hittell wrote books on a wide variety of topics, from religion to phrenology. He also wrote books on mining, the discovery of gold, San Francisco's history, and a Pacific Coast tour guide. For twenty-five years he was a journalist for the San Francisco's *Alta California*. But before all this, he went prospecting during the gold rush.

In the spring of 1850, Hittell and eleven others set off up the Cottonwood Creek in search of some rich diggings found by a man named Engles, who had been chased off by a tribe of Native Americans. The area they went into is about a hundred miles south of the Oregon border and about thirty miles west of the town of Cottonwood. It was here that they ran into the Wintu tribe.

His account is from an 1887 article he wrote for *Overland Monthly*.

PROSPECTING

Not understanding the geological influences under which the gold was distributed as we found it in the placers, the miners generally supposed it not improbable that spots would be found where a man could shovel out a bushel of gold dust in a day. Many hoped to get such claims, and for the sake of finding them would abandon others where they could make $40 or $60 a day. William Scott, who was at Sutter's Mill when the gold was found there, and a man of some intelligence, was working a year or two later in a claim that yielded $700 a day to himself and each of his partners, but they abandoned it to go to another ravine where they were told that men were making $1,100 a day and there was much unoccupied ground. When they reached the place they found that all the good claims were taken up, and when they returned to their old claim, they found that taken up too.

The Cottonwood [Creek] prospecting party, consisting of twelve men under Abraham Cunningham as captain—he still lives in Shasta County as a man highly respected—left the Middle Bar [of Clear Creek] on the second of February [1850]. As we were going into the midst of hostile Indians, six of us were armed with rifles—useful for getting game as well as for fighting Indians—and six had shovels and pans for prospecting. Each man carried bread supposed to be sufficient for ten days, and blankets; but as deer were abundant we hoped to get venison. A sharp axe, carried by turns, was to provide fire wood.

At the end of the first day's march we cut down a large oak tree. Its trunk for twenty feet made a back log for our camp fire, and the remainder of the tree supplied an abundance of wood, some of which was to be put on by anyone who woke in the night and felt the want of more heat. Our camping place was always near a multitude of manzanita bushes which we cut and piled up in a circular wall, through which the Indians could not shoot their arrows.

INDIANS

Early on the second day some Indians appeared on the hill tops on each side of the valley in which we were traveling. They watched us and frequently called out to each other, from height to height. Before noon we had to cross from one little valley to another, passing over a hill, the crest of which was bare, with chaparral on each side. We advanced to pass through that open space, which was perhaps fifty yards wide, and when within three hundred yards of it we heard a terrific yelling from that hill top as if five hundred Indians had collected there and were preparing to attack us. A few moments later we saw a string of Indians running along the brow of the hill across the open space from one clump of chaparral to the other, and this continued so long that we imagined that five hundred men at least must have passed in our sight. The meaning of their conduct was unmistakable; they meant fight.

Five hundred redskins with bows and arrows in the midst of their own mountainous country covered with chaparral and timber, against twelve white men of whom only six were armed with guns. We stopped to consider what we should do—retreat, stop and build a brush fortification,

This photograph of an Indian rancheria in the Sierra Nevada was taken sometime before 1866.

or advance. Cunningham ordered us to go on without delay; the greatest danger for us would follow any exhibition of fear.

We went forward at once, not without quicker heart-beating, as we neared the chaparral behind which the savages disappeared. No enemy showed himself to resist our advance, and when we reached the summit of the hill and looked down on the other side we saw perhaps three dozen Indians at a safe distance, running as fast as their legs could carry them, and beyond was a rancheria, a village, from which the squaws were hurrying with children and baskets into the chaparral.

We sat down to rest and consider whether there was an ambush, but we soon agreed that the few Indians whom we saw had run over the brow of the hill where we could see them, and had then run back out of sight so that they could make a long string and thus convey the idea of a large force. This explanation did not account for the noise, but we afterwards learned that they had wonderful voices, perhaps resulting from their habit of speaking to one another from mountain to mountain.

Surrounded

For two days we went forward with the Indians continually watching us and surrounding us, keeping out of rifle range however, so long as they could see where we were. They had been in the habit of stealing horses, oxen, provisions, clothing, and tools from the mines, and the Oregonians had sent out several expeditions to recapture the stolen property and punish the theft by shooting down every Indian within range of their rifles.

Our party was probably supposed to be out with such a purpose, and could not have been treated with more show of hostility. Nothing but fear of our superior weapons saved us from attack. But they misunderstood us. We had no grievances to avenge nor spite to gratify. Before starting we determined that we would make no unprovoked attack on the aborigines; our feelings and our interests were all in favor of peace. Several times on the third day, while following us in the hill and chaparral, the Indians lost sight of us, and trying to find us came very near us, where we saw them before they saw us.

Once a party of them were within ten steps of us, looking for us to their right while we sat in a clump of bushes at their left, amused at their movements. Something caused a loud laugh among us, and they, seeing us near, jumped and dodged in a most extraordinary manner, as if they expected to hear the rifles' crash at every instant. If they believed before that we were on the warpath, our conduct then set them to doubting and prepared them for more kindly thoughts of us.

Making Peace

The next morning we rested on a grassy hillside west of Duncan's Fork, and decided that we would make peace with the redskins if possible. Two unarmed men of our party went towards a few of them on the grassy hillside east of the creek, and called out to them "Amigo," Spanish for friend, and waved green boughs and a blue cloak as signs of amicable purpose. Gradually other redskins collected on the eastern hill until several hundred were visible.

When our patience was almost exhausted, a buck perhaps eighteen years old and a boy of ten came up to our two peacemakers and were induced to come over to our party. We shook hands with them, gave them presents, and did our best to gain their confidence. The young man made a speech with excellent voice and gestures. His manner would have done no discredit to an eminent white orator. There was no meaning for us in his words, but much in his looks, his tones, and his gestures. He pointed to his friends on the opposite hill, he put his hand on his breast, and then raised it towards the heavens as if swearing that he and his tribe had always been friends of the white man; and then pointing to the northeast where the miners were and to the southeast, while speaking angrily, he assured us, as we imagined, that the tribe to the southeast were the ones who did all the stealing. He spoke so loudly that his friends on the opposite hill heard and applauded him.

Alexander R. Andrews, one of our party and of the Kentucky Company, now a lawyer and prominent citizen of Shasta, says in his account of our expedition published in the *Shasta Directory for 1881*, that they were three-quarters of a mile away. After this speech was finished, a very old man and a boy trusted themselves in our power, and we made presents to them also, and before the middle of the afternoon they all deserted the eastern slope and came over to us, and from that time the most friendly relations prevailed between them and us.

GETTING TO WORK

Not having been able to separate, we had neither killed any deer nor prospected for gold, and now that we had made peace we could do both. We divided up into pairs, three of hunters and three of prospectors, each pair taking a separate course. Some Indians accompanied the hunters, and rendered excellent service in pointing out the places where the deer could be killed, and in tracking them when wounded.

That evening we had a full grown buck and two large fawns for supper. The heads, hides, hearts, lungs, and entrails were given to the Indians, who were evidently delighted with their share. The twelve white men ate every particle of their meat that evening for supper. They were hungry, and there was only a quarter of a deer for each man. We were astonished at our own appetites. The prospectors had found nothing of note. We did not give up our precaution of building a manzanita fort, which was a protection against the cold wind as well as against a possible surprise by the Indians.

The next day we again separated in pairs for hunting and prospecting, and in the evening we had two full grown deer, which we divided as before, and again our portion was entirely consumed for supper. We did not wait, however, to cook the liver, but taking Cunningham's advice and following his example, ate it raw with a little pepper and salt. Hunger overcame prejudice at the start, and we agreed that raw deer's liver from a freshly killed animal is a delicious morsel.

We had now been away from our cabins five days, and we had not only eaten our five deer, but all the bread that had been supposed to have been enough for ten days. The next day we separated without breakfast, to search for gold and deer, appointing as usual a place farther on where we should meet in the evening.

My companion was a Mr. Davis, and we were prospectors. About noon we became so hungry that we began to pick out and eat acorns from the holes in the bark of the oak and pine trees, in which they had been placed by the woodpeckers. The rains coming from the south had soaked and spoiled the acorns on that side of the trees, but on the north side the acorns were dry and sound, though presumably many of them were several years old. They were dry, hard, and bitter, but the sauce of hunger made them welcome. Having observed the Indians eat a kind of pepper grass, we tried it and found it good, and a pleasant variation from the bitter acorns.

RICH DIGGINGS

In the afternoon Davis and I found rich diggings. We came to a gully so steep that the bedrock was bare in places, and there in the clear water we could see the particles of gold, some weighing as much as a quarter of an ounce. In half an hour each had picked up on the point of his knife $45 worth—nearly three ounces. We went down the gully to where it was not so steep, and from a pan of surface dust washed out five dollars. We tried several other places and found as much. We came to the conclusion that we could make $500 a day in these gullies with a rocker.

We went to several other gullies and found prospects nearly as good, and that without going down to the bedrock—for we did not feel strong enough on our scanty diet to do any hard work. [French] Tuttle and

[Noah] Batchelder [or Batcheler], another pair of the prospectors, had also found good diggings in several large gullies, though like us they did not go down to the bedrock. They had, however, a much larger piece of the metal to show; it weighed an ounce, and it was in a shovelful of the top dirt which they threw away. A metallic ring struck their ears and a little search led to the finding of this piece, as long and wide as the bowl of a soup spoon, and in one place a quarter of an inch thick. Tuttle was confident he could wash $500 a day in his ravine, and Davis promised as much in ours; and more than $60 were shown as vouchers by the prospectors, who said there was an abundance of pay dirt but they had not anywhere gone through it to the bedrock.

Hungry as we were our party was very jovial that evening. We supposed that we were each sure of several hundred thousand dollars. The general estimate was $500,000. We discussed the methods of transporting our treasure to the East and the uses we would make of it. Occasionally one would go off to a pine tree and pick out some acorns.

WISHING FOR PORK AND BEANS

Andrews said that only one thing was needed to make his happiness perfect, and that was a good dinner of pork and beans. Some merriment was caused by recalling the fact that when at the Middle Bar he had been in the habit of saying that he would be perfectly happy if he could have a supper of ham and eggs and a dance with a Kentucky girl. When he had nothing better than acorns he thought pork and beans good enough for the highest enjoyment; but when he had an abundance of pork and beans, then he longed for ham and eggs. There was a sliding arrangement to his scale of felicity.

We made fun of our situation. When we found wormy acorns we offered them to our neighbors. We wondered whether Nebuchadnezzar's pasture was more palatable than ours. We agreed to gather the pepper grass seed when it ripened and send it to our Eastern relatives for the purpose of giving them a chance to go to grass.

Instead of starting for home the next morning we continued our journey another day, but when we met in the evening the hunters had killed no game and the prospectors had found no gold. We had to fall back on our acorns and grass. The Indians, who had come to see us every day and had furnished several men to accompany each pair of our hunters, seeing that we had nothing to eat, brought us a loaf of acorn bread and a basket of buckeye soup, both tasteless and full of sand, and to me less palatable than the raw acorns. We received their gifts with the show of gratitude due to their kindness.

We were all anxious to get back the next day to Clear Creek, so we started at daylight, and all reached the Middle Bar that evening, save one who arrived the next morning. For three days we had nothing to eat save acorns and grass, with a taste of acorn bread and buckeye soup. I prefer a square meal.

WORKING THE CLAIMS

Then began the preparations for moving to Cottonwood, now known as Arbuckle, where we arrived several weeks later, followed by some hundreds of Oregonians, who had heard at the Lower Springs of our rich diggings and wanted to share them. [*Note:* The town of Cottonwood is still called Cottonwood, but the area they were prospecting is known as the Arbuckle District.]

Our party, consisting of twelve prospectors and their respective partners, twenty-four in all, took up as claims the gullies that we had prospected, leaving the remainder of the country to the Oregonians. We decided to work our claims as a joint stock company, but we stuck together only one week. My partner and I took out $500 the first day, the next day $300, the third day $150, and decreasing sums on the following days. When we divided our joint stock gold there was little more than a tin cup full—not a pint cup—for each man.

When afterwards we worked together in couples, on separate account, the results were even less satisfactory. It seemed that in prospecting, we had not only struck the richest spots, but spots which were richer in the top dirt than on the bedrock.

February and March brought little rain; many of the gullies went dry soon after we reached our diggings; the Oregonians went back to the Lower Springs, after making war on the Indians, whom we could not afterwards conciliate; and before April we had returned to the Middle

Bar, not only without the $500,000 each, but poorer than if we had never undertaken our prospecting expedition.

When the prospectors first returned to Clear Creek for supplies, they told others of what they had found. Soon prospectors from all over flooded into the area and the Wintu tribe was driven away from their home.

In one of Hittell's books on mining, he writes of the various methods used to swindle buyers when a claim is sold.

SALTING MINES

Mining is a precarious business, and should be undertaken by inexperienced persons with great caution. It is impossible to know the cash value of a metalliferous lead or a placer claim, and the occupation is one wherein people are peculiarly liable to be carried away by excitements and by the hope of making fortunes suddenly [and] to pay much more for claims than they are really worth. There are also many modes of deceiving buyers.

Sellers of veins of auriferous or argentiferous quartz will procure specimens from richer veins, and represent them as coming from their own; or will select a few rich specimens of their ore and represent them as fair specimens of the whole, or when the rock is sent to the assayer, they will slip in some pure metal. Sometimes a rogue, to decrease the yield of auriferous quartz, will put grease into the battery, and placer miners not unfrequently "salt" their claims which they wish to sell, by putting in gold dust. If the claim contains stiff clay, it may be "salted" by shooting gold dust into it from a pistol.

The *Oroville Record* tells the following as a statement of events that happened about December 1860:

> *A party not a thousand miles from Oroville had a quartz ledge and mill which it was found desirable to dispose of. Procuring some really valuable quartz, in which the precious metal was plainly visible, they announced their willingness for parties desiring to purchase to test the ledge. This was accepted by "party of the second part," who proceeded to prospect quartz procured for the occasion, by the "party of the first part aforesaid."*

The party proposing to purchase knew the quartz was valuable on sight, but desiring to purchase cheap, were not particularly anxious to produce a rich prospect, and deposited a tallow candle or two in the arastra [a very primitive ore-crushing mill using two large stone blocks that were dragged by the beam in a circle around the post, usually powered by two mules attached to the ends of the beam]. The grease prevented amalgamation, and the rich quartz was duly crushed, then ground into impalpable powder, but produced a very diminutive prospect. The ledge was pronounced comparatively valueless, and was purchased cheap by the prospecting "party of the second part, aforesaid." Of course, the purchasers found no more valuable quartz, and were broken in a few months.

California's Strange Society

Henry Coke

Henry Coke was an aristocrat, novelist, and travel writer, the son of a British member of Parliament and First Earl of Leicester. Having entered the Naval Academy at the age of eleven, he served in the Royal Navy during the first Opium War with China. After attending Cambridge University, he then wrote a travel book on Vienna in the form of a journal.

At the age of twenty-three, he decided to travel to America and take the overland route to see the Wild West. He set off from the United Kingdom with a couple of friends in December 1849. Passing through various islands in the Caribbean, he made his way to St. Louis, arriving in May 1850. He and one friend then crossed the plains and the Rocky Mountains to Oregon, accompanied by seven other adventurers headed for the gold fields—two of whom drowned crossing rivers along the way. From Oregon they caught a ship that stopped in Hawaii before proceeding on to San Francisco, arriving in 1851. But as Coke was more interested in adventure and sightseeing than in searching for gold, he only remained in California for a few months.

Coke kept a journal of his journey, which was published in 1852 as *A Ride Over the Rocky Mountains to Oregon and California*. These excerpts are from that book.

ARRIVING IN SAN FRANCISCO

It is not quite three weeks since we left the Sandwich Islands [Hawaii]. The voyage is considered a short one, and here we are letting go the anchor in the bay of San Francisco. What an astonishing number of vessels there are going out, coming in, loading, and unloading! How magnificent is the bay!—one cannot see from shore to shore. The town, too—why it looks as big as Liverpool.

The day is rather wet, but it is impossible to stop on board. We cannot say that we are in California till we have landed; so to the shore we go. How shall I begin to describe what I saw? The place has all the characteristic features of an American town. Everything has the appearance of being new. The streets are paved with planks; and the people are busy, bearded, dirty, and heterogeneous. Yet there is something decidedly Californian about it. Perhaps it is the gambling-houses, perhaps the gold in the shop windows, perhaps. . . .

But here is a letter I wrote; it is the best description I can give. Unknown to me till long afterwards, it was published in the *Times* newspaper [probably the London *Times*]. Had I written it for that purpose, I should probably have expressed myself with more care; as it is, it was merely intended for the eyes of a private friend, and, without design, things were set down as they came uppermost.

So many books, so many letters, concerning California have appeared before the public within the last two years, that I will not venture to trespass on their patience now, either by an historical sketch of the country, or by a dissertation on its political condition, or by an idle exposition of my own speculations. The more enlightened reader I am incompetent to instruct; the general reader, if I may judge by myself, will be as well satisfied with a simple account of the common events of a Californian's every-day life, from which he may form the truest conceptions of the state of society, as with a complex analysis of State laws, or a dry list of tariffs, port dues, taxes, &c.

San Francisco, California. March 14th [1851].

It is now nearly a month since I arrived in San Francisco. During that time I have been busily employed, visiting all the different and most important mines in California. After the time and labour that it had cost me to reach this country, I fully expected that nothing could repay me; but I am agreeably surprised, and consider that I am now amply rewarded for all my troubles.

Even as a common-place traveller, I find in California a wide field of interest. The strange conglomeration of society; the practical results of an experimental system of self-government; the peculiarities of a constitution, framed not so much on the models of others as from individual causes and local necessities, are things which no other part of the world affords such perfect specimens of as California. Political economists and funded proprietors speculate on its immediate influences; while philosophers, on the other hand, prognosticating its ultimate destiny, look upon this country as the means of advancing civilisation and propagating Christianity from the eastern to the western shores of the Pacific.

Without, however, indulging in any such lucubrations, with which I have but small concern, I content myself with the ordinary avocation of gratifying curiosity and of being amused.

A FRONTIER CITY

On entering the bay of San Francisco, the first object that strikes one is the enormous mass of shipping. London and Liverpool are, of course, beyond comparison, but with the exception of these, and perhaps of New York, I know of no other port which contains so great a number of vessels. The town itself is equally remarkable. When one reflects that eighteen months ago a few scattered tents were the only habitations in the place, one looks with amazement on the city, which is daily increasing, and which already numbers over 30,000 inhabitants.

The site of the town is a steep sandy hill, but Yankee ingenuity is rapidly removing this inconvenience by levelling the hill and filling up the bay. The greater number of the buildings are upon piers stretching into the sea, and a lot of some forty feet square of "water surface" is worth about 5,000 dollars. In the very centre of the town are several large ships, dismasted and roofed over. Their strange-looking broadsides are decorated with the signs of different shops; and as they form a portion of the regular street, one wonders, at first, what eccentric characters have taken the trouble to paint their houses with two black stories and a white one in the middle.

Already there are several theatres, a French Vaudeville, and one Italian Opera! And notwithstanding the strong national propensity of the people for business, one of the principal features of San Francisco, and indeed of every town in California, is the gambling-houses. They are never closed, and they are always full. It would be difficult to give you a correct idea of these infernal regions, or to describe the strange scenes which daily take place in them. Picture to yourselves enormous rooms gaudily decorated, filled with some 400 or 500 people of all classes, without distinction of age, rank, or sex. "Monté," "faro," "rouge et noir," are the favourites among a variety of games. The tables are covered with money, and surmounted with ornamental lumps of gold and bags of gold dust. At one end of the room is, of course, a bar, at the other is a band. The excitement of the play, the effects of the liquor, the influence of the music, and above all the confusion of languages, is, as you may imagine, what the Yankees call "some."

The gambling card game of faro: All of the spades are laid out on the table, ace to king. Players place their bets on which card or cards they think will be a winning card. All plays are against the bank, not other players. The dealer then lays down two cards—a winning and losing card. Those who bet correctly win at one-to-one odds, and those who bet on the losing card lose. Bets on other cards don't count. If the winning and losing cards are the same—two fives, for example—the bank gets half of what's bet on that card. A board records which cards have been played. When only three cards are left in the deck, players bet on which order they will be played in. A correct guess wins four to one, unless the three cards contain a pair, in which case the payout is one to one. There is also a high card bet, in which the player bets the winning card will be higher than the losing card.

Everybody is armed, from the ruffian who transfers his treasures from the mine to the gambler's table, to the frail fair one who relieves the gambler's jacket for the benefit of her own.

Four times since I have been here—I wonder that it has happened no oftener—differences of opinion, concerning, no doubt, points of *honour,* have been summarily discussed and as summarily decided in those places by virtue of a "five-shooter." Three times out of the four the survivors experienced the pleasures of that prompt decision which they had so warmly advocated. In less than six hours after the quarrels the law of Judge Lynch had done its work [meaning the crowd lynched them], and order was again restored.

PASSING THROUGH TO THE MINES

Leaving San Francisco, I took my passage in a steamer to the city of Sacramento, a large town, about 150 miles up the river which bears the same name, and situated at the extreme point of inland navigation.

A day or two at this place sufficed to disgust me with a repetition of the scenes I had witnessed in San Francisco. Accordingly, by the first opportunity that offered I took my departure for Marysville, which, from its vicinity to the various branches of the Sacramento river, is the grand depot for all the miners of the wet "diggings" in Northern California, and consequently a point-of-interest to a sightseer.

After spending a pleasant evening with the editor of the *Marysville Herald*—who, by-the-by, happened to be a genuine cockney, serving the city of Marysville in the several capacities of editor, play-actor, concert-giver, and auctioneer—I started the next morning for the "Forks of the Yuba." A few hours' ride along the Spurs of the Sierra Nevada brought me at last within sight of the gold-hunters. Two or three hundred men were at work upon what had formerly been the bed of the river.

THE DIGGINGS

By the law of mutual agreement each miner is entitled to a certain portion of this "bar," as it is called, in which the gold is found. And as the precious metal cannot in such diggings be separated from the soil without the process of washing, the allotments are measured by thirty feet on the bank of the river, and so far back as the bed extends—thus giving to each man his allowance of water.

Generally speaking the original possessors have long since made their fortunes, and sold their claims to others for large or small sums, according to the richness of the soil. The result is that these claims are now falling into the hands of small companies of three or four, who, in their turn, will sell them, as immigration increases, to companies of six or eight, and so on, till the individual gains are so small that the price of labour falls and the capitalists become the sole proprietors of the mines.

Where three or four together possess a "claim" each attends to his own department of the labour—one loosens the soil, another fills the barrow or cart, a third carries it to the river, and the fourth washes it in the "rocker." If the dust is very fine, quicksilver is afterwards used to collect it from the black sand. For the most part the mining is above ground—i.e., the depth of the soil is seldom more than six feet above the rock. In some places there are what they call "coyote diggins": these produce the same kind of dust, and are worked like coal mines, having shafts sunk sometimes as deep as sixty feet.

The average weight of gold made by each miner throughout the "wet diggins," or diggings where water is used for washing the gold, is nearly half-an-ounce, or seven dollars a-day. To give you an instance, however, of the amount of metal in the soil, which I had from a miner on the spot: Three Englishmen bought a "claim" 30 feet by 100 feet, for 1,400 dollars. It had been twice before bought and sold for considerable sums, each party who sold it supposing it to be nearly exhausted. In three weeks the Englishmen paid their 1,400 dollars, and cleared 13 dollars a-day besides for their trouble. This "claim," which is not an unusually rich one, though perhaps it has been more successfully worked, has produced in eighteen months over 20,000 dollars, or 5,000*l.* [pounds sterling] worth of gold.

ROUGHING IT

After all one had heard of the dissipated habits and questionable characters of the miners, I was prepared to "rough it" during my visits to the mines, and when I found myself about to pass a night in a small tent designated the "miners" home, in which over forty of these gentlemen were assembled to drink, board, and lodge, I cannot say that I anticipated much pleasure in the prospect of sleeping four in a bed, or being at the "rude mercy" of a "crowd," of which I was the only one unarmed, but, strange to say, I never saw a more orderly congregation, or such good behaviour in such bad company, and the only thing that disturbed my peace was that one night the bunk in which I slept, not being sufficiently strong to support its unusual burden, yawned in the middle, and deposited its contents on the ground.

I returned to San Francisco, and thence I went to the "dry diggings" in the south. The country is here truly beautiful, and, like the plains of the great valley of the Sacramento, is exceedingly fertile, and possesses unlimited resources. Even in the present drought its valleys are watered by frequent rivulets, while throughout, the arid nature of the soil, combined with the uncertainty of the seasons, will prevent the Sacramento district ever becoming agricultural.

Its mineral wealth is, perhaps, the greatest in the world. The quartz rock, which is supposed to be the only permanent source from which gold will eventually be derived, extends north and south for more than a degree-and-a-half of latitude; and the quicksilver mines, now rendering from 3,000 lb. to 4,000 lb. of metal daily, threaten to destroy the previous monopoly of the Rothschilds.

At Mariposa, in the district of the quartz, a society possessing several "claims" have established, at a great expense, machinery for crushing the rock. They employ thirty men, whom they pay at the rate of 100 dollars each a-month. This society is now making a clear gain of 1,500 dollars a-day. This will show you what is to be expected when capital sets to work in the country. [. . .]

BACK IN SAN FRANCISCO

Fred and I, while at San Francisco, lived at the "El Dorado," the first hotel in the town. We had one bed-room between us, and generally dined at the *table d'hôte*. As in all American hotels, there were four meals a-day—breakfast, luncheon, dinner, and supper. The dinner was as good a one as could be got at the Astor House in New York. Plenty of everything, clean, and well-dressed. Venison, grizzly bear, Sandhill crane, snipes, quail, wild fowl, &c., were standing dishes in the game department. The beef and mutton always good, and, in short, excellent fare. For our board and lodging we paid eight dollars, not quite 2*l.* a day; wine of course is extra, and neither very good nor very cheap. As there is always a rush for places when dinner is announced, we used to secure, beforehand, a couple of seats at one end of the table.

FRONTIER JUSTICE IN MARYSVILLE

On my way to Marysville I stopped a couple of days at Sacramento. The weather was beginning to be cold. I had been rambling all the morning through the town, and was just returned to my hotel, and sat ruminating over a large stove in the bar-room, thinking Sacramento about the most comfortless place in the world. In the course of my walk I had observed a crowd collected round a large elm tree in the horse-market; on inquiring the cause of this assembly, I was told that a man had been lynched on one of the lower boughs of the elm at four o'clock this morning. A newspaper containing an account of the affair lay on a chair beside me, and, having taken it up, I was perusing the trial, when a ruffianly-looking individual interrupted me with "Say, stranger, let's have a look at that paper, will you?"

"When I have done with it," said I, and continued reading. This answer would have satisfied most Christians endowed with any moderate degree of patience: but not so the ruffian, he leant himself over the back of my chair, put one hand on my shoulder, and with the other held the paper, so that he could read as well as I.

"Well I guess you're readin about Jim, aint you?"

"Who's Jim?" said I.

"Him as they hung this morning," he answered, at the same time resuming his seat. "Jim was a partic'lar friend of mine, and I helped to hang him."

"Did you?" said I—"A friendly act—What was he hanged for?"

"When did *you* come to Sacramento city?"

"I only arrived this morning, and have not yet heard the particulars of this case."

"Oh! well! I reckon I'll tell you how it was then. You see, Jim was a Britisher, that is, he come from a place they call Botamy Bay, which belongs to Victoria, but aint exactly in the old country, I believe. When he first come to Californy, about six months back, he wasn't acquainted none with any boys hereaway, so he took to digging all by hisself. It was up at Cigar Bar whar he dug, and I happened to be a digging there too, and so it was we got to know one another. Jim hadn't been here a fortnight before one o' the boys lost about three hundred dollars that he'd made a *caché* of. Somehow suspicions fell on Jim. More than one of us thought he had been digging for bags instead of dust, and the man as lost the money swore he would have a turn with him, and so Jim took my advice and sloped."

"Well," said I, "he wasn't lynched for that, was he?"

"'Taint likely," said the ruffian; "for till the last week or ten days nobody knowed whar he'd gone to. Well! when he come to Sacramenty this time, he come with a pile and no mistake. And all day and all night Jim used to play at faro, and roulette, and a heap of other games. Nobody couldn't tell how he made his money last so long, nor whar he got it from, but certain sure everybody thought as how Jim was considerable of a loafer. Last of all, a blacksmith as lives in Broad-street, said he found out the way he done it, and asked me to come with him to show up Jim for cheating.

"Now whether it was that Jim suspected the blacksmith, I can't say, but he didn't cheat, and lost his money in consequence. This riled him very bad, and so, wanting to get quit of the blacksmith, he began to quarrel. The blacksmith was a quick-tempered man, and, after a good deal of abuse, could not keep his temper any longer, and struck Jim a blow on the mouth. Jim jumped from his seat, pulled a revolver from his pocket, and shot the blacksmith dead on the spot. I was the first man that laid hold of the murderer, and, if it had not been for me, I believe the people in the room would have torn him to pieces.

"'Send for Judge Parker,' shouted some.

"'Let's try him here,' said others.

"'I don't want to be tried at all,' said Jim; 'you all know damned well that I shot the man; and I know bloody well that you'll hang me. Give me till daylight, and then I'll die like a man.'

"But we all agreed that he ought not to be condemned without a proper trial, and as the report of the pistol had brought a crowd to the place, a jury was formed out of them that were present, and three judges were elected from the most respectable gentlemen in the town.

"The trial lasted nearly a couple of hours. Nobody doubted that he was guilty, or that he ought to be hanged for murder; but the question was, whether he should die by Lynch law, or be kept for a regular trial before the judges of the Criminal Court. The best speakers said that Lynch law was no law, and endangered the life of every innocent man; but the mob would have it that he was to die at once.

"So as it was just then about daylight, they carried him to the horse-market, set him on a table, and tied the rope round one of the lower branches of a big elm tree. All the time I kept by his side, and when he was getting on the table he asked me to lend him my revolver to shoot one of the jurymen, who had spoken violently against him. When I refused, he asked me to tie the knot so as it wouldn't slip.

"'It ain't no account,' said I, 'to talk in that way. Jim, old fellow, you're bound to die; and if they didn't hang you I'd shoot you myself.'

"'Well, then,' said he, 'give me hold of the rope, and I'll show you how little I care for death.'

"He seized the cord, pulled himself in an instant out of the reach of the crowd, and sat cross-legged on the bough. Half a dozen rifles were raised to bring him down, but, reflecting that he could not escape, they forbore to fire. He tied a noose in the rope, put it round his neck, slipped it up till it was pretty tight, and then stood up and addressed the mob. He didn't say much, except that he hated them all. He cursed the man he shot; he then cursed the world; and last of all he cursed himself, and, with a terrible oath, he jumped into the air, and with a jerk that shook the tree, swung backwards and forwards over the heads of the crowd."

A SAD REVERIE

I believe the narrator went on talking about himself; but, I confess, I paid no further attention to his story. The rude picture he had drawn of his desperate *friend* filled my mind with strange reflections.

"You see Jim was a Britisher," and spoke good broad-provincial English, too, no doubt. And so I traced his sad career from his happy English home. Happy home! perhaps, though, it was not a happy home—perhaps he had been one of a large family—a wanting, poverty-stricken family in a manufacturing district—and Jim had found no means of keeping body and soul together, but by shooting other people's pheasants, and getting his bread and water thereby in an English jail. Perhaps, too, when he came out of jail, he did not find bread any easier to be got at than before he went there, and so shot pheasants again, and went to jail again. And for the third offence a bench of magistrates, with "fair round bellies with good capons lined," thought a change of air would best suit Jim's complaint, and so the scoundrel got to "Botamy Bay, which belongs to Victoria."

Alas, poor England! do you *turn out* many of your sons in this fashion? Do many of them get to "Botamy Bay," and then get elsewhere, and then get hanged for knaves and scoundrels, as they get to be? They tell me that it is so; and lo! here is one, a veritable specimen of such things. But they say 'tis cant to talk in this manner. There must and will be food for the gallows supplied at all times, and by all countries.

Had Jim been called Jacques, and a Frenchman, doubtless I, for one, should not have been blue-be-devilled about England, and so let it pass. The reverie was an expensive one. I had, in the meanwhile, burnt a hole in my boot.

Is Cheating Smart?

One of my companions in the vehicle that took us down from Marysville was rather an amusing specimen of a Californian. He was a roughish fellow to talk to, but well to do in the world, at least respectably dressed, and was evidently treated by the driver and an occasional acquaintance that we passed on the road with that degree of deference which in this enlightened country is only conferred upon the "smart."

He began the conversation with me by asking how much I would take for the studs in my shirt, and upon being told they were not for sale in the first place, and in the second that no amount would buy them, as they were given to me by a friend, he answered that considering they were a present, and cost nothing, I ought to be the more ready to "trade," and that I might make my mind easy upon one subject, which was, that if he had a chance, and he meant to look out sharp for one, he would steal them as sure as he was born.

Such a declaration might have startled a person unused to the open and candid nature of such rascals, but the genus is so common, and is moreover so thoroughly appreciated anywhere in America, that I was not the least bit more astonished than if any other foreigner had offered me a cigar; but, merely taking the remark as a compliment to my studs, I buttoned my coat, that he might not be tempted with the opportunity, which I knew he would not fail to profit by if it occurred.

This little incident introduced a spirited discussion on the topic of "smartness." The Yankee was convinced that "Every man for himself and the Devil take the hindmost," was the only motto for a wise man in this world, and, as an instance of the wisdom of this dogma, he mentioned his own case; showing how from the lowest dregs of society he had risen to affluence; how he had used no other weapons to combat against the greatest reverses of fortune but the mother-wit that had taught him—that the easiest method of avoiding difficulties was to put your hands into the pockets of your friends.

Every man, he argued, would cheat his neighbour, if he knew how. What folly it was then not to be beforehand with the rest of the world, and cheat them in advance. The mistake people made was that they foolishly substituted the word "cheat," in the place of the word "smart." What was a crime with us Britishers was a creditable act with an American. And if a man's intellects were not given him for his own advantage he did not see for whom else they could be given.

CONNING ONE'S WAY TO SUCCESS

"Yourn warn't given you for the advantage of the man you sold the stage to, I guess—was it coachman?"

This appeal was made by a dirty-looking passenger to the driver.

"I reckon not—that was a smart job from beginning to end—that was," returned the coachman.

"What was it?" I asked; "I suppose you stole the coach from the man first, painted it a different colour, and then got a friend to sell it to him for a new one?"

"Not so bad as that neither, stranger. What I did I don't consider nothing out of the way of business; it's what any fool might do, and not be smart at that either. You see, when I first got to San Francisco, I had no more than a respectable suit of black, and five dollars in my pocket. I wanted to get to the diggings, but it would have cost me a deal more than five dollars to fit out for that expedition, so I made up my mind to stay where I was till I could afford to go.

"One day when I was walking up to the square, thinking how I should get any living without working to death for it, I saw an old friend of mine driving a mule-team. I asked him how he had managed to get money to buy the mules.

"'They're not mine,' says he; 'they belong to a gentleman of whom I hire them for a small sum.'

"'And what,' said I, 'did he see in your ugly face to make him so charitably inclined?'

"'He saw these gold spectacles, which I always mean to wear in future, as the best friends I ever had. I was like you when I landed; I had but five dollars in my pocket, and three of 'em I gave to a Jew for these specks. If they had been silver they would never have done the job.

"'Well, I mounts the specks, and off I goes to the charitable old boy of whom I had heard talk, and represented myself to him as a medical gentleman that had left a large family, and come out here to give the sick the benefit of my practice on purely philanthropical motives. Of course, I made a good circumstantial story, telling him that I should be glad of some easy job, as I wasn't accustomed to hard manual labour, and as soon as I had earned enough to live upon, should go and practise at the mines.

"'He heard my story to the end, looked at me, and then at the gold specks, and I am sartain sure if it had not been for those specks, and those specks hadn't been gold, he never would have believed a word I said.'

"'I wish then you would lend them to me, friend?'

"'I won't do that, but I will lend you something better. I must go to Sacramento for a couple of days, and until I return, you shall have the loan of this mule-team.'

"Here's luck, thought I; this team can't be worth more than ten dollars a day to their owner, and if I sell them, they can't be worth less than 500 dollars to me; so into the market they shall go."

"And you stole the mules?" we asked.

"I sold them leastwise, and borrowed the money."

"And you were not hanged for it?"

"Not that I know of," said he; "but to cut a long story short, and come to the matter of the stage which I begun about; the money that I got for the mules bought me a light wagon and four horses, and I persuaded a man who had another team to let me drive them in the wagon, and he was to have a share of the profits. We soon established a good business; I bought out my partner, and sold the whole concern for just five times what it cost me, and a mighty good thing the man who bought the business would have made of it, if he had not been a-dealing with a smart 'un. But there's where it is you see; he wasn't smart, and I was.

"I went to San Francisco, paid my friend the price of the mules which he had naturally been put in prison for stealing; gave him a hundred dollars to keep him quiet; bought a good stage and three fast teams; came back to San Jose, and in one week drove the old coach off the road; made two thousand dollars by the traffic, and sold the whole concern again for two thousand more. And here I am in a fair way to become a rich man; have invested 4,000 dollars at 40 per cent, which, though it is not great interest in these times, yet it is as safe as a mortgage on the most valuable property in California can make it.

"Gentlemen, as we are at the end of the journey let us liquor."

The Fast Life in San Francisco

J. D. Borthwick

J. D. Borthwick was a Scottish physician who set off to see Canada and the United States after receiving his inheritance at the age of twenty-one. Coming down with gold fever, he landed in California in the summer of 1851 at the age of twenty-six or twenty-seven. He wrote of his experiences during the gold rush in several magazine articles and eventually in several books. These excerpts are from two articles that were published in 1857 in *Hutchings' California Magazine*.

San Francisco painted by E. Godchaux in 1851

LIVING THE FAST LIFE

San Francisco [in 1851] exhibited an immense amount of vitality compressed into a small compass, and a degree of earnestness was observable in every action of a man's daily life. People lived more there in a week than they would in a year in most other places.

In the course of a month, or a year, in San Francisco, there was more hard work done, more speculative schemes were conceived and executed, more money was made and lost, there was more buying and selling, more sudden changes of fortune, more eating and drinking, more smoking, swearing, gambling, and tobacco-chewing, more crime and profligacy, and, at the same time, more solid advancement made by the people, as a body, in wealth, prosperity, and the refinements of civilization, than could be shown in an equal space of time by any community of the same size on the face of the earth.

The every-day jog-trot of ordinary human existence was not a fast enough pace for Californians in their impetuous pursuit of wealth. The longest period of time ever thought of was a month. Money was loaned, and houses were rented by the month: interest and rent being invariably payable monthly and in advance. All engagements were made by the month, during which period the changes and contingencies were so great that no one was willing to commit himself for a longer term. In the space of a month the whole city might be swept off by fire, and a totally new one might be flourishing in its place. So great was the constant fluctuation in the prices of goods, and so rash and speculative was the usual style of business, that no great idea of stability could be attached to anything, and the ever-varying aspect of the streets, as the houses were being constantly pulled down and rebuilt, was emblematic of the equally varying fortunes of the inhabitants. [...]

FIGHT!

Presently one would hear "Hullo there's a muss!" (Anglicé: a row), and men would be seen rushing to the spot from all quarters. Auction-rooms, gambling-rooms, stores, and drinking-shops would be emptied, and a mob collect in the street in a moment. The "muss" would probably be only a *difficulty* between two gentlemen, who had referred it to the arbitration of knives or pistols; but if no one was killed, the mob would disperse, to resume their various occupations, just as quickly as they had collected.

Some of the principal streets were planked, as was also, of course, that part of the city which was built on piles; but where there was no plank-ing, the mud was ankle-deep, and in many places there were mud-holes, rendering the street almost impassable.

California was often said to be famous for three things—rats, fleas, and empty bottles. The whole place swarmed with rats of an enormous size; one could hardly walk at night without treading on them. They destroyed an immense deal of property, and a good ratting terrier was worth his weight in gold dust. I knew instances, however, of first rate terriers in Sacramento City (which for rats beat San Francisco hollow) becoming at last so utterly disgusted with killing rats, that they ceased to consider it any sport at all, and allowed the rats to run under their noses without deigning to look at them.

As for the other industrious little animals, they were a terrible nuisance. I suppose they were indigenous to the sandy soil. It was quite a common thing to see a gentleman suddenly pull up the sleeve of his coat, or the leg of his trousers, and smile in triumph when he caught his little tormentor.

THE WELL-DRESSED MEN AND WOMEN

The few ladies who were already in San Francisco very naturally avoided appearing in public; but numbers of female toilettes [dresses], of the most extravagantly rich and gorgeous materials, swept the muddy streets, and added not a little to the incongruous variety of the scene.

There was in the crowd a large proportion of well-shaven men, in stove-pipe hats and broadcloth; but, however nearly a man might approach in appearance to the conventional idea of a gentleman, it is not to be supposed, on that account, that he either was or got the credit of being, a bit better than his neighbors. The man standing next him, in the guise of a laboring man, was perhaps his superior in wealth, character and education. Appearances, at least as far as dress was concerned, went for nothing at all. [. . .]

The numbers of the different classes forming the community were not in the proportion requisite to preserve its equilibrium. Transplanting one's self to California from any part of the world involved an outlay beyond the means of the bulk of the labouring classes; and to those who did come to the country, the mines were of course the great point of attraction; so that in San Francisco the numbers of the labouring and of the working classes generally, were not nearly equal to the demand. The consequence was that labourers' and mechanics' wages were ridiculously high; and, as a general thing, the lower the description of the labour, or of service, required, the more extravagant in proportion were the wages paid.

Jumping Ship

Sailors' wages were two and three hundred dollars per month, and there were hundreds of ships lying idle in the bay for the want of crews to man them even at these rates. Every ship, on her arrival, was immediately deserted by all hands; for, of all people, sailors were the most unrestrainable in their determination to go to the diggings; and it was there a common saying, of the truth of which I saw myself many examples, that sailors, black men, and Dutchmen were the luckiest men in the mines: a very drunken old salt was always particularly lucky.

Derelict ships in San Francisco's Yerba Buena Bay in 1853. More than eight hundred vessels were abandoned during the gold rush.

There was a great overplus of young men of education, who had never dreamed of manual labour, and who found that their services in their wonted capacities were not required in such a rough-and-ready, every-man-for-himself sort of a place. Hard work, however, was generally better paid than head work, and men employed themselves in any way, quite regardless of preconceived ideas of their own dignity.

It was one intense scramble for dollars—the man who got most was the best man—how he got them had nothing to do with it. No occupation was considered at all derogatory, and, in fact, everyone was too much occupied with his own affairs to trouble himself in the smallest degree about his neighbour.

A man's actions and conduct were totally unrestrained by the ordinary conventionalities of civilized life, and, so long as he did not interfere with the rights of others he could follow his own course, for good or for evil, with the utmost freedom.

Among so many temptations to err, thrust prominently in one's way, without any social restraint to counteract them, it was not surprising that many men were too weak for such a trial, and, to use an expressive, though not very elegant phrase, went to the devil. The community was composed of isolated individuals, each quite regardless of the good opinion of his neighbors. [...]

The Dark Side

Although employment, of one sort or another, and good pay, were to be had by all who were able and willing to work, there was nevertheless a vast amount of misery and destitution. Many men had come to the country with their expectations raised to an unwarrantable pitch, imagining that the mere fact of emigration to California would insure them a rapid fortune; but when they came to experience the severe competition in every branch of trade, their hopes were gradually destroyed by the difficulties of the reality. [...]

Drinking was the great consolation for those who had not moral strength to bear up under their disappointments. Some men gradually obscured their intellects by increased habits of drinking, and, equally gradually, reached the lowest stage of misery and want; while others went at it with more force, and drank themselves into delirium tremens before they knew where they were. There is something in the climate which superinduces it with less provocation than in other countries. But, though drunkenness was common enough, the number of drunken men one saw was small, considering the enormous consumption of liquor.

In San Francisco, where the ordinary rate of existence was even faster than in the Atlantic States, men required an extra amount of stimulant to keep it up, and this fashion of drinking was carried to excess. The saloons were crowded from early morning till late at night; and in each, two or three bar-keepers were kept unceasingly at work, mixing drinks for expectant groups of customers. They had no time even to sell segars, which were most frequently dispensed at a miniature tobacconist's shop in another part of the saloon. [. . .]

A WELL-ARMED CROWD

There were several very good American theatres, a French theatre, and an Italian opera, besides concerts, masquerades, a circus, and other public amusements. The most curious were certainly the masquerades. They were generally given in one of the large gambling saloons, and in the placards announcing that they were to come off, appeared conspicuously also the intimation of "No weapons admitted;" "A strong police will be in attendance."

The company was just such as might be seen in any gambling-room; and, beyond the presence of half-a-dozen masks in female attire, there was nothing to carry out the idea of a ball or a masquerade at all, but it was worthwhile to go, if only to watch the company arrive, and to see the practical enforcement of the weapon clause in the announcements.

Several doorkeepers were in attendance, to whom each man as he entered delivered up his knife or his pistol, receiving a check for it, just as one does for his cane or umbrella at the door of a picture-gallery. Most men draw a pistol from behind their back, and very often a knife along with it; some carried their bowie-knife down the back of their neck, or in their breast; demure, pious-looking men, in white neckcloths, lifted up the bottom of their waistcoat and revealed the butt of a revolver; others, after having already disgorged a pistol, pulled up the leg of their trousers and abstracted a huge bowie-knife from their boot; and there were men, terrible fellows, no doubt, but who were more likely to frighten themselves than anyone else, who produced a revolver from each trouser-pocket, and a bowie-knife from their belt.

If any man declared that he had no weapon, the statement was so incredible that he had to submit to be searched; an operation which was performed by the doorkeepers, who, I observed, were occasionally rewarded for their diligence by the discovery of a pistol secreted in some unusual part of the dress.

To Live by Luck

Henry David Thoreau

Henry David Thoreau's ideas were heavily influenced by his friend and mentor, Ralph Waldo Emerson. Thoreau became friends with Emerson in the mid-1830s, and as he was very interested in living close to nature, Emerson allowed him to camp out for two years on his property at Walden Pond. That, of course, is when Thoreau wrote his famous book, *Walden.* Thoreau is also famous for his essay "Civil Disobedience." On leaving his cabin near Walden Pond, Thoreau went to work for Emerson as a gardener, repairman, assistant, and tutor for Emerson's children, living in Emerson's house. They were also friends and neighbors with Nathaniel Hawthorne and Louisa May Alcott.

Oddly, both Thoreau and Emerson had very negative opinions about the gold rush. Instead of associating it with the individualism and freedom from the pressures of society that they both espoused, they saw it as being about greed and materialism. To them it didn't seem like working for a living, but more like a lottery where gold seekers gambled for riches. As Emerson put it: "It was a rush and a scramble of needy adventurers, and, in the western country, a general jail-delivery of all the rowdies of the rivers." These impressions probably mirrored those of many Easterners at the time; that is, those who had refrained from joining the rush themselves.

Thoreau kept a journal for much of his life; what follows he wrote on February 1, 1852.

A GOLDEN LOTTERY

The recent rush to California and the attitude of the world, even of its philosophers and prophets, in relation to it appears to me to reflect the greatest disgrace on mankind. That so many are ready to get their living by the lottery of gold-digging without contributing any value to society, and that the great majority who stay at home justify them in this both by precept and example! It matches the infatuation of the Hindus who have cast themselves under the car of Juggernaut.

I know of no more startling development of the morality of trade and all the modes of getting a living than the rush to California affords. Of what significance the philosophy, or poetry, or religion of a world that will rush to the lottery of California gold-digging on the receipt of the first news, to live by luck, to get the means of commanding the labor of others less lucky—i.e. of slaveholding—without contributing any value to society? And that is called enterprise, and the devil is only a little more enterprising!

The philosophy and poetry and religion of such a mankind are not worth the dust of a puffball. The hog that *roots* his own living, and so makes manure, would be ashamed of such company. If I could command the wealth of all the worlds by lifting my finger, I would not pay such a price for it. It makes God to be a moneyed gentleman who scatters a handful of pennies in order to see mankind scramble for them.

Going to California. It is only three thousand miles nearer to hell. I will resign my life sooner than live by luck. The world's raffle. A subsistence in the domains of nature a thing to be raffled for! No wonder that they gamble there. I never heard that they did anything else there. What a comment, what a satire, on our institutions! The conclusion will be that mankind will hang itself upon a tree. And who would interfere to cut it down. And have all the precepts in all the bibles taught men only this? and is the last and most admirable invention of the Yankee race only an improved muck-rake? patented too!

If one came hither to sell lottery tickets, bringing satisfactory credentials, and the prizes were seats in heaven, this world would buy them with a rush.

Did God direct us so to get our living, digging where we never planted, and He would perchance reward us with lumps of gold? It is a text, oh! for the Jonahs of this generation, and yet the pulpits are as silent as immortal Greece, silent, some of them, because the preacher is gone to California himself.

The gold of California is a touchstone which has betrayed the rotten-
ness, the baseness, of mankind. Satan, from one of his elevations, showed
mankind the kingdom of California, and they entered into a compact
with him at once.

While gold seeking may have been like a lottery, in that some miners got rich and
most didn't, many people did quite well establishing other types of businesses. And
Thoreau was particularly wrong about one thing: The gold hunters had to work long,
back-breaking hours in rough and dangerous conditions, often barely scratching out
a meager living. When the rush was over, most remained in the West. And they were
joined by many others who came to California to establish new lives.

As for contributing to society, the gold and silver pulled out of the ground helped
the Union win the Civil War, putting an end to legal slavery—something both Thoreau
and Emerson passionately favored.

A Woman at the Mines

Dame Shirley

Dame Shirley is the pseudonym of Louise Clappe (sometimes spelled Louisa Clapp). Louise, a tiny, well-educated thirty-year-old woman who sported blonde curls that dangled to her waist, was newly married to Dr. Fayette Clappe. As both of them suffered from ill heath, the couple thought a change of climate might help. Leaving behind their home in Amherst, Massachusetts, they set off for California by ship in 1849.

For more than a year, the couple lived in San Francisco. Because of its unique topography and being surrounded by water on three sides, San Francisco's summers are cool and foggy. Tiring of the fog, enchanted by the tales of gold, and because of their ill health, they decided to head to the sunnier climate inland—to the gold fields of the Feather River Valley in the Sierra Nevada.

Throughout her stay there, from September 1851 through November 1852, Louise wrote a series of captivating personal letters to her sister Mary Jane, who was also known as Molly. In 1854, California's first magazine, *The Pioneer,* began publishing these letters. Previously Louise had published some poems under the pen name "Shirley Lee," Lee being her mother's maiden name. For the letters, it was shortened to just "Shirley." Within some of the letters, she jokingly referred to herself as Dame Shirley and that's the name by which she's now remembered.

Dame Shirley's accounts remain the most popular of the gold rush. Here are a few selections from her letters.

HEADING TO RICH BAR
[September 13, 1851]

F. was just recovering from a brain-fever when he concluded to go to the mines; but, in spite of his excessive debility, which rendered him liable to chills at any hour of the day or night, he started on the seventh day of June—mounted on a mule, and accompanied by a jackass to carry his baggage, and a friend who kindly volunteered to assist him in spending his money—for this wildly beautiful spot.

F. was compelled by sickness to stop several days on the road. He suffered intensely, the trail for many miles being covered to the depth of twelve feet with snow, although it was almost midsummer when he passed over it. He arrived at Rich Bar the latter part of June, and found the revivifying effect of its bracing atmosphere far surpassing his most sanguine hopes. He soon built himself an office, which was a perfect marvel to the miners, from its superior elegance. It is the only one on the Bar, and I intend to visit it in a day or two, when I will give you a description of its architectural splendors.

It will perhaps enlighten you as to one peculiarity of a newly discovered mining district, when I inform you that although there were but two or three physicians at Rich Bar when my husband arrived, in less than three weeks there were *twenty-nine* who had chosen this place for the express purpose of practicing their profession.

Finding his health so almost miraculously improved, F. concluded, should I approve the plan, to spend the winter in the mountains. I had teased him to let me accompany him when he left in June, but he had at that time refused, not daring to subject me to inconveniences, of the extent of which he was himself ignorant. When the letter disclosing his plans for the winter reached me at San Francisco, I was perfectly enchanted. You know that I am a regular nomad in my passion for wandering.

Of course my numerous acquaintances in San Francisco raised one universal shout of disapprobation. Some said that I ought to be put into a strait-jacket, for I was undoubtedly mad to think of such a thing. Some said that I should never get there alive, and if I *did*, would not stay a month; and others sagely observed—with a profound knowledge of the habits and customs of the aborigines of California—that, even if the Indians *did not* kill me, I should expire of *ennui* or the cold before spring. One lady declared, in a burst of outraged modesty, that it was absolutely indelicate to think of living in such a large population of men, where, at the most, there were but two or three women. I laughed merrily at their mournful prognostications, and started gayly for Marysville, where I arrived in a couple of days, ready to commence my journey to Rich Bar.

THE DOCTOR'S OFFICE

Through the middle of Rich Bar runs the street, thickly planted with about forty tenements, among which figure round tents, square tents, plank hovels, log cabins, etc.—the residences varying in elegance and convenience from the palatial splendor of "The Empire" down to a "local habitation" formed of pine boughs and covered with old calico shirts.

To-day I visited the "office," the only one on the river. I had heard so much about it from others, as well as from F., that I really *did* expect something extra. When I entered this imposing place the shock to my optic nerves was so great that I sank helplessly upon one of the benches, which ran, divan-like, the whole length (ten feet!) of the building, and laughed till I cried. There was, of course, no floor. A rude nondescript in one corner, on which was ranged the medical library, consisting of half a dozen volumes, did duty as a table. The shelves, which looked like sticks snatched hastily from the wood-pile and nailed up without the least alteration, contained quite a respectable array of medicines. The white-canvas window stared everybody in the face, with the interesting information painted on it, in perfect grenadiers of capitals, that this was Dr. ——'s office.

At my loud laugh (which, it must be confessed, was noisy enough to give the whole street assurance of the presence of a woman) F. looked shocked, and his partner looked prussic acid. To him (the partner, I mean; he hadn't been out of the mines for years) the "office" was a thing sacred, and set apart for an almost admiring worship. It was a beautiful architectural ideal embodied in pine shingles and cotton cloth. Here he literally "lived, and moved, and had his being," his bed and his board. With an admiration of the fine arts truly praiseworthy, he had fondly decorated the walls thereof with sundry pictures from Godey's, Graham's, and Sartain's magazines, among which, fashion-plates with imaginary monsters sporting miraculous waists, impossible wrists, and fabulous feet, largely predominated.

During my call at the office I was introduced to one of the *finders* of Rich Bar—a young Georgian, who afterwards gave me a full description of all the facts connected with its discovery. This unfortunate had not spoken to a woman for two years, and, in the elation of his heart at the joyful event, he rushed out and invested capital in some excellent champagne, which I, on Willie's principle of "doing in Turkey as the Turkeys do," assisted the company in drinking, to the honor of my own arrival.

I mention this as an instance that nothing can be done in California without the sanctifying influence of the *spirit,* and it generally appears in a much more "questionable shape" than that of sparkling wine.

The Discovery and Wealth of Rich Bar

Mr. H. informed me that on the 20th of July, 1850, it was rumored at Nelson's Creek—a mining station situated at the Middle Fork of the Feather River, about eighty miles from Marysville—that one of those vague "Somebodies"—a near relation of the "They-Says"—had discovered mines of a remarkable richness in a northeasterly direction, and about forty miles from the first-mentioned place. Anxious and immediate search was made for "Somebody," but, as our Western brethren say, he "wasn't thar'." But his absence could not deter the miners when once the golden rumor had been set afloat.

A large company packed up their goods and chattels, generally consisting of a pair of blankets, a frying-pan, some flour, salt pork, brandy, pickax and shovel, and started for the new Dorado. They "traveled, and traveled, and traveled," as we used to say in the fairy-stories, for nearly a week, in every possible direction, when, one evening, weary and discouraged, about one hundred of the party found themselves at the top of that famous hill [Red Hill] which figures so largely in my letters, whence the river can be distinctly seen. Half of the number concluded to descend the mountain that night, the remainder stopping on the summit until the next morning.

On arriving at Rich Bar, part of the adventurers camped there, but many went a few miles farther down the river. The next morning, two men turned over a large stone, beneath which they found quite a sizable piece of gold. They washed a small panful of the dirt, and obtained from it two hundred and fifty-six dollars. Encouraged by this success, they commenced staking off the legal amount of ground allowed to each person for mining purposes, and, the remainder of the party having descended the hill, before night the entire bar was "claimed."

In a fortnight from that time, the two men who found the first bit of gold had each taken out six thousand dollars. Two others took out thirty-three pounds of gold in eight hours, which is the best day's work that has been done on this branch of the river. The largest amount ever taken from one panful of dirt was fifteen hundred dollars. In a little more than a week after its discovery, five hundred men had settled upon the Bar for the summer. Such is the wonderful alacrity with which a mining town is built.

Soon after was discovered, on the same side of the river, about half a mile apart, and at nearly the same distance from this place, the two bars, Smith and Indian, both very rich; also another, lying across the river, just opposite Indian, called Missouri Bar. There are several more, all within a few miles of here, called Frenchman's, Taylor's, Brown's, The Junction, Wyandott, and Muggin's; but they are, at present, of little importance as mining stations.

Those who worked in these mines during the fall of 1850 were extremely fortunate, but, alas! the monte fiend ruined hundreds! Shall I tell you the fate of the most successful of these gold-hunters? From poor men, they found themselves, at the end of a few weeks, absolutely rich. Elated with their good fortune, seized with a mania for monte, in less than a year these unfortunates, so lately respectable and intelligent, became a pair of drunken gamblers. One of them, at this present writing, works for five dollars a day and boards himself out of that; the other actually suffers for the necessaries of life—a too common result of scenes in the mines.

Snowed In

There were but few that dared to remain in the mountains during the winter, for fear of being buried in the snow, of which, at that time, they had a most vague idea. I have been told that in these sheltered valleys it seldom falls to the depth of more than a foot, and disappears almost invariably within a day or two. Perhaps there were three hundred that concluded to stay, of which number two thirds stopped on Smith's Bar, as the labor of mining there is much easier than it is here.

Contrary to the general expectation, the weather was delightful until about the middle of March. It then commenced storming, and continued to snow and rain incessantly for nearly three weeks. Supposing that the rainy season had passed, hundreds had arrived on the river during the previous month. The snow, which fell several feet in depth on the mountains,

A wagon train on the road into Lake Valley in the early 1860s

rendered the trail impassable, and entirely stopped the pack trains. Provisions soon became scarce, and the sufferings of these unhappy men were indeed extreme. Some adventurous spirits, with true Yankee hardihood, forced their way through the snow to the Frenchman's rancho, and packed flour *on their backs* for more than forty miles! The first meal that arrived sold for three dollars a pound. Many subsisted for days on nothing but barley, which is kept here to feed the pack-mules on.

One unhappy individual, who could not obtain even a little barley for love or money, and had eaten nothing for three days, forced his way out to the Spanish Rancho, fourteen miles distant, and in less than an hour after his arrival had devoured twenty-seven biscuits and a corresponding quantity of other eatables, and, of course, drinkables to match.

Don't let this account alarm you. There is no danger of another famine here. They tell me that there is hardly a building in the place that has not food enough in it to last its occupants for the next two years; besides, there are two or three well-filled groceries in town.

In October 1851, Dame Shirley and Dr. Clappe moved half a mile west to Indian Bar, where they built a log cabin. She noted, "I am the only petticoated astonishment on this Bar."

A Mineress
From our Log Cabin, Indian Bar; November 25, 1851

Nothing of importance has happened since I last wrote you, except that I have become a *mineress;* that is, if having washed a pan of dirt with my own hands, and procured therefrom three dollars and twenty-five cents in gold dust, which I shall inclose in this letter, will entitle me to the name. I can truly say, with the blacksmith's apprentice at the close of his first day's work at the anvil, that I am sorry I learned the trade, for I wet my feet, tore my dress, spoilt a pair of new gloves, nearly froze my fingers, got an awful headache, took cold, and lost a valuable breastpin, in this my labor of love. After such melancholy self-sacrifice on my part, I trust you will duly prize my gift. I can assure you that it is the last golden handiwork you will ever receive from Dame Shirley.

Apropos of lady gold-washers in general—it is a common habit with people residing in towns in the vicinity of the "Diggings" to make up pleasure-parties to those places. Each woman of the company will exhibit, on her return, at least twenty dollars of the *oro*, which she will gravely inform you she has just panned out from a single basinful of the soil. This, of course, gives strangers a very erroneous idea of the average richness of auriferous dirt.

I myself thought (now, don't laugh) that one had but to saunter gracefully along romantic streamlets on sunny afternoons, with a parasol and white kid gloves perhaps, and to stop now and then to admire the scenery, and carelessly rinse out a small panfull of yellow sand (without detriment to the white kids, however, so easy did I fancy the whole process to be), in order to fill one's workbag with the most beautiful and rare specimens of the precious mineral. Since I have been here I have discovered my mistake, and also the secret of the brilliant success of former gold-washeresses.

The miners are in the habit of flattering the vanity of their fair visitors by scattering a handful of "salt" (which, strange to say, is *exactly* the color of gold-dust, and has the remarkable property of often bringing to light very curious lumps of the ore) through the dirt before the dainty fingers touch it, and the dear creatures go home with their treasures, firmly believing that mining is the prettiest pastime in the world.

I had no idea of permitting such a costly joke to be played upon me; so I said but little of my desire to "go through the motions" of gold-washing, until one day, when, as I passed a deep hole in which several men were at work, my companion requested the owner to fill a small pan, which I had in my hand, with dirt from the bed-rock. This request was, of course, granted, and the treasure having been conveyed to the edge of the river, I succeeded, after much awkward maneuvering on my own part, and considerable assistance from friend H., an experienced miner, in gathering together the above-specified sum.

All the diggers of our acquaintance say that it is an excellent "prospect," even to come from the bed-rock, where, naturally, the richest dirt is found. To be sure, there are, now and then, "lucky strikes," such, for instance, as that mentioned in a former letter, where a person took out of a single basinful of soil two hundred and fifty-six dollars. But such luck is as rare as the winning of a hundred-thousand-dollar prize in a lottery. We are acquainted with many here whose gains have *never* amounted to much more than wages, that is, from six to eight dollars a day. And a claim which yields a man a steady income of ten dollars *per diem* is considered as very valuable.

The Crime
From our Log Cabin, Indian Bar, December 15, 1851

I little thought, dear M., that here, with the "green watching hills" as witnesses, amid a solitude so grand and lofty that it seems as if the faintest whisper of passion must be hushed by its holy stillness, I should have to relate the perpetration of one of those fearful deeds which, were it for no other peculiarity than its startling suddenness—so utterly at variance with all *civilized* law—must make our beautiful California appear to strangers rather as a hideous phantom than the flower-wreathed reality which she is.

Whether the life which a few men, in the impertinent intoxication of power, have dared to crush out was worth that of a fly, I do not know—perhaps not,—though God alone, methinks, can judge of the value of the soul upon which he has breathed. But certainly the effect upon the hearts of those who played the principal parts in the revolting scene referred to—a tragedy, in my simple judgment, so utterly useless—must be demoralizing in the extreme.

The facts in this sad case are as follows: Last fall, two men were arrested by their partners on suspicion of having stolen from them eighteen hundred dollars in gold-dust. The evidence was not sufficient to convict them, and they were acquitted. They were tried before a meeting of the miners—as at that time the law did not even *pretend* to wave its scepter over this place.

The prosecutors still believed them guilty, and fancied that the gold was hidden in a "coyote hole" near the camp from which it had been taken. They therefore watched the place narrowly while the suspected men remained on the Bar. They made no discoveries, however, and soon after the trial the acquitted persons left the mountains for Marysville.

A few weeks ago, one of these men returned, and has spent most of the time since his arrival in loafing about the different barrooms upon the river. He is said to have been constantly intoxicated. As soon as the losers of the gold heard of his return, they bethought themselves of the "coyote hole," and placed about its entrance some brushwood and stones in such a manner that no one could go into it without disturbing the arrangement of them. In the mean while the thief settled at Rich Bar, and pretended that he was in search of some gravel-ground for mining purposes.

A few mornings ago he returned to his boarding-place—which he had left some hour earlier—with a spade in his hand, and, as he laid it down, carelessly observed that he had "been out prospecting." The losers of the gold went, immediately after breakfast, as they had been in the habit of doing, to see if all was right at the "coyote hole." On this fatal day, they saw that the entrance had been disturbed, and going in, they found upon the ground a money-belt which had apparently just been cut open. Armed with this evidence of guilt, they confronted the suspected person and sternly accused him of having the gold in his possession. Singularly enough, he did not attempt a denial, but said that if they would not bring him to a trial (which of course they promised) he would give it up immediately. He then informed them that they would find it beneath the blankets of his *bunk*— as those queer shelves on which miners sleep, ranged one above another somewhat like the berths of a ship, are generally called. There, sure enough, were six hundred dollars of the missing money, and the unfortunate wretch declared that his partner had taken the remainder to the States.

The Trial

By this time the exciting news had spread all over the Bar. A meeting of the miners was immediately convened, the unhappy man taken into custody, a jury chosen, and a judge, lawyer, etc., appointed. Whether the men who had just regained a portion of their missing property made any objections to the proceedings which followed, I know not. If they had done so, however, it would have made no difference, as the *people* had taken the matter entirely out of their hands.

At one o'clock, so rapidly was the trial conducted, the judge charged the jury, and gently insinuated that they could do no less than to bring in with their verdict of guilty a sentence of *death!* Perhaps you know that when a trial is conducted without the majesty of the law, the jury are compelled to decide not only upon the guilt of the prisoner, but the mode of his punishment also. After a few minutes' absence, the twelve men, who had consented to burden their souls with a responsibility so fearful, returned, and the foreman handed to the judge a paper, from which he read the will of the *people,* as follows: "That William Brown, convicted of stealing, etc., should, in *one hour* from that time, be hung by the neck until he was dead."

By the persuasions of some men more mildly disposed, they granted him a respite of *three hours* to prepare for his sudden entrance into eternity. He employed the time in writing, in his native language (he is a Swede), to some friends in Stockholm. God help them when that fatal post shall arrive, for, no doubt, *he* also, although a criminal, was fondly garnered in many a loving heart.

The Execution

He had exhibited, during the trial, the utmost recklessness and *noncha-lance,* had drank many times in the course of the day, and when the rope was placed about his neck, was evidently much intoxicated. All at once, however, he seemed startled into a consciousness of the awful reality of his position, and requested a few moments for prayer.

The execution was conducted by the jury, and was performed by throwing the cord, one end of which was attached to the neck of the prisoner, across the limb of a tree standing outside of the Rich Bar grave-yard; when all who felt disposed to engage in so revolting a task lifted the poor wretch from the ground in the most awkward manner possible. The whole affair, indeed, was a piece of cruel butchery, though *that* was not intentional, but arose from the ignorance of those who made the preparations. In truth, life was only crushed out of him by hauling the writhing body up and down, several times in succession, by the rope, which was wound round a large bough of his green-leaved gallows. Almost everybody was surprised at the severity of the sentence, and many, with their hands on the cord, did not believe even *then* that it would be carried into effect, but thought that at the last moment the jury would release the prisoner and substitute a milder punishment.

It is said that the crowd generally seemed to feel the solemnity of the occasion, but many of the drunkards, who form a large part of the community on these bars, laughed and shouted as if it were a spectacle got up for their particular amusement. A disgusting specimen of intoxicated humanity, struck with one of those luminous ideas peculiar to his class, staggered up to the victim, who was praying at the moment, and, crowding a dirty rag into his almost unconscious hand, in a voice broken by a drunken hiccough, tearfully implored him to take his "hankercher," and if he were *innocent* (the man had not denied his guilt since first accused), to drop it as soon as he was drawn up into the air, but if *guilty,* not to let it fall on any account.

The body of the criminal was allowed to hang for some hours after the execution. It had commenced storming in the earlier part of the evening, and when those whose business it was to inter the remains arrived at the spot, they found them enwrapped in a soft white shroud of feathery snow-flakes, as if pitying Nature had tried to hide from the offended face of Heaven the cruel deed which her mountain-children had committed.

Afterthoughts

I have heard no one approve of this affair. It seems to have been carried on entirely by the more reckless part of the community. There is no doubt, however, that they seriously *thought* they were doing right, for many of them are kind and sensible men. They firmly believed that such an example was absolutely necessary for the protection of this community. Probably the recent case of Little John [accused of stealing $400 in gold dust, was sentenced to receive thirty-nine lashes and exile] rendered this last sentence more severe than it other-wise would have been. The "Squire," of course, could do nothing (as in criminal cases the *people* utterly refuse to acknowledge his authority) but protest against the whole of the proceedings, which he did in the usual legal manner.

If William Brown had committed a murder, or had even attacked a man for his money—if he had been a quarrelsome, fighting character, endangering lives in his excitement, it would have been a very different affair. But with the exception of the crime for which he perished (he *said* it was his first, and there is no reason to doubt the truth of his assertion), he was a harmless, quiet, inoffensive person.

Vigilante Justice

You must not confound this miners' judgment with the doings of the noble Vigilance Committee of San Francisco. They are almost totally different in their organization and manner of proceeding. The Vigilance Committee had become absolutely necessary for the protection of society. It was composed of the best and wisest men in the city. They used their power with a moderation unexampled in history, and they laid it down with a calm and quiet readiness which was absolutely sublime, when they found that legal justice had again resumed that course of stern, unflinching duty which should always be its characteristic. They took ample time for a thorough investigation of all the circumstances relating to the criminals who fell into their hands, and in *no* case have they hung a man who had not been proved beyond the shadow of a doubt to have committed at least *one* robbery in which life had been endangered, if not absolutely taken.

But by this time, dear M., you must be tired of the melancholy subject, and yet if I keep my promise of relating to you all that interests *us* in our new and strange life, I shall have to finish my letter with a catastrophe in many respects more sad than that which I have just recounted.

A Probable Murder

At the commencement of our first storm, a hard-working, industrious laborer, who had accumulated about eight hundred dollars, concluded to return to the States. As the snow had been falling but a few hours when he, with two acquaintances, started from Rich Bar, no one doubted that they would not reach Marysville in perfect safety. They went on foot themselves, taking with them one mule to carry their blankets. For some unexplained reason, they took an unfrequented route. When the express man came in, he said that he met the two companions of R. eight miles beyond Buck's Rancho, which is the first house one finds after leaving Rich Bar, and is only fourteen miles distant from here.

These men had camped at an uninhabited cabin called the "Frenchman's," where they had built a fire and were making themselves both merry and comfortable. They informed the express man that they had left their *friend* (?) three miles back, in a dying state; that the cold had been too much for him, and that no doubt he was already dead. They had brought away the money, and even the *blankets*, of the expiring wretch! They said that if they had stopped with him they would have been frozen themselves. But even if their story is true, they must be the most brutal of creatures not to have made him as comfortable as possible, with *all* the blankets, and, after they had built their fire and got warm, to have returned and ascertained if he were really dead.

On hearing the express man's report, several men who had been acquainted with the deceased started out to try and discover his remains. They found his violin, broken into several pieces, but *all* traces of the poor fellow himself had disappeared, probably forever.

In the mean while some travelers had carried the same news to Burke's Rancho, when several of the residents of that place followed the two men, and overtook them, to Bidwell's Bar, where they had them arrested on suspicion of murder. They protested their innocence, of course, and one of them said that he would lead a party to the spot where they had left the dying man. On arriving in the vicinity of the place, he at first stated that it was under one tree, then another, and another, and at last ended by declaring that is was utterly impossible for him to remember where they were camped at the time of R.'s death.

Barbarous Deeds

In this state of things, nothing was to be done but to return to B.'s, when, the excitement having somewhat subsided, they were allowed to proceed on their journey, the money—which they both swore R. had willed in his dying moments to a near relation of one of these very men—having been taken from them, in order to be sent by express to the friends of the deceased in the States.

Although they have been acquitted, many shake their heads doubtfully at the whole transaction. It seems very improbable that a man, accustomed all his life to hard labor and exposure, even although slightly unwell, as it is said he was at the time, should have sunk under the cold during a walk of less than twenty miles, amid a gentle fall of snow and rain, when, as it is well known, the air is comparatively mild. It is to be hoped, however, that the companions of R. were brutal rather than criminal, though the desertion of a dying friend under such circumstances, even to the last unfeeling and selfish act of removing from the expiring creature his blankets, is, in truth, almost as bad as actual murder.

I hope, in my next, that I shall have something more cheerful than the above chapter of horrors to relate. In the meanwhile, adios, and think as kindly as you can of the dear California, even though her lustrous skies gaze upon such barbarous deeds.

THE BEAUTIFUL SIERRAS
[April 10, 1852]

You would certainly wonder, were you seated where I now am, how anyone with a quarter of a soul *could* manufacture herself into a bore amid such surroundings as these. The air is as balmy as that of a midsummer's day in the sunniest valleys of New England. It is four o'clock in the evening, and I am sitting on a cigar-box outside of our cabin. From this spot

A miner's cabin on the American River sometime before 1866

not a person is to be seen, except a man who is building a new wing to the Humboldt. Not a human sound, but a slight noise made by the aforesaid individual in tacking on a roof of blue drilling to the room which he is finishing, disturbs the stillness which fills this purest air.

I confess that it is difficult to fix my eyes upon the dull paper, and my fingers upon the duller pen with which I am soiling it. Almost every other minute I find myself stopping to listen to the ceaseless river-psalm, or to gaze up into the wondrous depths of the California heaven; to watch the graceful movements of the pretty brown lizards jerking up their impudent little heads above a moss-wrought log which lies before me, or to mark the dancing water-shadow on the canvas door of the bakeshop opposite; to follow with childish eyes the flight of a golden butterfly, curious to know if it will crown with a capital of winged beauty that column of Nature's carving, the pine stump rising at my feet, or whether it will flutter down (for it is dallying coquettishly around them both) upon that slate-rock beyond, shining so darkly lustrous through a flood of yellow sunlight; or I lazily turn my head, wondering if I know the blue or red shirted miner who is descending the precipitous hill behind me.

In sooth, Molly, it is easy to be commonplace at all times, but I confess that, just at present, I find it difficult to be utilitarian; the saucy lizards, the great orange-dotted butterflies, the still, solemn cedars, the sailing smoke-wreath, and the vaulted splendor above, are wooing me so winningly to higher things. [...]

How to Find Gold
In the first place, then, as to the discovery of gold. In California, at least, it must be confessed that, in this particular, science appears to be completely at fault—or as an intelligent and well-educated miner remarked to us the other day, "I maintain that science is the blindest guide that one could have on a gold-finding expedition. Those men who judge by the appearance of the soil, and depend upon geological calculations, are invariably disappointed, while the ignorant adventurer, who digs just for the sake of digging, is almost sure to be successful."

I suppose that the above observation is quite correct, as all whom we have questioned upon the subject repeat, in substance, the same thing. Wherever geology has said that gold *must* be, there, perversely enough, it lies not; and wherever her ladyship has declared that it could *not* be, there has it oftenest garnered up in miraculous profusion the yellow splendor of its virgin beauty. It is certainly very painful to a well-regulated mind to see the irreverent contempt shown by this beautiful mineral to the dictates of science. But what better can one expect from the root of all evil? As well as can be ascertained, the most lucky of the mining Columbuses have been ignorant sailors, and foreigners, I fancy, are more successful than Americans.

Our countrymen are the most discontented of mortals. They are always longing for big strikes. If a claim is paying them a steady income, by which, if they pleased, they could lay up more in a month than they could in a year at home, still they are dissatisfied, and in most cases will wander off in search of better diggings. There are hundreds now pursuing this foolish course, who, if they had stopped where they first camped, would now have been rich men.

Sometimes a company of these wanderers will find itself upon a bar where a few pieces of the precious metal lie scattered upon the surface of the ground. Of course they immediately prospect it, which is accomplished by panning out a few basinfuls of the soil. If it pays, they claim the spot and build their shanties. The news spreads that wonderful diggings have been discovered at such a place. The monte-dealers—those worse than fiends— rush, vulture-like, upon the scene and erect a round tent, where, in gambling, drinking, swearing, and fighting, the *many* reproduce pandemonium in more than its original horror, while a *few* honestly and industriously commence digging for gold, and lo! as if a fairy's wand had been waved above the bar, a full-grown mining town hath sprung into existence.

Staking a Claim

But first, let me explain to you the claiming system. As there are no state laws upon the subject, each mining community is permitted to make its own. Here they have decided that no man may claim an area of more than forty feet square. This he stakes off, and puts a notice upon it, to the effect that he holds it for mining purposes. If he does not choose to work it immediately, he is obliged to renew the notice every ten days, for, without this precaution, any other person has a right to "jump" it, that is, to take it from him.

There are many ways of evading the above law. For instance, an individual can hold as many claims as he pleases if he keeps a man at work in each, for this workman represents the original owner. I am told, however, that the laborer himself can jump the claim of the very man who employs him, if he pleases so to do. This is seldom, if ever, done. The person who is willing to be hired generally prefers to receive the six dollars per diem, of which he is *sure* in any case, to running the risk of a claim not proving valuable. After all, the holding of claims by proxy is considered rather as a carrying out of the spirit of the law than as an evasion of it. But there are many ways of *really* outwitting this rule, though I cannot stop now to relate them, which give rise to innumerable arbitrations, and nearly every Sunday there is a miners' meeting connected with this subject.

Working a Claim

Having got our gold-mines discovered and claimed, I will try to give you a faint idea of how they work them. Here, in the mountains, the labor of excavation is extremely difficult, on account of the immense rocks which form a large portion of the soil. Of course no man can work out a claim alone. For that reason, and also for the same that makes partnerships desirable, they congregate in companies of four or six, generally designating themselves by the name of the place from whence the majority of the members have emigrated; as, for example, the Illinois, Bunker Hill, Bay State, etc., companies.

In many places the surface soil, or in mining phrase, the top dirt, pays when worked in a long-tom. This machine (I have never been able to discover the derivation of its name[7]) is a trough, generally about twenty feet in length and eight inches in depth, formed of wood, with the exception of six feet at one end, called the "riddle" (query, why "riddle"?[8]), which is made of sheet-iron perforated with holes about the size of a large marble. Underneath this colander-like portion of the long-tom is placed another trough, about ten feet long, the sides six inches, perhaps, in height, which, divided through the middle by a slender slat, is called the riffle-box.

It takes several persons to manage properly a long-tom. Three or four men station themselves with spades at the head of the machine, while at the foot of it stands an individual armed "wid de shovel an' de hoe." The spadesmen throw in large quantities of the precious dirt, which is washed down to the riddle by a stream of water leading into the long-tom through wooden gutters or sluices. When the soil reaches the riddle, it is kept constantly in motion by the man with the hoe. Of course, by this means, all the dirt and gold escapes through the perforations into the riffle-box below, one compartment of which is placed just beyond the

---

7 It is probably so called because of its vague similarity in shape to a type of cannon with that name.

8 It's probably called a riddle because it's riddled with holes. Some called it the grizzly. Normally the riddle was one to two feet long, not six feet.

riddle. Most of the dirt washes over the sides of the riffle-box, but the gold, being so astonishingly heavy, remains safely at the bottom of it.

When the machine gets too full of stones to be worked easily, the man whose business it is to attend to them throws them out with his shovel, looking carefully among them as he does so for any pieces of gold which may have been too large to pass through the holes of the riddle. I am sorry to say that he generally loses his labor. At night they pan out the gold which has been collected in the riffle-box during the day.

Many of the miners decline washing the top dirt at all, but try to reach as quickly as possible the bed-rock, where are found the richest deposits of gold. [. . .] When a company wish to reach the bed-rock as quickly as possible, they sink a shaft (which is nothing more nor less than digging a well) until they "strike it." [*Note:* Elsewhere in her letters, Dame Shirley says some of the shafts were sixty feet deep.] They then commence drifting coyote-holes, as they call them, in search of crevices, which, as I told you before, often pay immensely. These coyote-holes sometimes extend hundreds of feet into the side of the hill. Of course they are obliged to use lights in working them. They generally proceed until the air is so impure as to extinguish the lights, when they return to the entrance of the excavation and commence another, perhaps close to it. When they think that a coyote-hole has been faithfully worked, they clean it up, which is done by scraping the surface of the bed-rock with a knife—lest by chance they have overlooked a crevice—and they are often richly rewarded for this precaution.

Waterworks

Now I must tell you how those having claims on the hills procure the water for washing them. The expense of raising it in any way from the river is too enormous to be thought of for a moment. In most cases it is brought from ravines in the mountains. A company, to which a friend of ours belongs, has dug a ditch about a foot in width and depth, and more than three miles in length, which is fed in this way.

I wish that you could see this ditch. I never beheld a *natural* streamlet more exquisitely beautiful. It undulates over the mossy roots and the gray old rocks like a capricious snake, singing all the time a low song with the "liquidest murmur," and one might almost fancy it the airy and coquettish

Undine herself. When it reaches the top of the hill, the sparkling thing is divided into five or six branches, each one of which supplies one, two, or three long-toms. There is an extra one, called the waste-ditch, leading to the river, into which the water is shut off at night and on Sundays. This race (another and peculiar name for it) has already cost the company more than five thousand dollars.

They sell the water to others at the following rates. Those that have the first use of it pay ten per cent upon all the gold that they take out. As the water runs off from their machine (it now goes by the elegant name of "tailings"), it is taken by a company lower down, and as it is not worth so much as when it was clear, the latter pay but seven per cent. If any others wish the tailings, now still less valuable than at first, they pay four per cent on all the gold which they take out, be it much or little. The water companies are constantly in trouble, and the arbitrations on that subject are very frequent.

I think that I gave you a vague idea of fluming in a former letter. I will not, therefore, repeat it here, but will merely mention that the numerous fluming companies have already commenced their extensive operations upon the river. [***Note:*** Fluming involves diverting a river so the riverbed can be worked.]

As to the rockers, so often mentioned in story and in song, I have not spoken of them since I commenced this letter. The truth is, that I have seldom seen them used, though hundreds are lying ownerless along the banks of the river. I suppose that other machines are better adapted to mining operations in the mountains.

Nature's Great Lottery

Gold-mining is Nature's great lottery scheme. A man may work in a claim for many months, and be poorer at the end of the time than when he commenced, or he may take out thousands in a few hours. It is a mere matter of chance. A friend of ours, a young Spanish surgeon from Guatemala, a person of intelligence and education, told us that after working a claim for six months he had taken out but six ounces.

It must be acknowledged, however, that if a person work his claim himself, is economical and industrious, keeps his health, and is satisfied with small gains, he is bound to make money. And yet I cannot help remarking that almost all with whom we are acquainted seem to have *lost.* Some have had their claims jumped. Many holes, which had been excavated and prepared for working at a great expense, caved in during the heavy rains of the fall and winter.

Often, after a company has spent an immense deal of time and money in sinking a shaft, the water from the springs (the greatest obstacle which the miner has to contend with in this vicinity) rushes in so fast that it is impossible to work in them, or to contrive any machinery to keep it out, and for that reason only, men have been compelled to abandon places where they were at the very time taking out hundreds of dollars a day.

If a fortunate or an unfortunate (which shall I call him?) *does* happen to make a big strike, he is almost sure to fall into the hands of the professed gamblers, who soon relieve him of all care of it. They have not troubled the Bar much during the winter, but as the spring opens they flock in like ominous birds of prey. Last week one left here, after a stay of four days, with over a thousand dollars of the hard-earned gold of the miners. But enough of these best-beloved of Beelzebub, so infinitely worse than the robber or murderer—for, surely, it would be kinder to take a man's life than to poison him with the fatal passion for gambling.

CHANGES AT RICH BAR
[Indian Bar; May 1, 1852]

Nothing of importance has happened since I last wrote, except that the Kanaka [Hawaiian] wife of a man living at The Junction has made him the happy father of a son and heir. They say that she is quite a pretty little woman, only fifteen years old, and walked all the way from Sacramento to this place.

A few evenings ago a Spaniard was stabbed by an American. It seems that the presumptuous foreigner had the impertinence to ask very humbly and meekly that most noble representative of the Stars and Stripes if the latter would pay him a few dollars which he had owed him for some time. His high mightiness the Yankee was not going to put up with any such impertinence, and the poor Spaniard received for answer several inches of cold steel in his breast, which inflicted a very dangerous wound. Nothing was done and very little was said about this atrocious affair.

At Rich Bar they have passed a set of resolutions for the guidance of the inhabitants during the summer, one of which is to the effect that no foreigner shall work in the mines on that bar. This has caused nearly all the Spaniards to immigrate upon Indian Bar, and several new houses for the sale of liquor, etc., are building by these people. It seems to me that the above law is selfish, cruel, and narrow-minded in the extreme.

When I came here the Humboldt was the only public house on the Bar. Now there are the Oriental, Golden Gate, Don Juan, and four or five others, the names of which I do not know. On Sundays the swearing, drinking, gambling, and fighting which are carried on in some of these houses are truly horrible.

It is extremely healthy here. With the exception of two or three men who were drowned when the river was so high, I have not heard of a·death for months.

Nothing worth wasting ink upon has occurred for some time, except the capture of two grizzly-bear cubs by the immortal Yank. He shot the mother, but she fell over the side of a steep hill and he lost her. Yank intends to tame one of the cubs. The other he sold, I believe for fifty dollars. They are certainly the funniest-looking things that I ever saw, and the oddest possible pets.

In October 1852, Louise and her husband traveled to Marysville for three weeks to attend a political convention, as her husband was a delegate. When they returned home, they were shocked to find Indian Bar was rapidly becoming a ghost town.

End of the Dream
From our Log Cabin, Indian Bar; November 21, 1852.

I suppose, Molly dear—at least, I flatter myself—that you have been wondering and fretting a good deal for the last few weeks at not hearing from Dame Shirley. The truth is, that I have been wondering and fretting *myself* almost into a fever at the dreadful prospect of being compelled to spend the winter here, which, on every account, is undesirable.

To our unbounded surprise, we found, on our return from the American Valley, that nearly all the fluming companies had failed. Contrary to

A flume at Brown's Flat in Tuolumne County in the early 1860s

every expectation, on arriving at the bed-rock no gold made its appearance. But a short history of the rise, progress, and final fate of one of these associations, given me in writing by its own secretary, conveys a pretty correct idea of the result of the majority of the remainder.

"The thirteen men, of which the American Fluming Company consisted, commenced getting out timber in February. On the 5th of July they began to lay the flume. A thousand dollars were paid for lumber which they were compelled to buy. They built a dam six feet high and three hundred feet in length, upon which thirty men labored nine days and a half. The cost of said dam was estimated at two thousand dollars. This company left off working on the twenty-fourth day of September, having taken out, in *all*, gold-dust to the amount of forty-one dollars and seventy cents! Their lumber and tools, sold at auction, brought about two hundred dollars."

A very small amount of arithmetical knowledge will enable one to figure up what the American Fluming Company made by *their* summer's work. This result was by no means a singular one. Nearly every person on the river received the same step-mother's treatment from Dame Nature in this her mountain workshop.

Of course the whole world (*our* world) was, to use a phrase much in vogue here, "dead broke." The shopkeepers, restaurants, and gambling-houses, with an amiable confidingness peculiar to such people, had trusted the miners to that degree that they themselves were in the same money-less condition. Such a batch of woeful faces was never seen before, not the least elongated of which was F.'s, to whom nearly all the companies owed large sums.

Of course, with the failure of the golden harvest Othello's occupation was gone. The mass of the unfortunates laid down the shovel and the hoe, and left the river in crowds. It is said that there are not twenty men remaining on Indian Bar, although two months ago you could count them up by hundreds. [. . .]

F. has just entered, with the joyful news that the express man has arrived. He says that it will be impossible for mule trains to get in for some time to come, even if the storm is really over, which he does not believe. In many places on the mountains the snow is already five feet in depth, although he thinks that, so many people are constantly leaving for the valley, the path will be kept open, so that I can make the journey with comparative ease on his horse, which he has kindly offered to lend me, volunteering to accompany F., and some others who will make their exodus at the same time on foot. Of course I shall be obliged to leave my trunks, merely taking a change of linen in a carpet bag. We shall leave to-morrow, whether it rain or snow, for it would be madness to linger any longer.

My heart is heavy at the thought of departing forever from this place. I *like* this wild and barbarous life. I leave it with regret. The solemn fir-trees, whose "slender tops *are* close against the sky" here, the watching hills, and the calmly beautiful river, seem to gaze sorrowfully at me as I stand in the moonlighted midnight to bid them farewell. Beloved, unconventional wood-life; divine Nature, into whose benign eyes I never looked, whose many voices, gay and glad, I never heard, in the artificial heart of the busy world—I quit your serene teachings for a restless and troubled future. Yes, Molly, smile if you will at my folly, but I go from the mountains with a deep heart-sorrow. I took kindly to this existence, which to you seems so sordid and mean. Here, at least, I have been contented.

The "thistle-seed," as you call me, sent abroad its roots right lovingly into this barren soil, and gained an unwonted strength in what seemed to you such unfavorable surroundings. You would hardly recognize the feeble and half-dying invalid, who drooped languidly out of sight as night shut down between your straining gaze and the good ship *Manilla* as she wafted her far away from her Atlantic home, in the person of your *now* perfectly healthy sister.

Some large trees in Calaveras County during the early 1860s

Gold Made Misery My Companion

Alonzo Delano

The following continuation of Alonzo Delano's narrative is composed of excerpts from his letters. By 1851 things were changing once again, as tremendously inflated prices dropped because goods were flooding into California. This, in turn, sparked the rise of California's agricultural industry. While wintering for four months in San Francisco, Delano wrote the following in a letter dated January 15, 1851.

THE CRASH

Last year, from the 3rd of November till about the 1st of February, it was pouring down "from the flood gates of Heaven" like big guns. The rivers overflowed their banks and more than one quarter of the Valley was submerged. This year, up to the present time, there has not been near as much rain as is usual at home, and the weather has been luxuriously pleasant.

The climate on the Coast I think is healthy and decidedly desirable for a residence, and were it not for three especial reasons—a wife and two children at home—I should not think of returning. The valley of Santa Clara and the country around San Jose produce the finest vegetables in the world, as our markets, well supplied, abundantly testify, and when California shall have disenthralled herself of the immorality, the vice, and hordes of Mexican and Sydney villains, as well as a sprinkling from other countries, this portion of it will be desirable as a home.

But now we are in a crisis, the result of which must bring ruin and misfortune to a multitude of individuals, though it may end in substantial benefit to the country. A failure in the mines, as well as a failure in the city, throws men upon their individual resources; and as the best business which has been followed the past season has been that of horticulture, thousands, by a natural impulse, are looking to Mother Earth for her bounty to replenish their pockets. This, of course, will develop the agricultural resources of the country, as well as find a permanent and industrious population employment.

The country at this moment is overstocked with merchandise and provisions. In the mines, unless it may be in those most distant, there is more than can be sold during the winter; and this is the case in all the towns. Everything imported from the States is selling at a ruinous sacrifice, and as the want of rain in the mines prevents the dry diggings from being productive, less gold is obtained than was anticipated, a portion of which would go to pay for these goods. As soon as the upper towns and mines were supplied this fall, the price of many kinds of goods fell ninety per cent. Add to this the exorbitant rents demanded for any place to do business in, and you will not be surprised to hear of failures.

There seems to be a universal stagnation in trade, and although there may be millions to loan on good security, scarcely any businessman who is compelled to borrow can give the security required. A few days since I saw the invoice of a large lot of desirable goods for this market charged at Boston prices, and at higher rates than could be bought for here. Day before yesterday a finished house which had been sent out on speculation, which was said to have cost nearly four thousand dollars, was sold at auction to pay freight and brought eight hundred.

This is a very common occurrence; and when a man wants to build, he watches his chance to find a vessel selling off a cargo of lumber at auction to pay charges. Beautiful crushed sugar is selling at 12½ cts.; best quality of lard at 10 and 12½ cts.; sugar-cured hams, in prime order, at 1 ½ cts.; pickles in quart jars sold a few days since at $1.12½ cts. per dozen. Arrivals of cargoes of merchandise are almost of daily occurrence, and we are advised that heavy shipments are on the way, so that I see no reason why this state of things may not continue for months to come.

I received, a few weeks since, a large consignment of goods to sell on commission, and I have hardly sold enough to get back the small advances which I made upon them. Men are resorting to new methods of disposing of stocks, chiefly fancy goods, and that is by lottery. Heavy amounts of rich jewelry, and even a public house, are offered for sale in this way, tickets selling for from one to five dollars.

But one of the most recent humbugs which has been got up is the astonishing discovery of Gold Bluff, up towards Klamath River. The very sand is so rich that it contains about one-tenth gold—so they say. A vessel has just returned from there with specimens of sand, but the company, instead of loading their ship down with the precious metal, have formed a joint stock company with a capital of a hundred thousand dollars and are selling off shares at a hundred dollars a head. What fools—when they could have made so much more by a week's work in sifting gold at the Bluff—ahem! But fools are not all dead, and they are actually making large sales of shares. I have seen several gentlemen of intelligence who have visited the spot, who say that it is a ridiculous humbug.

Closing Shop and Returning to Mining
Grass Valley, Nevada County; June 11, 1851

Once more in the mountains—once more among the everlasting hills of California, the land of circumstance and of adventure. How truly may it be said that "no man knoweth what the morrow may bring forth."

When I last descended from the snow-capped peaks of the Snowy Mountains, I thought that it was for the last time and that my weary feet would no more climb their dizzy heights, nor my tongue again be parched by burning thirst. But, alas, a life of ease is not for me, and, until the sun of life goes down, I may hardly hope for rest. Yet "hope on, hope ever," and in California even hope for heaven. The desire for wealth brought me here, and the weary search for gold hath made misery often my companion; yet although I have not been completely successful and have run many risks, I am not discouraged and will still plod on.

Trade in the city became dull and fluctuating, and an opportunity occurring of selling out to advantage, it could not be neglected, for here you must go with the current. Stemming it is destruction; so I closed for the time my "merchandise."

Quartz Mining

About the same time the subject of quartz mining began to attract attention and my mining experience was sought. I examined a vein at Grass Valley, between Yuba and Bear rivers, made a favorable report, backed up by an offer to invest all I possessed in the world, and became a party in a quartz mining company. And this species of mining will be the text of my sermon.

Through the whole extent of the California mountains veins of quartz extend which have been found to contain gold in veins, in many instances visible to the naked eye, and which, upon assay, are found to yield astonishing results. It is believed generally that here is the matrix of gold and that from this source the gold of the gulches and streams comes by the decomposition of the rock as well as by being thrown out by volcanic force; and by the action of the elements it slides down to where it is found

Nevada City, looking north toward Sugarloaf Mountain, in the early 1860s

on the banks of streams and in low grounds. It is found in the rock from the finest particles, invisible to the naked eye, to that of spangles and in lumps such as are picked up in the gulch and river diggings.

In large masses of rock you trace a regular vein, generally in small spangles but sometimes in decayed or porous portions. It presents many fantastic shapes; I have seen it assume the shape of a tree, then of leaves, a heart, a human face, &c., &c. These veins of quartz vary in thickness from that of a knife-blade to three feet, and a few score feet may exhibit these changes; but twelve to eighteen inches may be a kind of maximum. They seem to have been forced up through strata of slate or of gray granite, which often present an appearance of decomposition. Sometimes they are in proximity with hornblende. Occasionally the quartz is found decomposed, and in its stead is a rich gravel and earth which yields from ten cents to five, ten, even fifty dollars to the pan. Gold Tunnel, at Nevada City, is of this character.

Gold Tunnel and Gold Hill

By the politeness of G. S. McMakin, Esq., one of the proprietors of that rich mine, I was enabled to make a thorough inspection of their tunnel. It lays in a small ravine worn by water and is, perhaps, sixty feet above the bed of Deer Creek, which flows at its base. In sinking a shaft for the purpose of coyote digging in October last, they struck the vein of quartz which was mostly decomposed, and in December they commenced a regular tunnel to follow the vein. The vein is of a reddish or iron brown, but all the earth which is excavated appears to be extremely rich.

Mr. McMakin took about half a pound of dirt indiscriminately in a pint cup from the side of the mine in my presence, and without using much care in washing, it had fifty cents, and in $1^{15}/_{16}$ of dirt in another instance he found two dollars and eighty cents. They have followed the vein an hundred and ten feet, and it is now about three feet thick, with a dip of forty-five degrees to the east. The base and surrounding rock is gray granite, partially decomposed. Occasionally a large boulder is found through which they blast. They are following the vein, not downward, but horizontally. There are other tunnels at Nevada City, but none so rich as this have been discovered, and in some the vein has not been struck.

Boulders uncovered by placer mining at Knapp's Ranch in Columbia in the early 1860s

At Grass Valley, five miles below Nevada City, are probably the most extensive quartz mining operations that exist at this moment in California. Late last fall a layer of quartz was struck in sinking a shaft for coyote digging on the top of a hill, since called Gold Hill, which was found to contain a large deposit of gold. The quartz here seems to lay in slabs and boulders, as if it had been raised and a mass of earth, falling in, filled the cavity, leaving the quartz near the surface; and consequently, although there is a large quantity of ore, there is not a regular vein, unless at a greater depth than it has been prospected. Across a small ravine south, and perhaps eighty rods distant from Gold Hill, is Massachusetts Hill, where the Sierra Nevada Quartz Mining Company is located.

On this hill the last-named company are in active operation and are opening their mine scientifically so that it may be worked for years. Here they struck a well-defined vein four inches thick and which increased in richness and thickness as they proceeded down, when at the depth of sixty feet the vein was eighteen inches thick, the dip being to the east at an angle of forty-five degrees. At this depth they came to water, but the vein can be followed north and south above the water. They then commenced a tunnel at the base of the hill about an hundred and fifty feet below its apex, and had proceeded only twenty feet when they struck what is supposed to be a lateral vein twelve inches thick of the same character of earth as at Gold Tunnel at Nevada City. They are continuing the tunnel through this vein in the direction of the vein, which they must reach within two hundred feet.

You may judge something of the character of the vein when I tell you that they employed from five to twenty men at an expense of five dollars per day in prospecting—have dug at least four hundred feet, and probably nine tenths of the labor in opening the mine has been unproductive of revenue; yet they have paid all expenses of labor, board, and tools, and acquisition of working territory from the mine itself, by crushing pieces of quartz by hand in a mortar and washing without quicksilver, and have at this moment ten thousand dollars' worth of rock and rich earth raised (estimating it at thirty dollars per ton, the price paid at the mills) clear of expense.

The mines in that vicinity do not sell their richest specimens to the crushing mills. It is only the refuse rock or that in which gold is not visible to the naked eye. The rich specimens the miners crush themselves by hand, and these yield one to ten dollars, and even two ounces to the pound. Indeed, I have one piece weighing nine ounces avoirdupois, which, by estimating its specific gravity, contains three ounces of gold.

I will at some convenient opportunity send you a specimen. One of the specimens, weighing fourteen pounds, from this vein, containing over six hundred dollars, was sold to go to the World's Fair, after being shown in New York.

Crushing Rocks

A year ago there was but a single shanty at Grass Valley; now there are two hundred wood houses, good hotels, stores, a sawmill, four steam crushing mills in operation, and four more in active progress of erection, and vast quantities of rock piled up ready for use. New veins, or rather new openings of the vein, are continually made, and it appears to be uniformly rich as a general thing, though some placers are richer than others. The mills in operation are too light and too imperfect. They should be not less than twenty horsepower, with stampers weighing two hundred and fifty to five hundred each. Those now operating are of from ten to twelve horsepower engines, with stampers weighing about one hundred pounds, though heavy mills are being erected. One by Walsh, Esq., is of sixty horsepower and no doubt will be effective.

But the greatest difficulty is in saving the gold; not more than one fifth is extracted or saved. The general average saved by the mills is five cents to the pound in the refuse rock. Repeated experiments have shown that four fifths of the gold is lost and that there is much more in the quartz which is passed off at the mill than is saved. This subject is occupying the attention of scientific men here, and I hope it will at home. But a small part will amalgamate with quicksilver; if fire is applied, no flux is

Columbia Gulch in the early 1860s

Hydraulic mining near French Corral in Nevada County, California, sometime before 1866. This type of mining was banned in 1884 because of the severe environmental damage it caused.

known which may be reduced to extensive practical use, and if dissolved by acids, the expense of the latter absorbs all the profits.

A New Era

A new era in gold-digging seems to have arisen. Although surface digging is still carried on with its usual labor and disappointments, with its very few successful ones, the mode of washing the earth has steadily improved and dirt that at first would not be touched with the pan is often made very profitable with the sluice. But the developments made in the quartz veins seem to make it as certain here as mining in Peru, Chile or Mexico, where mines have been worked for more than two hundred years, and it is thought that capital may be as safely invested in this species of mining as in railroad, factory, or bank stock, in shipping, farming, or merchandise. But this requires capital to commence with. Individual labor and poor machinery amounts to nothing and must, in general, prove a failure.

To open a mine properly it may cost twenty thousand dollars, though in some instances, by good luck, two thousand dollars may strike the vein; and then to purchase the requisite machinery thirty to forty thousand dollars more may be required before a dollar is returned, but by an expense of two or three thousand dollars a vein may be prospected and a degree of certainty arrived at which will justify a farther expenditure.

I append a calculation predicated upon what is actually done at some of the mines at Grass Valley. I will take a twelve-horsepower engine with poor crushers and imperfect machinery and exorbitant wages as a basis:

10 tons crushed in 24 hours is 20,000 lbs.
Yield per pound 5c.
Total per day $1,000.00
Expenses.
20 men at $10 per day, men boarding themselves, $200
Wear and tear and extras 100–300.00
Profit $700.00
One year, say days 300
$210,000.00

Leaving a profit of two hundred and ten thousand dollars per year. Men can be hired at from three to five dollars per day; and with proper machinery thirty and forty tons of rock can be crushed as well as ten, which, of course, increases your profits. Now, instead of estimating the yield at five cents make it one half or two and one half cents, and you will find you are doing rather a snug cash business; and then hit upon some method of saving all the gold, and instead of two and one half cents to the pound, you will have from fifteen to twenty-five cents at least.

God forbid that I should mislead anyone on this subject. I have suffered too much myself to wish even a dog to endure what I have, but I desire to give my countrymen the truth and the benefit of my experience without my hardships. It is an impression gaining favor here that quartz mining will become a legitimate business of California as much as wool-growing in the Western States, and I confess that I am compelled to adopt that opinion from what I have seen.

I have personally traced this vein by outcrops and excavations more than a hundred and fifty miles, and feel confident of its extent. It passes through the country in a southeast and northwest direction, following the main direction of the Sierra Nevada Mountains, and the general dip is to the east at an angle of forty-five degrees. There are evidences of silver in quantities, but I defer that subject until my information is more definite, although I have seen beautiful specimens of pure metal that had been melted like the lumps of gold which we find.

The awful fire at San Francisco has beggared hundreds and ruined thousands. I, too, come in for my share of loss and at present can only say as the fellow did when the saddle turned and threw him into the mud, "just like my damned luck."

Truly yours,

A. Delano

Sacramento City also had its fires. This one took place on the night of November 2–3, 1852. Since firefighters couldn't get enough water to fight large fires, they tried to create firebreaks by dynamiting city blocks in the path of the blaze, hoping it wouldn't leap over the blown-up buildings. In this way fires could sometimes be contained.

When the gold rush began, San Francisco was mainly a collection of tents and wooden structures, with occasional ships' hulls used as buildings. The rapidly growing town suffered seven major fires in just over a year and a half. The one Delano is referring to in his letter was the sixth major fire, which took place on May 4, 1851, in which three-fourths of the city burned down. It was thought the fire was deliberately set in a paint and upholstery store at 11 p.m. the night before, as a man was seen running from the store at the time the fire started. Between 1,500 and 2,000 houses were destroyed, along with most of business district. It's estimated that the damage amounted to $12 million.

A similar major fire, exactly one year earlier, on May 4, 1850, was also thought to be deliberate, as was one that occurred just seven weeks later, on June 22, 1851, which destroyed ten blocks and parts of six more, including the new city hall building, with a total estimated loss of $3 million.

After each of the major fires, large portions of the city had to be rebuilt. Many wooden structures were replaced with brick buildings, which were more fire resistant, but were later found to be dangerous during earthquakes.

Several volunteer fire departments were established, although they often competed against each other, sometimes resulting in brawls or riots. In one case a building in Chinatown burned down while two fire departments fought each other over the right to fight the fire. Delano included his observations about these fires and the increasing crime problem in his next letters.

THE NEED FOR LAW AND ORDER
[San Francisco; June 13, 1851]

We are in the midst of certainly a moral and nearly a political revolution. The outrages upon the order-loving people have been so great—so many murders, robberies, and incendiary conflagrations have been committed, not only here but throughout California, and so wretchedly has the law been administered—that the people have arisen in their might to protect themselves.

Since the great fire, eight different palpable attempts have been made to fire the city. It is no longer safe to walk the streets after dark unarmed, and we do not know when we lay down at night but that before the morning sun our dwellings may be burnt to ashes. The magistrates and police cannot execute the laws if they would. Lawyers are found who will make the technicalities and subtleties of the law subservient to the horde of villains who are in our midst, to screen them from justice. The penal colonies of Great Britain are emptying their hordes of convicts upon our shores, and every arrival from Sydney swells the number by hundreds. A mass meeting was held on the Plaza yesterday—another today, and another will be held tomorrow, to adopt some measures to protect ourselves and check the crime that is carrying murder and desolation to our citizens in their dwellings. [*Note:* This was the formation of the first Committee of Vigilance.] This is no fancy sketch. Ask any man who is returning from California—he will attest its truth.

A man was caught in the act of setting fire to the city a few days ago. He is in the hands of the law and will escape. Night before last a man was caught with a safe which he had stolen. He was seized, tried by the citizens fairly and impartially, found guilty, and hung [was hanged] before daylight.

There are thousands upon the Plaza today, and with a small exception, the feeling of self-defense was the ruling one. A few attempted to stem the popular current, and a gang of bullies and rowdies attempted to put down the movement on the part of the people, and at one time there were indications of a severe fight. But the people triumphed—resolutions passed which amounted to little else than revolution, and tomorrow another mass meeting is to be held. [. . .]

The city is nearly rebuilt since the fire. I am once more in my old office—rather, in a new one, where the old one stood. I find my actual loss by the fire was a little over twelve hundred dollars, but as luck would have it, it didn't break me. It came a little hard, as it was money loaned out. Quartz mining is still good and will be for ages.

Business, I mean merchandising, is good for nothing. Goods are lower than in New York—even in the mines it does not pay as a general thing. Men dare not employ capital, and there is neither confidence nor credit.

LAWLESS GANGS OF DESPERADOS
[Grass Valley, Sierra Nevada Quartz Mines; June 29, 1851]

The determination of the people in the cities to protect themselves against the lawless gangs of desperados who are bringing ruin upon the whole country is extending itself to the mining districts. Sensible that such felons will take refuge in the mines when an asylum is no longer afforded them in the cities, the miners are associating for the purpose of punishing crime, and Vigilance Committees are organizing. One was formed here last night, and we are ready to pay our respects to all scoundrels who may be inclined to pay us a visit. Repugnant as this course is to Americans who are brought up in the school of law and order, there is no other way to save our lives and to protect our property, for the technicalities of the law have been perverted to screen the guilty and protect them in their career of crime so long that nothing is left but a resolution in fact to put the law into the hands of the people to protect themselves. You will learn by the public prints the infamous use made of the pardoning power by Governor McDougal in granting a full and free pardon to a murderer—a wanton and deliberate murderer. It is but a sample of the manner in which the law has been administered by those entrusted with its execution.

———— ❦ ————

[San Francisco; August 1, 1851]

In the cities, as well as in the mountain wilds, it is unsafe for men to go unarmed, and particularly after nightfall; and even in thoroughfares in the largest towns, men are compelled to take the middle of the street, fearful that the first man they meet may be an assassin or robber with a sling shot or pistol.

For a long time this was patiently endured. That reverence for existing law which is almost an intuitive feeling with Americans endured there, to await its action, in the hope that its just administration would rid society of its pests and excrescences; but when at length it was seen that the executive itself, if not in actual collusion with crime, pardoned it in its most glaring deformity; that criminals almost universally escaped punishment; that in more than two hundred murders in less than a year but a single legal execution had taken place in the whole State, that the police force was wholly inefficient and sometimes even connected with the commission of crime; that witnesses notoriously perjured themselves to screen their companions in guilt and prove an alibi; that public officers were guilty of peculation [embezzlement] and malfeasance; and that for the guilty to be in any event condemned to prison was only affording an easy mode to escape punishment by the insecurity of the jails and the negligence of the jailors; in short, when it was found that under the administration of the law, the insecurity of life and property increased instead of diminished, the people became aroused to a sense of their own wrongs and, convinced that there was no other mode of redress, resolved to take the punishment of their aggressors into their own hands, not in opposition to law and order, but to aid the law to do what of itself it could not do, protect the honest part of the community.

Not a morning paper appeared in San Francisco that did not herald the perpetration of some robbery or murder the previous night in the city, and it was the same from the mines and different parts in the whole country. In distant counties, goaded on to desperation by repeated acts of violence, the citizens occasionally tumultuously arose and seized the perpetrator, when the constituted authorities would interfere, generally with success, and the criminal almost invariably would escape punishment, till at length it became a byword and reproach when an arrest was made: "He will escape by the law."

Up to the present moment, although within the past year at least forty murders have been committed in San Francisco and its immediate vicinity, there has never been a legal execution. In several glaring cases the perpetrators were admitted to merely nominal bail, without the ceremony of incarceration, and were free to continue their assaults and depredations.

Incendiarism [arson] was so common that when the citizen laid down at night, his papers and valuables, as well as clothes, were placed in a situation where they could be seized at a moment's warning, and the thought was constant that before daylight should appear he might be a houseless, homeless, ruined man.

These things could no longer be endured. Self-preservation rendered it imperative that the first law of nature should be observed, and that unless some united effort was made, society must resolve itself into its primitive elements and brute force be the only defense against aggression and violence. Every ship from the penal colonies of Great Britain only added numbers to the English convicts already here, while the vicious of all nations seemed by instinct to find a rendezvous on our shores, so that

California contained hordes of the most accomplished villains who had passed through every grade of crime and were prepared to practice their infernal arts upon the honest and industrious part of the community at the moment of their arrival.

The True Purifiers of Society

Under this state of things an association was organized in San Francisco, composed of its best and most prominent citizens, which soon swelled to a thousand, encouraged and approved by nine tenths of the whole community, who were determined to bring palpable offenders to prompt and speedy justice.

Their first act was to take into custody a thief who was caught in the act of stealing a safe. He was fairly tried before a jury immediately summoned, full proof of guilt was adduced, and without noise or parade he was taken to the plaza about midnight and hung on the piazza of the Adobe.

The second day after, a public meeting was called at which thousands of citizens were assembled, who, with but one single dissenting voice (from a lawyer), ratified by vote the acts of the Vigilance Committee (as it was called).

A second meeting took place the following day at which a series of resolutions were introduced, the object of which was to sustain the Committee in purifying the city from the pest of society and censuring the uncertain and tardy administration of justice by the officers of the law. An attempt was made to prevent the passage of these resolutions by a prominent member of the Legislature, backed up by a gang of rowdies and gamblers whom he had rallied around him and who endeavored to interfere with the meeting by violent and unfair means. But the resolutions passed by overwhelming acclamation—a revolution had in fact taken place.

The Vigilance Committee were looked upon as the true purifiers of society, instead of the courts; yet in no case did the former impede the acts of the latter in its administration of justice; its only aim was to punish speedily those who were not secured by the police, without going through with the technicalities of the law, its insecurity and uncertainty; and yet they punished no criminal without a fair trial, without full and positive proof of guilt.

The effect of this association was speedily felt. After the execution of Jenkins, numbers of known thieves and burglars left the city, and the Recorder's dock, instead of being filled every morning with criminals, fell off at once to a few cases of drunkenness and disorderly conduct. Determined to effect a thorough renovation, the Committee gave notice to notorious villains to leave the city in five days, and when they refused to obey, they were seized and placed in durance [incarcerated] until they could be sent out of the country. Ships from the penal colonies were boarded and the characters of the passengers enquired into, and when they were satisfactorily proven to be convicts, they were not suffered to land, but compelled to return in the same vessel which brought them out.

As a matter of course there was opposition to the measures of the Vigilance Committee. The constituted authorities, sworn to administer the law (which, even if willing, they had been unable to do), looked upon these acts of the Committee as a breach of the law; the gamblers, thieves, their aiders and abettors, their counselors, who were deriving a revenue in shielding them from justice, weak men who had but little at stake or who could be influenced by the specious reasoning of those directly interested in opposing justice and speedy punishment, formed a party in opposition to the people, for the Vigilance Committee was now the only recognized organ of the people as a body.

Yet in spite of the remonstrances of the Courts, the maligners of those interested, and the doubts of the weak, the Committee steadily persevered in their work, and a feeling of security began to be felt which had not been done for a year and a half before. Even the pulpit came forward to the rescue, and ministers of the gospel were heard from the sacred desk to approve of the acts of the Vigilance Committee, under the peculiar circumstances of the case.

The example of San Francisco was speedily followed in all other towns in California, and Vigilance Committees were formed even in the mountains, at nearly every extensive digging, and at this moment, while the constituted authorities are endeavoring to throw impediments in the way of these Committees, thus indirectly encouraging the commission of crime which they cannot punish, these associations are calmly and steadily pursuing their object, and are restoring a degree of confidence in the community which has not been felt for many months.

In addition to other benefits, these associations have had the effect of instigating the Courts to renewed energy and more prompt execution of law and of justice; and when the time shall arrive that there is sufficient honesty and power in the Courts to faithfully discharge their duties in repressing crime and bring offenders to justice, they will at once resign the right of abrogating to themselves the power of punishing the guilty and leave it with those whose duty it is to protect the honest against fraud and violence.

Executions

By the indefatigable energy of the Vigilance Committee, a notorious robber was arrested and the proof was so satisfactory that he was condemned to death. Previous to his execution, Stuart confessed his crimes, and brought to light what had long been suspected, that organized bands of desperadoes existed, that certain lawyers were engaged to protect them with the chicanery of the law, and men of standing were implicated as aiders and abettors in their nefarious practices.

Upon the execution of Stuart in open day at the instance of the committee, the authorities expressed themselves as being highly indignant of what they termed an outrage (on what?—their authority?—certainly not on justice). A grand jury was impaneled at the instance of the Judge, who charged them that an awful outrage had been committed in thus hanging a man contrary to law, although the felon had confessed himself guilty of the blackest crimes, and they were directed to bring in a true bill of indictment. The Mayor, too, came out with a proclamation on the subject, but the Committee, disregarding those impotent offerings of spleen, calmly and deliberately pursued the even tenor of their way, determined that justice should overtake the guilty.

A few days ago at Sacramento City, a young man just from the mines, named Wilson, was robbed in open daylight by four desperadoes who decoyed him to an unfrequented part of the city. An alarm was raised, and in half an hour the robbers were in the hands of the Vigilance Committee.

The authorities interfered and promised most solemnly that they should be tried immediately without delay, and they were finally given up. It became known the following day that the trial had been postponed four days by the interference of the lawyers, when the people assembled and in a determined manner called upon the executors of the law to redeem their promises, and told them decidedly that unless they proceeded at once with the trial, they would take the prisoners themselves.

Seeing that the people were not to be put off with promises, they then went on with the examination according to law, and a week has been dragged along, during which one has been sentenced to ten years' imprisonment, two to be hung, and one remains to be tried. The testimony is positive, as the robbery was witnessed by several individuals; yet, had not the Courts been urged on by the people, weeks would have, in all probability, been consumed; and it is not at all improbable that the villains might have escaped.

And such is the present condition of California. With a beautiful climate, abounding in the elements of wealth and of comfort, it is on the verge of anarchy from the imbecility of its rulers; and were it not for the stern determination of the honest part of community to rid the country of its hideous excrescences, it would soon resolve into the primitive condition of society when justice and protection could only be given by the power of the sword and the will of the strong.

You will think the picture too highly drawn. You will think I am excited. On the contrary, I am of a dispassionate temperament, and the portrait may be judged by every public account which you receive through the press, as well as at the hands of returning Californians.

Yours,

A. D.

Back to Mining
Grass Valley; August 30, 1851

Once more a miner—once more a delver in earth in search of its hidden treasures. Speculation, merchandise, literary efforts, idling, and the various employments which men are forced into in this unparalleled country, unparalleled for good and evil, have again settled into primitive operations, and I am again a mountaineer, my castle a cabin, my frills a red shirt, my hope in the mines, and my heart with my family beyond the Missouri. But gracious heaven! what a change two years has produced.

When I detailed to you, in my first letters, the toils and hardships of the miner exemplified in my own experience, I little thought that in so brief a space of time such a mighty change would occur. Where we then climbed mountains weary and fainting under the heavy loads we carried on our backs, where by difficult paths a mule brought us our hard and homely fare, where the bare means of existence was all we expected—now good roads are opened with daily stages running over them from the principal towns in the Valley; these roads are lined with comfortable houses for the accommodation of travellers, where the luxuries of life may be had in profusion, and a vast number of teams loaded with all the necessaries and comforts for man are constantly passing. Villages and towns are springing up among the hills, which exhibit the life and bustle of trading towns, and society, though by no means purified of its excrescences, begins to assume the form of civilization. Immense works are undertaken which might daunt the resolution of wealthy capitalists at home, and are carried through with success.

In short, in every direction you behold a sublime spectacle of the energy and indomitable perseverance of a free people, who think and act for themselves, and make science and art their slaves in securing the talisman of Earth—gold. Rivers and creeks are turned from their channels and carried by canals miles along mountains, over hills, across gulches, by means of aqueducts, for forty miles or more, thus distributing the indispensable element to the miner for separating the gold from the earth and opening to man rich deposits which could not be worked without water. [...]

A year ago there were no inhabitants here. Occasionally a solitary miner might be seen resting his weary limbs in the shade of a magnificent pine, or while prospecting under the weight of his blankets, mining tools and transient supply of pork and hard bread, keeping a cautious watch with his hand on his trusty rifle to guard against surprise, not knowing but in another instant an arrow from the bow of some lurking treacherous savage might terminate his toil and earthly career at one and the same moment.

Now in this immediate vicinity there are probably two thousand men at work, with all the comforts of life within their reach, and the only danger is from the robber and midnight assassin, and these are now held in check. Families are coming in, and although female influence is but little felt, still the germ is laid, and the lower mines will soon present that feature in the happiness of isolated man.

Christmas and New Year's in Mud Springs

Andrew Gilmore

Twenty-two-year-old Andrew Gilmore headed west to seek his fortune, accompanied by his brother Nathan, in 1851. The two ended up in Mud Springs, which was about five miles southwest of Placerville. In 1855, the residents of Mud Springs decided the town would be better off if they changed the name to the more attractive El Dorado.

Placerville's Main Street in the early 1860s

Placerville was originally named Dry Diggins, but by 1849 it had become popularly known as Hangtown because of the many executions that took place there. Then, in 1854, the town's fathers renamed it Placerville.

On their arrival, the Gilmores were initially quite surprised. Having come from a religious community in Indiana, they always considered Sunday to be a day of worship. Not so in gold country. Here it was just a day off from work and "was the day when gambling halls, saloons, dancehalls did their best business." The Gilmores quickly realized they were not in Indiana anymore.

Still, they were there with a singular purpose in mind and they immediately set to work. In the winter of 1851–52, Andrew wrote the following letter to another of his brothers, who had stayed at home.

A VERY GOOD DAY
Pine Cottage; December 24th, [1851], Wdns. Nite

Dear Brother:

'Tis night, the labors of another day are over and I have seated myself very comfortably on my stool by the side of the table to talk with you a while with my pen as this is the only way by which we can now converse. As I have been hard at work today and feel quite tired, I shall not trouble you with many lines tonight.

Nath has gone to bed. A. and Joe are at our next door neighbors and they are all well as a matter of course. I am consequently sitting here all alone, by myself and nobody to bother me. I said that I had been at work today. Well, I have, and I will tell you what I have done.

We got up very early this morning and ate breakfast before daylight, and then Aaron and I went to work to washing mud. We have a long-tom to wash in. Joe and I dig up the mud and then throw it in the tom while A. washes it. It is pretty muddy disagreeable work, I can assure you.

Well, we worked all day only stopping to eat dinner and we made $32.00. Nath is working in a tunnel. But that was not all my day's work either, for after coming home I went to work, though I was very tired, and washed five of the dirtiest kind of shirts. These at 25 cts. a shirt (the price of washing in this country) would make $1.25 and this added to $10.66⅔ would, according to the simple rule of addition, make my day's work $11.91⅔, which I'll venture to say is more than you have made today. Yes, and it's more than I make every day tho' it is the least day's work I have done this week.

Dry Diggings in the Rainy Season

These are dry diggings. I would have you to understand that they can only be worked in the wet season. It seems to be a notion entertained generally among you that during the wet season no work can be done in the mines and that it pours down rain constantly during the winter. Both of these notions are far from being correct. During the rainy season, if you might call it such, is the only time that these diggings can be worked to any advantage, as you must know that in all mining operations water is essentially necessary unless it should be in the diggings where you could pick up slugs the size of your foot.

Such diggings I have frequently heard of but I have never yet been fortunate enough to find them. Mining operations are never suspended but are carried on during all seasons of the year and in all kinds of weather. As for the weather: that is nearly the same from one end of the year to the other, there being but few days but what a person can work. It does not rain one-tenth as much here in the winter as it does in Indiana. At least, it did not last winter, and this winter so far has not been as wet as last. For the last three days it has rained more than at any time before during the present winter.

We have an abundance of water now to wash in any of the ravines, but I fear it will not last long as it has cleared away and looks as though we were going to have another dry spell of two or three weeks. The water quits running almost as soon as it quits raining, so that as the old saying goes, we have to make hay while the sun shines, or rather we have to make gold when it rains. We don't mind showers but draw on our oilcloth suits and work away bidding defiance to rain. We can come in at night almost as dry as if we have been sitting by the fire all day.

We can average when we have plenty of water about $8 per day and these diggings have all been worked over once or twice before, so that you may judge they were, in the first instance, tolerably rich. I believe that all of the reports that were published with reference to the richness of the mines when they were first discovered were true for it seems to me that at that time a man could as easily make from one to three ounces per day as we can now make one-half an ounce. At least, I believe that with my present knowledge of mining and with the present machines for separating the gold from the dirt, I could have made an independent fortune in a few weeks.

At that time they had nothing but pans or cradles to wash in. But now great improvements have been made in the machines for washing. With the tom we can wash six times as much dirt in a day as in a cradle. Consequently, dirt that is only one-sixth as rich as dirt that would pay for washing in a cradle would pay for toming.

The boys are all in bed asnoring away, so good night.

CHRISTMAS IN THE RAIN
Thursday night—[December] 25th

"Christmas Gift to You." Oh, I wish that I could be at home today. I think we would have a Christmas party. We would have the old gobbler roasted with a score of fat hens, pound cakes, pies, and lots of other good things. But the best of all would be the pleasure of seeing you all. Probably if we live we may be with you next Christmas.

I will tell you what kind of a day it has been and what we have been doing. It has been the most rainy day I believe that I have ever seen in this country. In fact, it would pass very well in old "Put" [Putman County, Indiana] for a wet day and we are most assuredly not sorry to see it, for we now feel confident from the quantity of rain that has fallen today that we will have an abundance of water to wash for some time to come, and it has still strong indications of continuing. This morning we got up quite early as usual and Aaron had breakfast over by daylight. As we had no invitations to any Christmas parties: and feeling no inclination to go on a "bust," we thought we might spend the day as profitably by going down to our diggings and working like fine fellows, even if it was Christmas and awful rainy at that. So Aaron and I encased ourselves in our waterproof suits and went to work, while Nath and Joe went to town to buy a new tom and also to wash some dirt that we have thrown up near our old cabin. A. and I worked until three o'clock in the afternoon, when it commenced raining so hard that it raised the water so much that we were obliged to quit. We made $11.25 each, which was a tolerably good rainy day's work. Nath and Joe bought a tom for which they paid $14. They washed a short time and made $9.

It is getting late and I must go to bed. It is very dark and cloudy but not raining any tonight. Good night.

REWORKING THE DIGGINGS
Saturday night. [December 27]

The week's work is over and I am not sorry either. We have been working faithfully every day this week and are consequently glad when Saturday night comes, knowing that on the morrow we will get to rest. The night is dark and cloudy. Some rain occasionally patters on the roof of our romantic little pine log cabin that is pleasantly situated among the stately pines. It is thundering in the southwest, which is an indication that we are going to have more rain.

It thunders but seldom in this country. We have rain now to our satisfaction. Every little ravine that was as dry as the floor this time last week is now running water enough to turn a mill. I have never seen it rain as it has done this week since I have been here.

It is now a little like what I imagined the rainy season was and if it will only continue this way there will be more gold taken out of the dry diggings this winter than there ever has been. Last winter being such a dry winter there was no water to wash of any consequence. Consequently a great many of the dry ravines have never been worked any since the winter of 1849.

Any diggings that were worked in 1849 will pay well for working over again. In fact, sometimes they even pay better the second time than the first. A great many of the ravines here have been worked over three or four times and the last time has paid good wages. Aaron and I have been washing today dirt that has all been washed once before and we made $31. Probably next winter somebody else will wash this same dirt over again but I think if they do they will not get very much for I think we certainly saved the most of the gold. But I suppose the persons who washed the dirt before us thought they were getting all of it.

When these diggings were first worked they used rockers altogether to wash in, and it was impossible to save the fine gold with these machines.

In fact, no machine has yet been made that will save all the gold, but a tom comes the nearest. For you must know that gold exists in particles as fine as flour almost and consequently those fine particles being as light as the sand will be washed by the water away with the sand. These diggings are paying much better than they did last winter and I think I might safely put down the average of miners here at present at $8 per day. That is a very low estimate.

Business here now is very brisk. Since the rain, provisions have advanced 5¢ in the lb. but fortunately we laid in a supply of the most important articles before the rain. Provisions are only about one-half as high as they were last winter. Our living now costs us about $4.50 a week each. At the boarding houses in town they charge $10 per week. For a single meal at the public houses—$1.00.

A NEW YEAR
Thurs. nite, Jan. 1st, 1852

This is New Year evening. I take up my pen to write a little more toward filling these pages. The year 1851 is now received with the past. Its months, weeks, and days have flown into oblivion. They are beyond our reach, past recalling, but a new year is now before us for enjoyment and improvement. If our lives are spared we should endeavor to spend it better than the one that has just closed.

The day has been cloudy and rather sultry. I am perfectly comfortable with scarcely any fire tonight, so that you may judge that it is not very cold. It has rained but very little since last Saturday, though mostly cloudy. It is sprinkling occasionally tonight. We have been looking for a letter for some time but have not received any. The latest we have from home were written in September.

Saturday night, [January] 3rd

I have just finished washing the dishes and doing up the household affairs and have taken my seat at the table to write some more. I'll tell you how we manage our housekeeping affairs as that may be an interesting item.

Well, you see we take it by turns, each one taking charge of the culinary department a week at a time, so in that way all have a fairer chance of testing our skill in the management of the pots. We are now pretty expert hands, I can assure you. If you will just come over and take breakfast with us in the morning I'll agree to bake for you some as good light biscuits as you ever ate. I will give you excellent coffee (though we haven't got any cream), besides lots of other good things. In the cooking line we are hard to beat.

Without changing the subject or anything of the kind, but did you ever hear the frogs croaking in January? Well, if you were here tonight you could hear them. It never gets so cold here but that the frogs are always able to croak.

This is one of the most beautiful nights I ever saw, warm enough to be comfortable without any fire. It is perfectly clear and calm, the moon shining most brilliantly to disclose the outlines of the neighboring hills and mountains that are covered with the verdant pines. Oh, a moonlight scene in this country is beautiful beyond description. The tall, green pines look more beautiful in the soft moonlight than at any other time.

—◦—

Thursday night, the 8th [of January]

I resume my pen to close this letter so as to start it out the next mail, which will close shortly. I have delayed finishing it, hoping that we would receive a letter from home, but none has yet come.

The weather is clear and beautiful. No appearance of rain. The water in the ravines has quit running and we now have none to wash with. But I hope that we will have rain before many days. It seems now just like spring. The rains have started the grass to growing and the hills that a few weeks since were parched with the long dry summer are now quite green. The oaks are the principal trees that have shed their leaves. The other trees and shrubs of the forest are fresh and green. [. . .]

Your affectionate brother,

A. H. Gilmore

San Francisco and Its Corrupt Government

Mifflin Wistar Gibbs

California's 1849 constitution outlawed slavery in the state, but some Southerners brought slaves with them from states where slavery was still legal. Once within the state, the slave would have legally been free, but they were sometimes afraid to press the issue and continued in their same role as before. Over the next few years there were a number of court cases involving slavery and the national Fugitive Slave Law. This became a hot issue in California, as it was throughout the rest of country. Things came to a boil in the years leading up to the Civil War. As the pro-slavery forces fought against the abolitionists, the laws were altered so that even a legally freed slave was under threat of being returned to slavery.

The gold rush offered everyone a chance at riches. As a result there were a number of wealthy African Americans in the state who assisted slaves to escape. There were also African American organizations, as well as largely Caucasian abolitionist groups and lawyers, that helped slaves and former slaves in every way they could.

Mifflin Wistar Gibbs became one of the leading citizens who was directly involved in this early civil rights movement. He was an African American born in Philadelphia. At the age of eight, after his father died, he was forced to quit school and go to work. He eventually became involved in the abolitionist movement and worked on the Underground Railroad. When he was twenty-seven—following a lecture tour of western New York with Frederick Douglass—he sailed from New York, arriving in San Francisco in September 1850.

While Gibbs's struggles for civil rights are interesting, they are not the focus of the following selections, as they were not directly related to the gold rush. Here he relates his experiences on arriving in San Francisco, practically penniless, and offers his unique take on the rise of the second Committee of Vigilance. This is from his book *Shadow and Light,* which was published in 1902.

OFF TO CALIFORNIA

The war with Mexico, discovery of gold in California in 1848, the acquisition of new territory, and the developments of our hitherto undeveloped Western possessions, stimulated the financial pulse, and permeated every avenue of industry and speculative life. While in New York State I met several going and returning gold seekers, many giving dazzling accounts of immense deposits of gold in the new Eldorado; and others, as ever the case with adventurers, gave gloomy statements of peril and disaster.

A judicious temperament, untiring energy, a lexicon of endeavor, in which there is no such word as "fail," is the only open sesame to hidden opportunities in a new country. Fortune, in precarious mood, may sometime smile on the inert, but she seldom fails to surrender to pluck, tenacity, and perseverance. As the Oxford men say, it is the one pull more of the oar that proves the "beefiness of the fellow;" it is the one march more that wins the campaign; the five minutes more persistent courage that wins the fight.

I returned to Philadelphia, and with some friendly assistance, sailed, in 1850, from New York, as a steerage passenger for San Francisco. Arriving at Aspinwall, the point of debarkation, on the Atlantic side, boats and boatsmen were engaged to transport passengers and baggage up the "Chagress," a small and shallow river. Crossing the Isthmus to Panama, on the Pacific side, I found Panama very cosmopolitan in appearance, for mingled with the sombrero-attired South American could be seen denizens from every foreign clime. [. . .]

PENNILESS IN SAN FRANCISCO

Having made myself somewhat presentable upon leaving the steerage of the steamer, my trunk on a dray, I proceeded to an unprepossessing hotel kept by a colored man on Kearny street. The cursory view from the outside, and the further inspection on the inside, reminded me of the old lady's description of her watch, for she said, "it might look pretty hard on the outside, but the inside works were all right." And so thought its jolly patrons. Seated at tables, well supplied with piles of gold and silver, where numerous disciples of that ancient trickster Pharaoh, being dubious perhaps of the propriety of adopting the literal orthography of his name, and abbreviated it to Faro.

Getting something for nothing, or risking the smaller in hope of obtaining the greater, seems a passion inherent in human nature, requiring a calm survey of the probabilities, and oftimes the baneful effects to attain a moral resistance. It is the "ignus fatu[u]s" [will-o'-the-wisp] that has lured many promising ones and wrecked the future of many lives. The effervescent happiness of some of the worshipers at this shrine was conspicuous. The future to them seemed cloudless. It was not so with me. I had a secret not at all complacent, for it seemed anxious to get out, and while unhappy from its presence, I thought it wise to retain it.

When I approached the bar I asked for accommodation, and my trunk was brought in. While awaiting this preparatory step to domicile, and gazing at the prints and pictures more or less "blaser" that adorned the bar, my eye caught a notice, prominently placed, in gilt letters. I see it now: "Board twelve dollars a week in advance."

It was not the price, but the stipulation demanded that appalled me. Had I looked through a magnifying glass the letters could not have appeared larger. With the brilliancy of a search light they seemed to ask, "Who are you and how are you fixed?" I responded by "staring fate in the face," and going up to the bar asked for a cigar. How much? Ten cents. I had sixty cents when I landed; had paid fifty for trunk drayage, and I was now a moneyless man—hence my secret.

Would there be strict enforcement of conditions mentioned in that ominous card. I was unacquainted with the Bohemian "song and dance" parlance in such extremities, and wondered would letting my secret come out, let a dinner come in. Possibly, I may have often been deceived when appealed to, but that experience has often been fruitful to friendless hunger. Finally the bell rang, and a polite invitation from the landlord placed me at the table. There is nothing so helpful to a disconsolate man as a good dinner. It dissipates melancholy and stimulates persistency. Never preach high moral rectitude or the possibilities of industry to a hungry man. First give him something to eat, then should there be a vulnerable spot to such admonition you will succeed. If not, he is an incorrigible.

After dinner I immediately went out, and after many attempts to seek employment of any kind, I approached a house in course of construction and applied to the contractor for work. He replied he did not need help. I asked the price of wages. Ten dollars a day. I said you could much oblige me by giving me, if only a few days' work, as I have just arrived. After a few moments' thought, during which mayhap charity and gain held conference, which succumbed, it is needless to premise, for we sometimes ascribe selfish motives to kindly acts, he said that if I choose to come for nine dollars a day I might. It is unnecessary for me to add that I chose to come.

When I got outside the building an appalling thought presented itself; whoever heard of a carpenter announcing himself ready for work without his tools. A minister may be without piety, a lawyer without clients, a politician impolitic, but a carpenter without tools, never! It would be prima facie evidence of an imposter. I went back and asked what tools I must bring upon the morrow; he told me and I left. But the tools, the tools, how was I to get them. My only acquaintance in the city was my landlord. But prospects were too bright to reveal to him my secret. I wended my way to a large tent having an assortment of hardware and was shown the tools needed. I then told the merchant that I had no money, and of the place I had to work the next morning. He said nothing for a moment, looked me over, and then said: "All right take them." I felt great relief when I paid the merchant and my landlord on the following Saturday.

Why do I detail to such length these items of endeavor; experiences which have had similarity in many lives? For the reason that they seem to contain data for a moral, which if observed may be useful. Never disclose your poverty until the last gleam of hope has sunk beneath the horizon of your best effort, remembering that invincible determination holds the key to success, while advice and assistance hitherto laggard, now with hasty steps greets you within the door.

I was not allowed to long pursue carpentering. White employees finding me at work on the same building would "strike." On one occasion the contractor came to me and said, "I expect you will have to stop, for this house must be finished in the time specified; but, if you can get six or eight equally good workmen, I will let these fellows go. Not that I have any special liking for your people. I am giving these men all the wages they demand, and I am not willing to submit to the tyranny of their dictation if I can help it." [. . .] I could not find the men he wanted or subsequent employment of that kind.

All classes of labor were highly remunerative, blacking boots not excepted. I after engaged in this, and other like humble employments, part of which was for Hon. John C. Frémont, "the path finder overland to California."

Saving my earnings, I joined a firm already established in the clothing business. After a year or more so engaged, I became a partner in the firm of Lester & Gibbs, importers of fine boots and shoes.

The following section is interesting because it is written from the point of view of a judge. After leaving California, Gibbs worked at a variety of occupations, but he usually quickly became a civic leader. In Victoria, British Columbia, he became the first black man elected to the city council. In Little Rock, Arkansas, he studied law, passed the bar and became an attorney, then a municipal judge. His years of involvement with the Republican Party—which was the more liberal party at the time—led to a variety of appointed positions, including United States Consul to Madagascar. It was after all of this that he wrote this next section about San Francisco's second Committee of Vigilance, which formed in 1856.

The establishment of the Vigilance Committee raises the question: When you have an openly criminal government, are you justified in taking matters into your own hands by becoming a vigilante? Is it OK to break the law to restore law and order, by overthrowing the local elected government? Are illegal means permitted when legal avenues are unavailable? In a broader context, are there situations where the ends justify the means? Those were the questions that confronted San Franciscans, including Gibbs, twice during the gold rush.

The first Committee of Vigilance, formed in 1851, had about 700 members. That group tried and hanged four people, flogged one, and exiled twenty-eight. The second Committee of Vigilance was formed in 1856, with around 6,000 members. Again, four men were hanged and elected officials were forced to resign. Both committees were disbanded after three months and both forced the replacement of corrupt Democrat politicians—then the more conservative pro-slavery party—with Republicans.

No doubt drawing on his experience as a lawyer and a judge, along with his personal experience in San Francisco, Gibbs wrote the following.

Sharpshooters of San Francisco's second Committee of Vigilance, photographed on May 15, 1856

A CROOKED JUSTICE SYSTEM

A rush to newly discovered gold fields bring in view every trait of human character, the more vicious standing out in bold relief, and stamping their impress upon the locality. This phase and most primitive situation can be accounted for partly by the cupidity of mankind, but mainly that the first arrivals are chiefly adventurers. Single men, untrammeled by family cares, traders, saloonists, gamblers, and that unknown quantity of indefinite quality, ever present, content to allow others to fix a status of society, provided they do not touch on their own special interests, and that other, the unscrupulous but active professional politician, having been dishonored at home, still astute and determined, seeks new fields for booty, obtain positions of trust and then consummate peculation [embezzlement] and outrage under the forms of law. But the necessity for the honest administration of the law eventually asserts itself for the enforcement of order.

It was quaintly said by a governor of Arkansas that he believed that a public official should be "reasonably honest." Even should that limited standard of official integrity be invaded, the people with an honest ballot need not be long in rectifying the evil by legal means. But cannot something be said in palliation [mitigation] of summary punishment by illegal means, when it is notorious and indisputable that all machinery for the execution of the law and the maintenance of order, the judges, prosecuting attorneys, sheriff, and drawers of jurors, and every other of court of law, are in the hands of a despotic cabal who excessively tax, and whose courts convict all those who oppose them, and exonerate by trial the most farcical, the vilest criminal, rob and murder in broad day light, often at the bidding of their protectors.

Such a status for a people claiming to be civilized seems difficult to conceive, yet the above was not an hypothesis of condition, but the actual one that existed in California and San Francisco, especially from 1849 to 1855. Gamblers and dishonest politicians from other States held the government, and there was no legal redress. Every attempt of the friends of law and order to elect honest men to office was met at the polls by vituperation and assault.

One of the means for thinning out the ranks of their opponents at the polls they found very efficient. It was to scatter their "thugs" along the line of waiting voters and known opposers, and quickly and covertly inject the metal part of a shoemaker's awl in the rear, but most fleshy part, of his adversary's anatomy, making sitting unpleasant for a time. There was usually uncertainty as to the point of compass from which the hint came to leave, but none as to the fact of its arrival. Hence the reformer did not stand on the order of his going, but generally left the line. These votes, of course, were not thrown out, for the reason they never got in. It diminished, but did not abolish the necessity of stuffing ballot boxes.

In the West I once knew an old magistrate named Scott, noted for his impartiality, but only called Judge Scott by non-patrons of his court, who had never come within the purview of his administration, to others he was known as "old Necessity," for it was said he knew no law. Revolutions, the beneficial results of which will ever live in the history of mankind, founded as they were on the rights of human nature and desire for the establishment and conservation of just government, have ever been the outgrowth of necessity.

Patient in protest of misgovernment, men are prone to "bear the ill they have" until, like the accumulation of rills on mountain side, indignation leaps the bounds of legal form and prostrate law to find their essence and purpose in reconstruction. At the time of which I write, there seemed nothing left for the friends of law, bereft as they were of all statutory means for its enforcement, but making a virtue of this necessity by organizing a "vigilance committee" to wrench by physical strength that unobtainable by moral right. There had been no flourish of trumpets, no herald of the impending storm, but the pent up forces of revolution in inertion, now fierce for action, discarded restraint. Stern, but quiet had been the preparation for a revolution which had come, as come it ever will, with such inviting environments. It was not that normal status, the usual frailties of human nature described by Hooker as "stains and blemishes that will remain till the end of the world, what form of government, soever, may take place, they grow out of man's nature." But in this event the stains and blemishes were effaced by a common atrocity.

A Citizen Army

Sitting at the back of my store on Clay street a beautiful Sunday morning, one of those mornings peculiar to San Francisco, with its balmy breezes and Italian skies, there seemed an unusual stillness, such a quiet as precedes the cyclone in tropical climes, only broken occasionally by silvery peals of the church bells. When suddenly I heard the plank street resound with the tramp of a multitude. No voice or other sound was heard but the tramp of soldiery, whose rhythm of sound and motion is ever a proclamation that thrills by its intensity, whether conquest or conservation be its mission. I hastened to the door and was appalled at the sight. In marching column, six or eight abreast, five thousand men carrying arms with head erect, a resolute determination born of conviction depicted in lineament of feature and expression.

Hastily improvised barracks in large storehouses east of Montgomery street, fortified by hundreds of gunny sacks filled with sand, designated "Fort Gunney," was the quarters for committee and soldiers. The committee immediately dispatched deputies to arrest and bring to the Fort the leaders of this cabal of misgovernment.

The effort to do so gave striking evidence of the cowardice of assassins. Men whose very name had inspired terror, and whose appearance in the corridors of hotels or barrooms hushed into silence the free or merry expression of their patrons, now fled and hid away "like damned ghosts at the smell of day" from the popular uprising of the people. The event which precipitated the movement—the last and crowning act of this oligarchy—was the shooting of James King, of William, a banker and publisher of a paper dedicated to the exposure and denunciation of this ring of dishonest officials and assassins. It was done in broad daylight on Montgomery Street, the main thoroughfare of the city. Mr. King, of William County, Maryland, was a terse writer, a gentleman highly esteemed for integrity and devotion to the best interests of his adopted State.

Many of the gang who had time and opportunity hid on steamers and sailing vessels to facilitate escape, but quite a number were arrested and taken to Fort Gunny for trial. One or two of the most prominent took refuge in the jail—a strong and well-appointed brick building—where, under the protection of their own hirelings in fancied security [they] considered themselves safe.

City Supervisor James Casey shot newspaper editor James King in 1856 because King revealed that Casey had previously been an inmate in New York's Sing Sing Prison. King's murder resulted in the formation of the second Committee of Vigilance.

A deputation of the committee from the fort placed a cannon at proper distance from the entrance to the jail. With a watch in his hand, the captain of the squad gave the keepers ten minutes to open the doors and deliver the culprits. I well remember the excitement that increased in intensity as the allotted period diminished; the fuse lighted, and two minutes to spare; the door opened; the delivery was made, and the march to Fort Gunny began.

A trial court had been organized at which the testimony was taken, verdict rendered, and judgment passed. From a beam projecting over an upper story window, used for hoisting merchandise, the convicted criminals were executed.

The means resorted to for the purification of the municipality were drastic, but the ensuing feeling of personal safety and confidence in a new administration appeared to be ample justification. Much has been said and written in defense and in condemnation of revolutionary methods for the reformation of government. It cannot but be apparent that when it is impossible to execute the virtuous purposes of government, the machinery having passed to notorious violators, who use it solely for vicious purpose, there seems nothing left for the votaries of order than to seize the reins with strong right arm and restore a status of justice that should be the pride and glory of all civilized people.

James Casey was executed by the vigilantes in 1856, along with Charles Cora, who had shot a US marshal.

Flush Times in California

Ulysses S. Grant

Ulysses S. Grant was the greatest Union general of the Civil War, and was elected president of the United States. While he was a good president, his reputation suffered from his defense of corrupt appointees, and because of the 1873–1879 economic depression. Accusations of Grant's drunkenness as a general, and of being a ruthless butcher of men, are false, unjustified slanders made by men who were trying to discredit him. Yet they unfortunately still persist in the public mind today.

After fighting as a cavalryman during the Mexican-American War, Grant was stationed in Fort Vancouver in the Oregon Territory, crossing the isthmus of Panama and arriving in San Francisco early in September 1852. He wrote the following in his book, *Personal Memoirs of U. S. Grant.*

DENIZENS OF THE RUSH

San Francisco at that day was a lively place. Gold, or placer digging as it was called, was at its height. Steamers plied daily between San Francisco and both Stockton and Sacramento. Passengers and gold from the southern mines came by the Stockton boat; from the northern mines by Sacramento. In the evening when these boats arrived, Long Wharf—there was but one wharf in San Francisco in 1852—was alive with people crowding to meet the miners as they came down to sell their "dust" and to "have a time."

Of these some were runners for hotels, boarding houses or restaurants; others belonged to a class of impecunious adventurers, of good manners and good presence, who were ever on the alert to make the acquaintance of people with some ready means, in the hope of being asked to take a

Lumber on San Francisco's Mission Street wharf is shown in a picture taken before 1866.

meal at a restaurant. Many were young men of good family, good education and gentlemanly instincts. Their parents had been able to support them during their minority, and to give them good educations, but not to maintain them afterwards.

From 1849 to 1853 there was a rush of people to the Pacific coast, of the class described. All thought that fortunes were to be picked up, without effort, in the gold fields on the Pacific. Some realized more than their most sanguine expectations; but for one such there were hundreds disappointed, many of whom now fill unknown graves; others died wrecks of their former selves, and many, without a vicious instinct, became criminals and outcasts.

STRANGER THAN FICTION

Many of the real scenes in early California life exceed in strangeness and interest any of the mere products of the brain of the novelist. Those early days in California brought out character. It was a long way off then, and the journey was expensive. The fortunate could go by Cape Horn or by the Isthmus of Panama; but the mass of pioneers crossed the plains with their ox-teams. This took an entire summer. They were very lucky when they got through with a yoke of worn-out cattle.

All other means were exhausted in procuring the outfit on the Missouri River. The immigrant, on arriving, found himself a stranger, in a strange land, far from friends. Time pressed, for the little means that could be realized from the sale of what was left of the outfit would not support a man long at California prices. Many became discouraged. Others would take off their coats and look for a job, no matter what it might be. These succeeded as a rule. There were many young men who had studied professions before they went to California, and who had never done a day's manual labor in their lives, who took in the situation at once and went to work to make a start at anything they could get to do.

Some supplied carpenters and masons with material—carrying plank, brick, or mortar, as the case might be; others drove stages, drays, or baggage wagons, until they could do better. More became discouraged early and spent their time looking up people who would "treat," or lounging about restaurants and or gambling houses where free lunches were furnished daily. They were welcomed at these places because they often brought in miners who proved good customers.

My regiment spent a few weeks at Benicia barracks, and then was ordered to Fort Vancouver, on the Columbia River, then in Oregon Territory. During the winter of 1852–3 the territory was divided, all north of the Columbia River being taken from Oregon to make Washington Territory.

Prices for all kinds of supplies were so high on the Pacific coast from 1849 until at least 1853—that it would have been impossible for officers of the army to exist upon their pay, if it had not been that authority was given them to purchase from the commissary such supplies as he kept, at New Orleans wholesale prices. A cook could not be hired for the pay of a captain. The cook could do better.

THE RAPIDLY EVOLVING CITY

The death of Colonel Bliss, of the Adjutant General's department, which occurred July 5th, 1853, promoted me to the captaincy of a company then stationed at Humboldt Bay, California. The notice reached me in September of the same year, and I very soon started to join my new command.

There was no way of reaching Humboldt at that time except to take passage on a San Francisco sailing vessel going after lumber. Redwood, a species of cedar, which on the Pacific coast takes the place filled by white pine in the East, then abounded on the banks of Humboldt Bay. There were extensive saw-mills engaged in preparing this lumber for the San Francisco market, and sailing vessels, used in getting it to market, furnished the only means of communication between Humboldt and the balance of the world.

I was obliged to remain in San Francisco for several days before I found a vessel. This gave me a good opportunity of comparing the San Francisco of 1852 with that of 1853. As before stated, there had been but one wharf in front of the city in 1852—Long Wharf. In 1853 the town had grown out into the bay beyond what was the end of this wharf when I first saw it. Streets and houses had been built out on piles where the year before the largest vessels visiting the port lay at anchor or tied to the wharf. There was no filling under the streets or houses. San Francisco presented the same general appearance as the year before; that is, eating, drinking, and gambling houses were conspicuous for their number and publicity. They were on the first floor, with doors wide open. At all hours of the day and night in walking the streets, the eye was regaled, on every block near the water front, by the sight of players at faro. Often broken places were found in the street, large enough to let a man down into the water below. I have but little doubt that many of the people who went to the Pacific coast in the early days of the gold excitement, and have never been heard from since, or who were heard from for a time and then ceased to write, found watery graves beneath the houses or streets built over San Francisco Bay.

Besides the gambling in cards there was gambling on a larger scale in city lots. These were sold "On Change," much as stocks are now sold on Wall Street. Cash, at time of purchase, was always paid by the broker; but the purchaser had only to put up his margin. He was charged at the rate of two or three per cent a month on the difference, besides commissions. The sand hills, some of them almost inaccessible to foot-passengers, were surveyed off and mapped into fifty *vara* lots—a *vara* being a Spanish yard. These were sold at first at very low prices, but were sold and resold for higher prices until they went up to many thousands of dollars. The brokers did a fine business, and so did many such purchasers as were sharp enough to quit purchasing before the final crash came.

As the city grew, the sand hills back of the town furnished material for filling up the bay under the houses and streets, and still further out. The temporary houses, first built over the water in the harbor, soon gave way to more solid structures. The main business part of the city now is on solid ground, made where vessels of the largest class lay at anchor in the early days.

I was in San Francisco again in 1854. Gambling houses had disappeared from public view. The city had become staid and orderly.

My family, all this while, was at the East. It consisted now of a wife and two children. I saw no chance of supporting them on the Pacific coast out of my pay as an army officer. I concluded, therefore, to resign, and in March applied for a leave of absence until the end of the July following, tendering my resignation to take effect at the end of that time. I left the Pacific coast very much attached to it, and with the full expectation of making it my future home. That expectation and that hope remained uppermost in my mind until the Lieutenant-Generalcy bill was introduced into Congress in the winter of 1863–4. The passage of that bill, and my promotion, blasted my last hope of ever becoming a citizen of the further West.

Lost in Snow

Anonymous

Bodie is a gold-mining town on the far eastern side of the Sierra Nevada, about one hundred miles southeast of Reno, Nevada. It sits in a gently sloping valley in the hills above Mono Lake, near the Nevada border. It is now, arguably, the best preserved ghost town in California.

The town was named after Wakeman Body (pronounced, and sometimes spelled, Bodey). The town's name is spelled "Bodie" because a man misspelled it when painting a sign and the residents decided they preferred this spelling. Bodie's mines were quartz mines, requiring large-scale operations, and two stamp mills were built there, but the mines closed by 1868.

Then, in 1875, one of the mines caved in, revealing a good deposit of gold, and Bodie jumped back to life. A large, twenty-stamp mill was built to crush the rocks, and the investors made a lot of money. The mines pulled as much as $600,000 worth of gold in a single month. The tiny camp soon had around 2,000 buildings, with an estimated population between 5,500 and 8,000. This was an authentic Wild West town, with more than sixty saloons, a Chinese quarter, gambling halls, prostitutes, gunfights, murders, and stagecoach robberies.

When one family decided to move from San Jose to Bodie in 1879, a newspaper reported that the three-year-old daughter said at the end of her evening prayer, "Good-bye, God; we are going to Bodie in the morning." This prompted one indignant Bodie newspaper editor to suggest the punctuation was wrong and the quotation should read, "GOOD. By God we are going to Bodie in the morning."

Eventually there were nine mills, with a total of 159 stamps, but they weren't able to produce enough ore to keep all the mills going, so some closed and the others only operated part time. As winter drew near in 1880, many of the rougher elements were drawn away to other boomtowns—such as Tombstone, Arizona, and Butte, Montana. The population dropped to about a thousand and the tough town evolved into a calmer, more family-friendly community. Bodie's two churches were then built.

Diminishing returns forced the mines to close by 1913. Several attempts to work the mines in the 1920s and 1930s failed. The last one was forced to close by the government during World War II, since mining for gold was deemed nonessential to the war effort. In 1932, most of the town's buildings burned down, and only about 110 remain standing today—still containing many of the household items, pool tables, carriages, and even unused coffins that were left behind when the town was abandoned. The deepest mines tunneled to a depth of 1,200 feet. In all, Bodie's mines produced an estimated $34 million worth of gold and silver bullion.

The following selection is about the initial discovery of gold at Bodie. In 1859, four prospectors set out into the hills above Mono Lake to search for new diggings. They were Terence Brodigan, John Doyle, Tim Garraty, and Wakeman Body. In a remote valley they discovered quartz outcroppings that would soon become the Bodie mines.

Since winter was approaching, the miners made a pact not to reveal their discovery until the spring, but Wakeman Body returned to the spot soon afterward with E. S. "Black" Taylor and they were caught in a November snowstorm.

This is what remains of the ghost town of Bodie, after much of it was destroyed by fires in 1892 and 1932.
PHOTOGRAPH BY JOHN RICHARD STEPHENS

What follows is from a series of travel articles that appeared on the front page of San Francisco's *Daily Alta California* in 1860. The anonymous reporter signed the articles with the pseudonym "Indication." For some reason the journalist misspelled Body's name as "Boda;" this error has been corrected in the following text.

A Miner's Camp

Mr. [E. S. "Black"] Taylor occupies one of four mining camps, situated on the west side of one of those cozy looking little valleys, which, with its rich carpet of grass and clover, contrast so finely with the barren, bleak looking mountains around, with their sandy and stony surfaces, and scattering bunches of sage and other brush wood. The place is shadeless with the exception of a bunch of willows hard by, from the foot of which issues a cold spring of pure water. The valley runs in a northerly direction, and along its eastern side there is a branch, of ditch-like appearance, which affords a scanty supply of water for mining purposes.

Quartz Ledges

On the east side of the Valley may be seen the outcroppings of two quartz ledges, one on the top of the mountain range nearby, and the other on the slope beyond. From a sag in these mountains, opposite the lower part of the Valley, the pay dirt is obtained, and is carried in sacks a few hundred yards down a little gulch running from it, to the branch to be washed.

The gold is small and rough, and occasionally mixed with quartz, showing that it has been dropped from the adjacent ledge. On the opposite side of this sag, gold of a similar kind is obtained in like manner, the pay dirt being had from the head of a small gulch, running eastwardly from the sag, and doubtless dropped from the other ledge, mentioned as running along the slope.

Here there is one Mining camp, known as "The Frenchman's." These places are said to pay remarkably well, whenever there is sufficient water to work them to advantage. They are of quite limited extent however, and have been mentioned thus particularly on account of the quartz ledges, which are supposed to supply them, as they have been extensively taken up, and are believed to be rich.

Mr. Taylor is engaged in running a tunnel immediately under the sag, so as to prospect the one next to the valley where he lives, and is altogether

The eastern side of the Sierra Nevada near Bodie
PHOTOGRAPH BY JOHN RICHARD STEPHENS

sanguine of success. Being an old practical miner, and well acquainted with the locality, it will probably not be long before the quality of the ledge will be known.

THE FATE OF BODY

These diggings were called after the name of their original discoverer, a Mr. Body, whose melancholy fate, last winter [November 1859], I do not recollect having seen in print, and will, therefore, give some account of it, Mr. Taylor being our informant.

Body had attempted to bring in some supplies on a sled, the snow being deep, and the weather intensely cold. A snow storm coming on, he was compelled to abandon them, and make his way to the camp, which he succeeded in finding.

During an interruption in the storm, accompanied by Mr. Taylor, he went in quest of the sled, and the two were soon lost in one of those sudden and terrible snow storms so often witnessed in this elevated region during the winter months. After wandering for two days and nights in search of their camp, poor Body's mind began to wander and his strength to fail, and Mr. Taylor being a strong and athletic man carried him on his shoulders, still hoping to find the camp, until his strength began to fail him, and he finally became so much exhausted that he was compelled to leave him on the way. This he did after making the best provision for him that he could under the circumstances.

He then made another desperate effort to reach the camp, in the hope of obtaining relief for his exhausted companion, and after wandering for several hours in his fruitless search, he found himself again on the precise spot where he had left him. He found him apparently asleep, his eyes half closed and his features calm and placid; but there was no arousing him from his slumbers, for he was sleeping the sleep of death.

With his own approaching fate prefigured before him in the lifeless and frozen form of his companion, and with heavy heart and failing strength, he resolved on making a last desperate effort, and, shaking off the drowsy demands of exhausted nature, started off again in search of his camp. His athletic frame had already begun to yield to the demands of hunger, fatigue, and cold, and it was with great difficulty that he could drag his numbed and weary limbs along through the deep snow, and perhaps with still greater difficulty that he could resist the almost overpowering demands of exhausted nature for repose.

After searching thus for hours he at last came upon a spot which he recognized, and which he pointed out to me, and to his great joy found that he was in sight of his camp, and not more than a half mile distant from it. Such was his exhaustion, however, that although his position was sufficiently elevated to overlook the camp, he was some twelve hours in crawling down to it, through the snow.

After hearing his plain, straight-forward narrative of the terrors of that adventure and looking around in vain for other evidences of fuel for the winter than mere brush wood, we came to the conclusion that those elevated regions would never furnish us with an abode in winter, at least, and that we should have left their inhospitable climate, with all their golden allurements, and have sought some more genial spot, where snow storms were less frequent, as well as less violent and the cold less intense.

A BAD BARGAIN

Mr. Taylor informed us that he was the original discoverer of the once celebrated "Rich Bar," on South-east Feather River, California, and not knowing the value of his claim there, he disposed of it for $3,000, not more than a twentieth of its subsequent value. This he lost in an attempt to send it from San Francisco to the States, through the failure of the rotten concern that had charge of it.

We wish him better luck next time, and if straight-forwardness of disposition, unflagging energy, and persevering industry can accomplish anything where he is now, he seems to be entitled to and we hope may receive the full benefit of their success.

Bidding adieu to our hospitable host, on the morning of the 19th, a ride of eight or ten miles brought us again in view of Lake Mono.

W. S. Body remained buried beneath the snow until spring, when Taylor and some other miners found most of his bones, scattered by coyotes, and buried them in a grave. Black Taylor was killed by Indians a few months after the above article was published.

The Strangest Population

Mark Twain

England has Shakespeare, Russia has Pushkin, and the United States has Twain.

Mark Twain—the nom de plume of Samuel Clemens—is best known as the author of *The Adventures of Huckleberry Finn, The Adventures of Tom Sawyer, The Prince and the Pauper, A Connecticut Yankee in King Arthur's Court,* and "The Celebrated Jumping Frog of Calaveras County"—the latter story set in the gold country of California. William Faulkner labeled him "the father of American literature." He was also one of America's greatest humorists.

Twain is the quintessential American author. At a time when the nation was still divided from the Civil War, everyone could identify with him. His writing and speeches helped to reunite the country.

When the Civil War broke out, Twain found himself an informal volunteer fighting for the Confederacy, but after two weeks he "resigned" and took off for the Nevada Territory and California, where he tried his hand as a prospector and miner. Unsuccessful, he turned to writing and created his famous pen name. It was his jumping frog story that launched his career as a humorist. Even though his form of humor almost landed him in several duels, he quickly became an international celebrity and remains tremendously popular today.

Twain said that at one point, he and his two mining partners struck a rich vein of silver that would have made them millionaires, but each relied on the other two to work their claim in the ten days required by law. None of them did and they lost the claim, making another group of prospectors very rich. It was then that Twain decided to move on from Nevada Territory. In this piece from *Roughing It* (1872) he writes of his days in California searching for gold.

After squandering his money in San Francisco, thinking one of his many claims would strike it rich, Mark Twain found himself penniless—that is, except for a well-worn dime he held on to so he would not actually be penniless.

Endless Summer

In Sacramento it is fiery Summer always, and you can gather roses, and eat strawberries and ice-cream, and wear white linen clothes, and pant and perspire, at eight or nine o'clock in the morning, and then take the cars, and at noon put on your furs and your skates, and go skimming over frozen Donner Lake, seven thousand feet above the valley, among snow banks fifteen feet deep, and in the shadow of grand mountain peaks that lift their frosty crags ten thousand feet above the level of the sea. There is a transition for you. Where will you find another like it in the Western hemisphere?

And some of us have swept around snow-walled curves of the Pacific Railroad in that vicinity, six thousand feet above the sea, and looked down as the birds do, upon the deathless Summer of the Sacramento Valley, with its fruitful fields, its feathery foliage, its silver streams, all slumbering in the mellow haze of its enchanted atmosphere, and all infinitely soft-ened and spiritualized by distance—a dreamy, exquisite glimpse of fairy-land, made all the more charming and striking that it was caught through a forbidden gateway of ice and snow, and savage crags and precipices.

Vanished Cities

It was in this Sacramento Valley, just referred to, that a deal of the most lucrative of the early gold mining was done, and you may still see, in places, its grassy slopes and levels torn and guttered and disfigured by the avaricious spoilers of fifteen and twenty years ago. You may see such disfigurements far and wide over California—and in some such places, where only meadows and forests are visible—not a living creature, not a house, no stick or stone or remnant of a ruin, and not a sound, not even a whisper to disturb the Sabbath stillness—you will find it hard to believe that there stood at one time a fiercely-flourishing little city, of two thou-sand or three thousand souls, with its newspaper, fire company, brass band, volunteer militia, bank, hotels, noisy Fourth of July processions and speeches, gambling hells crammed with tobacco smoke, profanity, and rough-bearded men of all nations and colors, with tables heaped with gold dust sufficient for the revenues of a German principality—streets crowded and rife with business—town lots worth four hundred dollars a front foot—labor, laughter, music, dancing, swearing, fighting, shooting, stabbing—a bloody inquest and a man for breakfast every morning—*everything* that delights and adorns existence—all the appointments and appurtenances of a thriving and prosperous and promising young city,—and *now* nothing is left of it all but a lifeless, homeless solitude. The men are gone, the houses have vanished, even the *name* of the place is forgotten. In no other land, in modern times, have towns so absolutely died and disappeared, as in the old mining regions of California.

TWO HUNDRED THOUSAND YOUNG MEN

It was a driving, vigorous, restless population in those days. It was a *curious* population. It was the *only* population of the kind that the world has ever seen gathered together, and it is not likely that the world will ever see its like again. For observe, it was an assemblage of two hundred thousand *young* men—not simpering, dainty, kid-gloved weaklings, but stalwart, muscular, dauntless young braves, brimful of push and energy, and royally endowed with every attribute that goes to make up a peerless and magnificent manhood—the very pick and choice of the world's glorious ones. No women, no children, no gray and stooping veterans—none but erect, bright-eyed, quick-moving, strong-handed young giants—the strangest population, the finest population, the most gallant host that ever trooped down the startled solitudes of an unpeopled land.

And where are they now? Scattered to the ends of the earth—or prematurely aged and decrepit—or shot or stabbed in street affrays—or dead of disappointed hopes and broken hearts—all gone, or nearly all—victims devoted upon the altar of the golden calf—the noblest holocaust that ever wafted its sacrificial incense heavenward. It is pitiful to think upon.

It was a splendid population—for all the slow, sleepy, sluggish-brained sloths staid at home—you never find that sort of people among pioneers—you cannot build pioneers out of that sort of material. It was that population that gave to California a name for getting up astounding enterprises and rushing them through with a magnificent dash and daring and a recklessness of cost or consequences, which she bears unto this day—and when she projects a new surprise, the grave world smiles as usual and says, "Well, that is California all over."

But they were rough in those times! They fairly reveled in gold, whisky, fights, and fandangoes, and were unspeakably happy. The honest miner raked from a hundred to a thousand dollars out of his claim a day, and what with the gambling dens and the other entertainments, he hadn't a cent the next morning, if he had any sort of luck. They cooked their own bacon and beans, sewed on their own buttons, washed their own shirts—blue woolen ones; and if a man wanted a fight on his hands without any annoying delay, all he had to do was to appear in public in a white shirt or a stove-pipe hat, and he would be accommodated. For those people hated aristocrats. They had a particular and malignant animosity toward what they called a "biled shirt."

It was a wild, free, disorderly, grotesque society! Men—only swarming hosts of stalwart men—nothing juvenile, nothing feminine, visible anywhere!

A Woman Sighted

In those days miners would flock in crowds to catch a glimpse of that rare and blessed spectacle, a woman! Old inhabitants tell how, in a certain camp, the news went abroad early in the morning that a woman was come! They had seen a calico dress hanging out of a wagon down at the camping-ground—sign of emigrants from over the great plains. Everybody went down there, and a shout went up when an actual, bona fide dress was discovered fluttering in the wind! The male emigrant was visible. The miners said, "Fetch her out!"

He said, "It is my wife, gentlemen—she is sick—we have been robbed of money, provisions, everything, by the Indians—we want to rest."

"Fetch her out! We've got to see her!"

"But, gentlemen, the poor thing, she—"

"Fetch her out!"

He "fetched her out," and they swung their hats and sent up three rousing cheers and a tiger; and they crowded around and gazed at her, and touched her dress, and listened to her voice with the look of men who listened to a *memory* rather than a present reality—and then they collected twenty-five hundred dollars in gold and gave it to the man, and swung their hats again and gave three more cheers, and went home satisfied.

Kissing a Child

Once I dined in San Francisco with the family of a pioneer, and talked with his daughter, a young lady whose first experience in San Francisco was an adventure, though she herself did not remember it, as she was only two or three years old at the time. Her father said that, after landing from the ship, they were walking up the street, a servant leading the party with the little girl in her arms. And presently a huge miner, bearded, belted, spurred, and bristling with deadly weapons—just down from a long campaign in the mountains, evidently barred the way, stopped the servant, and stood gazing, with a face all alive with gratification and astonishment.

Then he said, reverently, "Well, if it ain't a child!" And then he snatched a little leather sack out of his pocket and said to the servant, "There's a hundred and fifty dollars in dust, there, and I'll give it to you to let me kiss the child!"

That anecdote is *true*.

But see how things change. Sitting at that dinner-table, listening to that anecdote, if I had offered double the money for the privilege of kissing the same child, I would have been refused. Seventeen added years have far more than doubled the price.

A Genuine Live One

And while upon this subject I will remark that once in Star City, in the Humboldt Mountains [Nevada Territory], I took my place in a sort of long, post-office single file of miners, to patiently await my chance to peep through a crack in the cabin and get a sight of the splendid new sensation—a genuine, live Woman! And at the end of half of an hour my turn came, and I put my eye to the crack, and there she was, with one arm akimbo, and tossing flap-jacks in a frying-pan with the other.

And she was one hundred and sixty-five years old (Being in calmer mood, now, I voluntarily knock off a hundred from that.—M.T.), and hadn't a tooth in her head.

Miners, along with two women, in 1858

DECAYED MINING CAMPS AND MINERS

By and by, an old friend of mine, a miner, came down from one of the decayed mining camps of Tuolumne, California, and I went back with him. We lived in a small cabin on a verdant hillside, and there were not five other cabins in view over the wide expanse of hill and forest. Yet a flourishing city of two or three thousand population had occupied this grassy dead solitude during the flush times of twelve or fifteen years before, and where our cabin stood had once been the heart of the teeming hive, the centre of the city. When the mines gave out the town fell into decay, and in a few years wholly disappeared—streets, dwellings, shops, everything—and left no sign. The grassy slopes were as green and smooth and desolate of life as if they had never been disturbed.

The mere handful of miners still remaining had seen the town spring up, spread, grow, and flourish in its pride; and they had seen it sicken and die, and pass away like a dream. With it their hopes had died, and their zest of life. They had long ago resigned themselves to their exile, and ceased to correspond with their distant friends or turn longing eyes toward their early homes. They had accepted banishment, forgotten the world and been forgotten of the world. They were far from telegraphs and railroads, and they stood, as it were, in a living grave, dead to the events that stirred the globe's great populations, dead to the common interests of men, isolated and outcast from brotherhood with their kind.

It was the most singular, and almost the most touching and melancholy exile that fancy can imagine. One of my associates in this locality, for two or three months, was a man who had had a university education; but now for eighteen years he had decayed there by inches, a bearded, rough-clad, clay-stained miner, and at times, among his sighings and soliloquizings, he unconsciously interjected vaguely remembered Latin and Greek sentences—dead and musty tongues, meet vehicles for the thoughts of one whose dreams were all of the past, whose life was a failure; a tired man, burdened with the present, and indifferent to the future; a man without ties, hopes, interests, waiting for rest and the end.

POCKET MINING

In that one little corner of California is found a species of mining which is seldom or never mentioned in print. It is called "pocket mining" and I am not aware that any of it is done outside of that little corner. The gold is not evenly distributed through the surface dirt, as in ordinary placer mines, but is collected in little spots, and they are very wide apart and exceedingly hard to find, but when you do find one you reap a rich and sudden harvest. There are not now more than twenty pocket miners in that entire little region. I think I know every one of them personally.

I have known one of them to hunt patiently about the hill-sides every day for eight months without finding gold enough to make a snuff-box—his grocery bill running up relentlessly all the time—and then find a pocket and take out of it two thousand dollars in two dips of his shovel. I have known him to take out three thousand dollars in two hours, and go and pay up every cent of his indebtedness, then enter on a dazzling spree that finished the last of his treasure before the night was gone. And the next day he bought his groceries on credit as usual, and shouldered his pan and shovel and went off to the hills hunting pockets again, happy and content.

This is the most fascinating of all the different kinds of mining, and furnishes a very handsome percentage of victims to the lunatic asylum.

THE SEARCH

Pocket hunting is an ingenious process. You take a spadeful of earth from the hill-side and put it in a large tin pan and dissolve and wash it gradually away till nothing is left but a teaspoonful of fine sediment. Whatever gold was in that earth has remained, because, being the heaviest, it has sought the bottom. Among the sediment you will find half a dozen yellow particles no larger than pin-heads. You are delighted. You move off to one side and wash another pan. If you find gold again, you move to one side further, and wash a third pan. If you find *no* gold this time, you are delighted again, because you know you are on the right scent. You lay an imaginary plan, shaped like a fan, with its handle up the hill—for just where the end of the handle is, you argue that the rich deposit lies hidden, whose vagrant grains of gold have escaped and been washed down the hill, spreading farther and further apart as they wandered.

And so you proceed up the hill, washing the earth and narrowing your lines every time the absence of gold in the pan shows that you are outside the spread of the fan; and at last, twenty yards up the hill your lines have converged to a point—a single foot from that point you cannot find any gold.

Your breath comes short and quick, you are feverish with excitement; the dinner-bell may ring its clapper off, you pay no attention; friends may die, weddings transpire, houses burn down, they are nothing to you; you sweat and dig and delve with a frantic interest—and all at once you strike it! Up comes a spadeful of earth and quartz that is all lovely with soiled lumps and leaves and sprays of gold. Sometimes that one spadeful is all—$500. Sometimes the nest contains $10,000, and it takes you three or four days to get it all out. The pocket-miners tell of one nest that yielded $60,000 and two men exhausted it in two weeks, and then sold the ground for $10,000 to a party who never got $300 out of it afterward.

The hogs are good pocket hunters. All the summer they root around the bushes, and turn up a thousand little piles of dirt, and then the miners long for the rains; for the rains beat upon these little piles and wash them down and expose the gold, possibly right over a pocket. Two pockets were found in this way by the same man in one day. One had $5,000 in it and the other $8,000. That man could appreciate it, for he hadn't had a cent for about a year.

Sitting on Gold

In Tuolumne lived two miners who used to go to the neighboring village in the afternoon and return every night with household supplies. Part of the distance they traversed a trail, and nearly always sat down to rest on a great boulder that lay beside the path. In the course of thirteen years they had worn that boulder tolerably smooth, sitting on it.

By and by two vagrant Mexicans came along and occupied the seat. They began to amuse themselves by chipping off flakes from the boulder with a sledge-hammer. They examined one of these flakes and found it rich with gold. That boulder paid them $800 afterward. But the aggravating circumstance was that these men knew that there must be more gold where that boulder came from, and so they went panning up the hill and found what was probably the richest pocket that region has yet produced. It took three months to exhaust it, and it yielded $120,000.

The two American miners who used to sit on the boulder are poor yet, and they take turn about in getting up early in the morning to curse those Mexicans—and when it comes down to pure ornamental cursing, the native American is gifted above the sons of men.

I have dwelt at some length upon this matter of pocket mining because it is a subject that is seldom referred to in print, and therefore I judged that it would have for the reader that interest which naturally attaches to novelty.

The Miner's Cat

One of my comrades there—another of those victims of eighteen years of unrequited toil and blighted hopes—was one of the gentlest spirits that ever bore its patient cross in a weary exile: grave and simple Dick Baker, pocket-miner of Dead-Horse Gulch. He was forty-six, gray as a rat, earnest, thoughtful, slenderly educated, slouchily dressed, and clay-soiled, but his heart was finer metal than any gold his shovel ever brought to light—than any, indeed, that ever was mined or minted.

Whenever he was out of luck and a little down-hearted, he would fall to mourning over the loss of a wonderful cat he used to own (for where women and children are not, men of kindly impulses take up with pets, for they must love something). And he always spoke of the strange sagacity of that cat with the air of a man who believed in his secret heart that there was something human about it—may be even supernatural.

I heard him talking about this animal once. He said:

"Gentlemen, I used to have a cat here, by the name of Tom Quartz, which you'd a took an interest in I reckon—most anybody would, I had him here eight year—and he was the remarkablest cat *I* ever see. He was a large gray one of the Tom specie, an' he had more hard, natchral sense than any man in this camp—'n' a *power* of dignity—he wouldn't let the Gov'ner of Californy be familiar with him. He never ketched a rat in his life—'peared to be above it.

"He never cared for nothing but mining. He knowed more about mining, that cat did, than any man *I* ever, ever see. You couldn't tell *him* noth'n' 'bout placer diggin's—'n' as for pocket mining, why he was just born for it. He would dig out after me an' Jim when we went over the hills prospect'n', and he would trot along behind us for as much as five mile, if we went so fur. An' he had the best judgment about mining ground—why you never see anything like it.

"When we went to work, he'd scatter a glance around, 'n' if he didn't think much of the indications, he would give a look as much as to say, 'Well, I'll have to get you to excuse *me*,' 'n' without another word he'd hyste his nose into the air 'n' shove for home. But if the ground suited him, he would lay low 'n' keep dark till the first pan was washed, 'n' then he would sidle up 'n' take a look, an' if there was about six or seven grains of gold he was satisfied—he didn't want no better prospect 'n' that—'n' then he would lay down on our coats and snore like a steamboat till we'd struck the pocket, an' then get up 'n' superintend. He was nearly lightnin' on superintening.

"Well, bye an' bye, up comes this yer quartz excitement. Everybody was into it—everybody was pick 'n' blast 'n' instead of shovelin' dirt on the hill side—everybody was put 'n' down a shaft instead of scrapin' the surface. Noth'n' would do Jim, but we must tackle the ledges, too, 'n' so we did.

"We commenced put 'n' down a shaft, 'n' Tom Quartz he begin ta wonder what in the Dickens it was all about. *He* hadn't ever seen any mining like that before, 'n' he was all upset, as you may say—he couldn't come to a right understanding of it no way—it was too many for *him*. He was down on it, too, you bet you—he was down on it powerful—'n' always appeared to consider it the cussedest foolishness out. But that cat, you know, was *always* agin new fangled arrangements—somehow he never could abide 'em. *You* know how it is with old habits.

"But by an' by Tom Quartz begin to git sort of reconciled a little, though he never *could* altogether understand that eternal sinkin' of a shaft an' never pannin' out anything. At last he got to comin' down in the shaft, hisself, to try to cipher it out. An' when he'd git the blues, 'n' feel kind o' scruffy, 'n' aggravated 'n' disgusted—knowin' as he did, that the bills was runnin' up all the time an' we warn't makin' a cent—he would curl up on a gunny sack in the corner an' go to sleep. Well, one day when the shaft was down about eight foot, the rock got so hard that we had to put in a blast—the first blast 'n' we'd ever done since Tom Quartz was born. An' then we lit the fuse 'n' dumb out 'n' got off 'bout fifty yards—'n' forgot 'n' left Tom Quartz sound asleep on the gunny sack. In 'bout a minute we seen a puff of smoke bust up out of the hole, 'n' then everything let go with an awful crash, 'n' about four million ton of rocks 'n' dirt 'n' smoke 'n' splinters shot up 'bout a mile an' a half into the air, an' by George, right in the dead centre of it was old Tom Quartz a goin' end over end, an' a snortin' an' a sneez'n', an' a clawin' an' a reachin' for things like all possessed. But it warn't no use, you know, it warn't no use.

"An' that was the last we see of *him* for about two minutes 'n' a half, an' then all of a sudden it begin to rain rocks and rubbage, an' directly he come down ker-whop about ten foot off f'm where we stood. Well, I reckon he was p'raps the orneriest lookin' beast you ever see. One ear was sot back on his neck, 'n' his tail was stove up, 'n' his eye-winkers was swinged off, 'n' he was all blacked up with powder an' smoke, an' all sloppy with mud 'n' slush f'm one end to the other.

"Well sir, it warn't no use to try to apologize—we couldn't say a word. He took a sort of a disgusted look at hisself, 'n' then he looked at us—an' it was just exactly the same as if he had said—'Gents, may be *you* think it's smart to take advantage of a cat that ain't had no experience of quartz minin', but *I* think *different*'—an' then he turned on his heel 'n' marched off home without ever saying another word.

"That was jest his style. An' may be you won't believe it, but after that you never see a cat so prejudiced agin quartz mining as what he was. An' by an' bye when he *did* get to goin' down in the shaft agin, you'd 'a been astonished at his sagacity. The minute we'd tetch off a blast 'n' the fuse'd begin to sizzle, he'd give a look as much as to say: 'Well, I'll have to git you to excuse *me*,' an' it was surpris'n' the way he'd shin out of that hole 'n' go f'r a tree. Sagacity? It ain't no name for it. 'Twas *inspiration!*"

I said, "Well, Mr. Baker, his prejudice against quartz-mining *was* remarkable, considering how he came by it. Couldn't you ever cure him of it?"

"*Cure him!* No! When Tom Quartz was sot once, he was *always* sot— and you might a blowed him up as much as three million times 'n' you'd never a broken him of his cussed prejudice agin quartz mining."

The affection and the pride that lit up Baker's face when he delivered this tribute to the firmness of his humble friend of other days, will always be a vivid memory with me.

EMPTY POCKETS

At the end of two months we had never "struck" a pocket. We had panned up and down the hillsides till they looked plowed like a field; we could have put in a crop of grain, then, but there would have been no way to get it to market. We got many good "prospects," but when the gold gave out in the pan and we dug down, hoping and longing, we found only emptiness—the pocket that should have been there was as barren as our own—at last we shouldered our pans and shovels and struck out over the hills to try new localities.

We prospected around Angel's Camp, in Calaveras county, during three weeks, but had no success. Then we wandered on foot among the mountains, sleeping under the trees at night, for the weather was mild, but still we remained as centless as the last rose of summer. That is a poor joke, but it is in pathetic harmony with the circumstances, since we were so poor ourselves. In accordance with the custom of the country, our door had always stood open and our board welcome to tramping miners—they drifted along nearly every day, dumped their paust shovels by the threshold and took "pot luck" with us—and now on our own tramp we never found cold hospitality. Our wanderings were wide and in many directions; and now I could give the reader a vivid description of the Big Trees and the marvels of the Yo Semite [Yosemite]—but what has this reader done to me that I should persecute him? I will deliver him into the hands of less conscientious tourists and take his blessing. Let me be charitable, though I fail in all virtues else.

Part Two: Fiction

All Gold Cañon

Jack London

Jack London wrote such adventure classics as *The Call of the Wild* and *White Fang*, both of which take place during the Klondike gold rush in Canada's Yukon Territory during the late 1890s.

London was born in San Francisco in 1876 and raised in poverty. At one time involved in petty theft, he switched sides to work in law enforcement. After returning from a voyage to Japan as a sailor, he became a hobo and toured the country. He began high school at the age of nineteen, and the following year attended one semester at the University of California. Much of his education came from reading books. In 1897, he headed off to the Klondike. It was then that he turned to writing, although he was unsuccessful until he began writing stories about the Yukon.

In all, he wrote close to fifty books in seventeen years, dying at the age of forty while suffering from the effects of alcoholism and uremia, among other ailments. His stories remain tremendously popular, largely for capturing the American ideal of rugged individualism.

This story, set in a remote canyon in California's Sierra Nevada, explores some of the hazards of greed and the lust for gold.

It was the green heart of the cañon, where the walls swerved back from the rigid plan and relieved their harshness of line by making a little sheltered nook and filling it to the brim with sweetness and roundness and softness. Here all things rested. Even the narrow stream ceased its turbulent down-rush long enough to form a quiet pool. Knee-deep in the water, with drooping head and half-shut eyes, drowsed a red-coated, many-antlered buck.

On one side, beginning at the very lip of the pool, was a tiny meadow, a cool, resilient surface of green that extended to the base of the frowning wall. Beyond the pool a gentle slope of earth ran up and up to meet the opposing wall. Fine grass covered the slope—grass that was spangled with flowers, with here and there patches of color, orange and purple and golden. Below, the cañon was shut in. There was no view. The walls leaned together abruptly and the cañon ended in a chaos of rocks, moss-covered and hidden by a green screen of vines and creepers and boughs of trees. Up the cañon rose far hills and peaks, the big foothills, pine-covered and remote. And far beyond, like clouds upon the border of the sky, towered minarets of white, where the Sierra's eternal snows flashed austerely the blazes of the sun.

There was no dust in the cañon. The leaves and flowers were clean and virginal. The grass was young velvet. Over the pool three cottonwoods sent their snowy fluffs fluttering down the quiet air. On the slope the blossoms of the wine-wooded manzanita filled the air with springtime odors, while the leaves, wise with experience, were already beginning their vertical twist against the coming aridity of summer. In the open spaces on the slope, beyond the farthest shadow-reach of the manzanita, poised the mariposa lilies, like so many flights of jewelled moths suddenly arrested and on the verge of trembling into flight again. Here and there that woods harlequin, the madrone, permitting itself to be caught in the act of changing its pea-green trunk to madder-red, breathed its fragrance into the air from great clusters of waxen bells. Creamy white were these bells, shaped like lilies-of-the-valley, with the sweetness of perfume that is of the springtime.

There was not a sigh of wind. The air was drowsy with its weight of perfume. It was a sweetness that would have been cloying had the air been heavy and humid. But the air was sharp and thin. It was as starlight transmuted into atmosphere, shot through and warmed by sunshine, and flower-drenched with sweetness.

An occasional butterfly drifted in and out through the patches of light and shade. And from all about rose the low and sleepy hum of mountain bees—feasting Sybarites that jostled one another good-naturedly at the board, nor found time for rough discourtesy. So quietly did the little stream drip and ripple its way through the cañon that it spoke only in faint and occasional gurgles. The voice of the stream was as a drowsy whisper, ever interrupted by dozings and silences, ever lifted again in the awakenings.

The motion of all things was a drifting in the heart of the cañon. Sunshine and butterflies drifted in and out among the trees. The hum of the bees and the whisper of the stream were a drifting of sound. And the drifting sound and drifting color seemed to weave together in the making of a delicate and intangible fabric which was the spirit of the place. It was a spirit of peace that was not of death, but of smooth-pulsing life, of quietude that was not silence, of movement that was not action, of repose that was quick with existence without being violent with struggle and travail. The spirit of the place was the spirit of the peace of the living, somnolent with the easement and content of prosperity, and undisturbed by rumors of far wars.

The red-coated, many-antlered buck acknowledged the lordship of the spirit of the place and dozed knee-deep in the cool, shaded pool. There seemed no flies to vex him and he was languid with rest. Sometimes his ears moved when the stream awoke and whispered; but they moved lazily, with foreknowledge that it was merely the stream grown garrulous at discovery that it had slept.

But there came a time when the buck's ears lifted and tensed with swift eagerness for sound. His head was turned down the cañon. His sensitive, quivering nostrils scented the air. His eyes could not pierce the green screen through which the stream rippled away, but to his ears came the voice of a man. It was a steady, monotonous, singsong voice. Once the buck heard the harsh clash of metal upon rock. At the sound he snorted with a sudden start that jerked him through the air from water to meadow, and his feet sank into the young velvet, while he pricked his ears and again scented the air. Then he stole across the tiny meadow, pausing once and again to listen, and faded away out of the cañon like a wraith, soft-footed and without sound.

The clash of steel-shod soles against the rocks began to be heard, and the man's voice grew louder. It was raised in a sort of chant and became distinct with nearness, so that the words could be heard:

"Tu'n around an' tu'n yo' face
Untoe them sweet hills of grace
    (D' pow'rs of sin yo' am scornin'!).
Look about an' look aroun'
Fling yo' sin-pack on d' groun'
    (Yo' will meet wid d' Lord in d' mornin'!)."

A sound of scrambling accompanied the song, and the spirit of the place fled away on the heels of the red-coated buck. The green screen was burst asunder, and a man peered out at the meadow and the pool and the sloping side-hill. He was a deliberate sort of man. He took in the scene with one embracing glance, then ran his eyes over the details to verify the general impression. Then, and not until then, did he open his mouth in vivid and solemn approval:

"Smoke of life an' snakes of purgatory! Will you just look at that! Wood an' water an' grass an' a side-hill! A pocket-hunter's delight an' a cayuse's paradise! Cool green for tired eyes! Pink pills for pale people ain't in it. A secret pasture for prospectors and a resting-place for tired burros. It's just booful!"

He was a sandy-complexioned man in whose face geniality and humor seemed the salient characteristics. It was a mobile face, quick-changing to inward mood and thought. Thinking was in him a visible process. Ideas chased across his face like wind-flaws across the surface of a lake. His hair, sparse and unkempt of growth, was as indeterminate and colorless as his complexion. It would seem that all the color of his frame had gone into his eyes, for they were startlingly blue. Also, they were laughing and merry eyes, within them much of the naiveté and wonder of the child; and yet, in an unassertive way, they contained much of calm self-reliance and strength of purpose founded upon self-experience and experience of the world.

From out the screen of vines and creepers he flung ahead of him a miner's pick and shovel and gold-pan. Then he crawled out himself into the open. He was clad in faded overalls and black cotton shirt, with hobnailed brogans on his feet, and on his head a hat whose shapeless-ness and stains advertised the rough usage of wind and rain and sun and camp-smoke. He stood erect, seeing wide-eyed the secrecy of the scene and sensuously inhaling the warm, sweet breath of the cañon-garden through nostrils that dilated and quivered with delight. His eyes narrowed to laughing slits of blue, his face wreathed itself in joy, and his mouth curled in a smile as he cried aloud:

"Jumping dandelions and happy hollyhocks, but that smells good to me! Talk about your attar o' roses an' cologne factories! They ain't in it!"

He had the habit of soliloquy. His quick-changing facial expressions might tell every thought and mood, but the tongue, perforce, ran hard after, repeating, like a second Boswell.

The man lay down on the lip of the pool and drank long and deep of its water. "Tastes good to me," he murmured, lifting his head and gazing across the pool at the side-hill, while he wiped his mouth with the back of his hand. The side-hill attracted his attention. Still lying on his stomach, he studied the hill formation long and carefully. It was a practised eye that traveled up the slope to the crumbling cañon-wall and back and down again to the edge of the pool. He scrambled to his feet and favored the side-hill with a second survey.

"Looks good to me," he concluded, picking up his pick and shovel and gold-pan.

He crossed the stream below the pool, stepping agilely from stone to stone. Where the side-hill touched the water he dug up a shovelful of dirt and put it into the gold-pan. He squatted down, holding the pan in his two hands, and partly immersing it in the stream. Then he imparted to the pan a deft circular motion that sent the water sluicing in and out through the dirt and gravel. The larger and the lighter particles worked to the surface, and these, by a skilful dipping movement of the pan, he spilled out and over the edge. Occasionally, to expedite matters, he rested the pan and with his fingers raked out the large pebbles and pieces of rock.

The contents of the pan diminished rapidly until only fine dirt and the smallest bits of gravel remained. At this stage he began to work very deliberately and carefully. It was fine washing, and he washed fine and finer, with a keen scrutiny and delicate and fastidious touch. At last the pan seemed empty of everything but water; but with a quick semi-circular flirt that sent the water flying over the shallow rim into the stream, he disclosed a layer of black sand on the bottom of the pan. So thin was this layer that it was like a streak of paint. He examined it closely. In the midst of it was a tiny golden speck. He dribbled a little water in over the depressed edge of the pan. With a quick flirt he sent the water sluicing across the bottom, turning the grains of black sand over and over. A second tiny golden speck rewarded his effort.

The washing had now become very fine—fine beyond all need of ordinary placer-mining. He worked the black sand, a small portion at a time, up the shallow rim of the pan. Each small portion he examined sharply, so that his eyes saw every grain of it before he allowed it to slide over the edge and away. Jealously, bit by bit, he let the black sand slip away. A golden speck, no larger than a pin-point, appeared on the rim, and by his manipulation of the water it returned to the bottom of the pan. And in such fashion another speck was disclosed, and another. Great was his care of them. Like a shepherd he herded his flock of golden specks so that not one should be lost. At last, of the pan of dirt nothing remained but his golden herd. He counted it, and then, after all his labor, sent it flying out of the pan with one final swirl of water.

But his blue eyes were shining with desire as he rose to his feet. "Seven," he muttered aloud, asserting the sum of the specks for which he had toiled so hard and which he had so wantonly thrown away. "Seven," he repeated, with the emphasis of one trying to impress a number on his memory.

He stood still a long while, surveying the hillside. In his eyes was a curiosity, new-aroused and burning. There was an exultance about his bearing and a keenness like that of a hunting animal catching the fresh scent of game.

He moved down the stream a few steps and took a second panful of dirt.

Again came the careful washing, the jealous herding of the golden specks, and the wantonness with which he sent them flying into the stream.

"Five," he muttered, and repeated, "five."

He could not forbear another survey of the hill before filling the pan farther down the stream. His golden herds diminished. "Four, three, two, two, one," were his memory tabulations as he moved down the stream. When but one speck of gold rewarded his washing, he stopped and built a fire of dry twigs. Into this he thrust the gold-pan and burned it till it was blue-black. He held up the pan and examined it critically. Then he nodded approbation. Against such a color-background he could defy the tiniest yellow speck to elude him.

Still moving down the stream, he panned again. A single speck was his reward. A third pan contained no gold at all. Not satisfied with this, he panned three times again, taking his shovels of dirt within a foot of one another. Each pan proved empty of gold, and the fact, instead of discouraging him, seemed to give him satisfaction. His elation increased with each barren washing, until he arose, exclaiming jubilantly: "If it ain't the real thing, may God knock off my head with sour apples!"

Returning to where he had started operations, he began to pan up the stream. At first his golden herds increased—increased prodigiously. "Fourteen, eighteen, twenty-one, twenty-six," ran his memory tabulations. Just above the pool he struck his richest pan—thirty-five colors.

"Almost enough to save," he remarked regretfully as he allowed the water to sweep them away.

The sun climbed to the top of the sky. The man worked on. Pan by pan, he went up the stream, the tally of results steadily decreasing.

"It's just booful, the way it peters out," he exulted when a shovelful of dirt contained no more than a single speck of gold. And when no specks at all were found in several pans, he straightened up and favored the hillside with a confident glance.

"Ah, ha! Mr. Pocket!" he cried out, as though to an auditor hidden somewhere above him beneath the surface of the slope. "Ah, ha! Mr. Pocket! I'm a-comin', I'm a-comin', an' I'm shorely gwine to get yer! You heah me, Mr. Pocket? I'm gwine to get yer as shore as punkins ain't cauliflowers!"

He turned and flung a measuring glance at the sun poised above him in the azure of the cloudless sky. Then he went down the cañon, following the line of shovel-holes he had made in filling the pans. He crossed the stream below the pool and disappeared through the green screen. There was little opportunity for the spirit of the place to return with its quietude and repose, for the man's voice, raised in ragtime song, still dominated the cañon with possession.

After a time, with a greater clashing of steel-shod feet on rock, he returned. The green screen was tremendously agitated. It surged back and forth in the throes of a struggle. There was a loud grating and clanging of metal. The man's voice leaped to a higher pitch and was sharp with imperativeness. A large body plunged and panted. There was a snapping and ripping and rending, and amid a shower of falling leaves a horse burst through the screen. On its back was a pack, and from this trailed broken vines and torn creepers. The animal gazed with astonished eyes at the scene into which it had been precipitated, then dropped its head to the grass and began contentedly to graze. A second horse scrambled into view, slipping once on the mossy rocks and regaining equilibrium when its hoofs sank into the yielding surface of the meadow. It was riderless, though on its back was a high-horned Mexican saddle, scarred and discolored by long usage.

The man brought up the rear. He threw off pack and saddle, with an eye to camp location, and gave the animals their freedom to graze. He unpacked his food and got out frying-pan and coffee-pot. He gathered an armful of dry wood, and with a few stones made a place for his fire.

"My!" he said, "but I've got an appetite. I could scoff iron-filings an' horseshoe nails an' thank you kindly, ma'am, for a second helpin'."

He straightened up, and, while he reached for matches in the pocket of his overalls, his eyes traveled across the pool to the side-hill. His fingers had clutched the match-box, but they relaxed their hold and the hand came out empty. The man wavered perceptibly. He looked at his preparations for cooking and he looked at the hill.

"Guess I'll take another whack at her," he concluded, starting to cross the stream.

"They ain't no sense in it, I know," he mumbled apologetically. "But keepin' grub back an hour ain't goin' to hurt none, I reckon."

A few feet back from his first line of test-pans he started a second line. The sun dropped down the western sky, the shadows lengthened, but the man worked on. He began a third line of test-pans. He was crosscutting the hillside, line by line, as he ascended. The center of each line produced the richest pans, while the ends came where no colors showed in the pan. And as he ascended the hillside the lines grew perceptibly shorter. The regularity with which their length diminished served to indicate that somewhere up the slope the last line would be so short as to have scarcely length at all, and that beyond could come only a point. The design was growing into an inverted "V." The converging sides of this "V" marked the boundaries of the gold-bearing dirt.

The apex of the "V" was evidently the man's goal. Often he ran his eye along the converging sides and on up the hill, trying to divine the apex, the point where the gold-bearing dirt must cease. Here resided "Mr. Pocket"—for so the man familiarly addressed the imaginary point above him on the slope, crying out: "Come down out o' that, Mr. Pocket! Be right smart an' agreeable, an' come down!"

"All right," he would add later, in a voice resigned to determination. "All right, Mr. Pocket. It's plain to me I got to come right up an' snatch you out bald-headed. An' I'll do it! I'll do it!" he would threaten still later.

Each pan he carried down to the water to wash, and as he went higher up the hill the pans grew richer, until he began to save the gold in an empty baking powder can which he carried carelessly in his hip-pocket. So engrossed was he in his toil that he did not notice the long twilight of oncoming night. It was not until he tried vainly to see the gold colors in the bottom of the pan that he realized the passage of time. He straightened up abruptly. An expression of whimsical wonderment and awe overspread his face as he drawled: "Gosh darn my buttons! if I didn't plumb forget dinner!"

He stumbled across the stream in the darkness and lighted his long-delayed fire. Flapjacks and bacon and warmed-over beans constituted his supper. Then he smoked a pipe by the smouldering coals, listening to the night noises and watching the moonlight stream through the cañon. After that he unrolled his bed, took off his heavy shoes, and pulled the blankets up to his chin. His face showed white in the moonlight, like the face of a corpse. But it was a corpse that knew its resurrection, for the man rose suddenly on one elbow and gazed across at his hillside.

"Good night, Mr. Pocket," he called sleepily. "Goodnight."

He slept through the early gray of morning until the direct rays of the sun smote his closed eyelids, when he awoke with a start and looked about him until he had established the continuity of his existence and identified his present self with the days previously lived.

To dress, he had merely to buckle on his shoes. He glanced at his fireplace and at his hillside, wavered, but fought down the temptation and started the fire.

"Keep yer shirt on, Bill; keep yer shirt on," he admonished himself. "What's the good of rushin'? No use in gettin' all het up an' sweaty. Mr. Pocket'll wait for you. He ain't a-runnin' away before you can get your breakfast. Now, what you want, Bill, is something fresh in yer bill o' fare. So it's up to you to go an' get it."

He cut a short pole at the water's edge and drew from one of his pockets a bit of line and a draggled fly that had once been a royal coachman.

"Mebbe they'll bite in the early morning," he muttered, as he made his first cast into the pool. And a moment later he was gleefully crying: "What'd I tell you, eh? What'd I tell you?"

He had no reel, nor any inclination to waste time, and by main strength, and swiftly, he drew out of the water a flashing ten-inch trout. Three more, caught in rapid succession, furnished his breakfast. When he came to the stepping-stones on his way to his hillside, he was struck by a sudden thought, and paused.

"I'd just better take a hike down-stream a ways," he said. "There's no tellin' who may be snoopin' around."

But he crossed over on the stones, and with a "I really oughter take that hike," the need of the precaution passed out of his mind and he fell to work.

At nightfall he straightened up. The small of his back was stiff from stooping toil, and as he put his hand behind him to soothe the protesting muscles, he said: "Now what d'ye think of that? I clean forgot my dinner again! If I don't watch out, I'll sure be degeneratin' into a two-meal-a-day crank."

"Pockets is the hangedest things I ever see for makin' a man absent-minded," he communed that night, as he crawled into his blankets. Nor did he forget to call up the hillside, "Good night, Mr. Pocket! Good night!"

Rising with the sun, and snatching a hasty breakfast, he was early at work. A fever seemed to be growing in him, nor did the increasing richness of the test-pans allay this fever. There was a flush in his cheek other than that made by the heat of the sun, and he was oblivious to fatigue and the passage of time. When he filled a pan with dirt, he ran down the hill to wash it; nor could he forbear running up the hill again, panting and stumbling profanely, to refill the pan.

He was now a hundred yards from the water, and the inverted "V" was assuming definite proportions. The width of the pay-dirt steadily decreased, and the man extended in his mind's eye the sides of the "V" to their meeting place far up the hill. This was his goal, the apex of the "V," and he panned many times to locate it.

"Just about two yards above that manzanita bush an' a yard to the right," he finally concluded.

Then the temptation seized him. "As plain as the nose on your face," he said, as he abandoned his laborious cross-cutting and climbed to the indicated apex. He filled a pan and carried it down the hill to wash. It contained no trace of gold. He dug deep, and he dug shallow, filling and washing a dozen pans, and was unrewarded even by the tiniest golden speck. He was enraged at having yielded to the temptation, and berated himself blasphemously and pridelessly. Then he went down the hill and took up the cross-cutting.

"Slow an' certain, Bill; slow an' certain," he crooned. "Short-cuts to fortune ain't in your line, an' it's about time you know it. Get wise, Bill; get wise. Slow an' certain's the only hand you can play; so go to it, an' keep to it, too."

As the cross-cuts decreased, showing that the sides of the "V" were converging, the depth of the "V" increased. The gold-trace was dipping into the hill. It was only at thirty inches beneath the surface that he could get colors in his pan. The dirt he found at twenty-five inches from the surface, and at thirty-five inches yielded barren pans. At the base of the "V," by the water's edge, he had found the gold colors at the grass roots. The higher he went up the hill, the deeper the gold dipped. To dig a hole three feet deep in order to get one test-pan was a task of no mean magnitude;

while between the man and the apex intervened an untold number of such holes to be dug.

"An' there's no tellin' how much deeper it'll pitch," he sighed, in a moment's pause, while his fingers soothed his aching back.

Feverish with desire, with aching back and stiffening muscles, with pick and shovel gouging and mauling the soft brown earth, the man toiled up the hill. Before him was the smooth slope, spangled with flowers and made sweet with their breath. Behind him was devastation. It looked like some terrible eruption breaking out on the smooth skin of the hill. His slow progress was like that of a slug, befouling beauty with a monstrous trail.

Though the dipping gold-trace increased the man's work, he found consolation in the increasing richness of the pans. Twenty cents, thirty cents, fifty cents, sixty cents, were the values of the gold found in the pans, and at nightfall he washed his banner pan, which gave him a dollar's worth of gold-dust from a shovelful of dirt.

"I'll just bet it's my luck to have some inquisitive one come buttin' in here on my pasture," he mumbled sleepily that night as he pulled the blankets up to his chin.

Suddenly he sat upright. "Bill!" he called sharply. "Now, listen to me, Bill; d'ye hear! It's up to you, to-morrow mornin', to mosey round an' see what you can see. Understand? To-morrow morning, an' don't you forget it!"

He yawned and glanced across at his side-hill. "Good night, Mr. Pocket," he called.

In the morning he stole a march on the sun, for he had finished breakfast when its first rays caught him, and he was climbing the wall of the cañon where it crumbled away and gave footing. From the outlook at the top he found himself in the midst of loneliness. As far as he could see, chain after chain of mountains heaved themselves into his vision. To the east his eyes, leaping the miles between range and range and between many ranges, brought up at last against the white-peaked Sierras—the main crest, where the backbone of the Western world reared itself against the sky. To the north and south he could see more distinctly the cross-systems that broke through the main trend of the sea of mountains. To the west the ranges fell away, one behind the other, diminishing and fading into the gentle foothills that, in turn, descended into the great valley which he could not see.

And in all that mighty sweep of earth he saw no sign of man nor of the handiwork of man—save only the torn bosom of the hillside at his feet. The man looked long and carefully. Once, far down his own cañon, he thought he saw in the air a faint hint of smoke. He looked again and decided that it was the purple haze of the hills made dark by a convolution of the cañon wall at its back.

"Hey, you, Mr. Pocket!" he called down into the cañon. "Stand out from under! I'm a-comin', Mr. Pocket! I'm a-comin'!"

The heavy brogans on the man's feet made him appear clumsy-footed, but he swung down from the giddy height as lightly and airily as a mountain goat. A rock, turning under his foot on the edge of the precipice, did not disconcert him. He seemed to know the precise time required for the turn to culminate in disaster, and in the meantime he utilized the false footing itself for the momentary earth-contact necessary to carry him on into safety. Where the earth sloped so steeply that it was impossible to stand for a second upright, the man did not hesitate. His foot pressed the impossible surface for but a fraction of the fatal second and gave him the bound that carried him onward. Again, where even the fraction of a second's footing was out of the question, he would swing his body past by a moment's hand-grip on a jutting knob of rock, a crevice, or a precariously rooted shrub. At last, with a wild leap and yell, he exchanged the face of the wall for an earth-slide and finished the descent in the midst of several tons of sliding earth and gravel.

His first pan of the morning washed out over two dollars in coarse gold. It was from the centre of the "V." To either side the diminution in the values of the pans was swift. His lines of cross-cutting holes were growing very short. The converging sides of the inverted "V" were only a few yards apart. Their meeting-point was only a few yards above him. But the pay-streak was dipping deeper and deeper into the earth. By early afternoon he was sinking the test-holes five feet before the pans could show the gold-trace.

For that matter, the gold-trace had become something more than a trace; it was a placer mine in itself, and the man resolved to come back after he had found the pocket and work over the ground. But the increasing richness of the pans began to worry him. By late afternoon the worth of the pans had grown to three and four dollars. The man scratched his head perplexedly and looked a few feet up the hill at the manzanita bush that marked approximately the apex of the "V." He nodded his head and said oracularly: "It's one o' two things, Bill: one o' two things. Either Mr. Pocket's spilled himself all out an' down the hill, or else Mr. Pocket's so rich you maybe won't be able to carry him all away with you. And that'd be an awful shame, wouldn't it, now?" He chuckled at contemplation of so pleasant a dilemma.

Nightfall found him by the edge of the stream, his eyes wrestling with the gathering darkness over the washing of a five-dollar pan.

"Wisht I had an electric light to go on working," he said.

He found sleep difficult that night. Many times he composed himself and closed his eyes for slumber to overtake him; but his blood pounded with too strong desire, and as many times his eyes opened and he murmured wearily, "Wisht it was sun-up."

Sleep came to him in the end, but his eyes were open with the first paling of the stars, and the gray of dawn caught him with breakfast finished and climbing the hillside in the direction of the secret abiding-place of Mr. Pocket.

The first cross-cut the man made, there was space for only three holes, so narrow had become the pay-streak and so close was he to the fountain-head of the golden stream he had been following for four days.

"Be ca'm, Bill; be ca'm," he admonished himself, as he broke ground for the final hole where the sides of the "V" had at last come together in a point.

"I've got the almighty cinch on you, Mr. Pocket, an' you can't lose me," he said many times as he sank the hole deeper and deeper.

Four feet, five feet, six feet, he dug his way down into the earth. The digging grew harder. His pick grated on broken rock. He examined the rock. "Rotten quartz," was his conclusion as, with the shovel, he cleared the bottom of the hole of loose dirt. He attacked the crumbling quartz with the pick, bursting the disintegrating rock asunder with every stroke.

He thrust his shovel into the loose mass. His eye caught a gleam of yellow. He dropped the shovel and squatted suddenly on his heels. As a farmer rubs the clinging earth from fresh-dug potatoes, so the man, a piece of rotten quartz held in both hands, rubbed the dirt away.

"Sufferin' Sardanopolis!" he cried. "Lumps an' chunks of it! Lumps an' chunks of it!"

It was only half rock he held in his hand. The other half was virgin gold. He dropped it into his pan and examined another piece. Little yellow was to be seen, but with his strong fingers he crumbled the rotten quartz away till both hands were filled with glowing yellow. He rubbed the dirt away from fragment after fragment, tossing them into the gold-pan. It was a treasure-hole. So much had the quartz rotted away that there was less of it than there was of gold. Now and again he found a piece to which no rock clung—a piece that was all gold. A chunk, where the pick had laid open the heart of the gold, glittered like a handful of yellow jewels, and he cocked his head at it and slowly turned it around and over to observe the rich play of the light upon it.

"Talk about yer Too Much Gold diggin's!" the man snorted contemptuously. "Why, this diggin' 'd make it look like thirty cents. This diggin' is All Gold. An' right here an' now I name this yere cañon 'All Gold cañon,' b' gosh!"

Still squatting on his heels, he continued examining the fragments and tossing them into the pan. Suddenly there came to him a premonition of danger. It seemed a shadow had fallen upon him. But there was no shadow. His heart had given a great jump up into his throat and was choking him. Then his blood slowly chilled and he felt the sweat of his shirt cold against his flesh.

He did not spring up nor look around. He did not move. He was considering the nature of the premonition he had received, trying to locate the source of the mysterious force that had warned him, striving to sense the imperative presence of the unseen thing that threatened him. There is an aura of things hostile, made manifest by messengers too refined for the senses to know; and this aura he felt, but knew not how he felt it. His was the feeling as when a cloud passes over the sun. It seemed that between him and life had passed something dark and smothering and menacing; a gloom, as it were, that swallowed up life and made for death—his death.

Every force of his being impelled him to spring up and confront the unseen danger, but his soul dominated the panic, and he remained squatting on his heels, in his hands a chunk of gold. He did not dare to look around, but he knew by now that there was something behind him and above him. He made believe to be interested in the gold in his hand. He examined it critically, turned it over and over, and rubbed the dirt from it. And all the time he knew that something behind him was looking at the gold over his shoulder.

Still feigning interest in the chunk of gold in his hand, he listened intently and he heard the breathing of the thing behind him. His eyes searched the ground in front of him for a weapon, but they saw only the uprooted gold, worthless to him now in his extremity. There was his pick, a handy weapon on occasion; but this was not such an occasion. The man realized his predicament. He was in a narrow hole that was seven feet deep. His head did not come to the surface of the ground. He was in a trap.

He remained squatting on his heels. He was quite cool and collected; but his mind, considering every factor, showed him only his helplessness. He continued rubbing the dirt from the quartz fragments and throwing the gold into the pan. There was nothing else for him to do. Yet he knew that he would have to rise up, sooner or later, and face the danger that breathed at his back. The minutes passed, and with the passage of each minute he knew that by so much he was nearer the time when he must stand up, or else—and his wet shirt went cold against his flesh again at the thought—or else he might receive death as he stooped there over his treasure.

Still he squatted on his heels, rubbing dirt from gold and debating in just what manner he should rise up. He might rise up with a rush and claw his way out of the hole to meet whatever threatened on the even footing above ground. Or he might rise up slowly and carelessly, and feign casually to discover the thing that breathed at his back. His instinct and every fighting fibre of his body favored the mad, clawing rush to the surface. His intellect and the craft thereof, favored the slow and cautious meeting with the thing that menaced and which he could not see. And while he debated, a loud, crashing noise burst on his ear. At the same instant he received a stunning blow on the left side of the back, and from the point of impact felt a rush of flame through his flesh. He sprang up in the air, but halfway to his feet collapsed. His body crumpled in like a leaf withered in sudden heat, and he came down, his chest across his pan of gold, his face in the dirt and rock, his legs tangled and twisted because of the restricted space at the bottom of the hole. His legs twitched convulsively several times. His body was shaken as with a mighty ague. There was a slow expansion of the lungs, accompanied by a deep sigh. Then the air was slowly, very slowly, exhaled, and his body as slowly flattened itself down into inertness.

Above, revolver in hand, a man was peering down over the edge of the hole. He peered for a long time at the prone and motionless body beneath him. After a while the stranger sat down on the edge of the hole so that he could see into it, and rested the revolver on his knee. Reaching his hand into a pocket, he drew out a wisp of brown paper. Into this he dropped a few crumbs of tobacco. The combination became a cigarette, brown and squat, with the ends turned in. Not once did he take his eyes from the body at the bottom of the hole. He lighted the cigarette and drew its smoke into his lungs with a caressing intake of the breath. He smoked slowly. Once the cigarette went out and he relighted it. And all the while he studied the body beneath him.

In the end he tossed the cigarette stub away and rose to his feet. He moved to the edge of the hole. Spanning it, a hand resting on each edge, and with the revolver still in the right hand, he muscled his body down into the hole. While his feet were yet a yard from the bottom he released his hands and dropped down.

At the instant his feet struck bottom he saw the pocket-miner's arm leap out, and his own legs knew a swift, jerking grip that overthrew him. In the nature of the jump his revolver hand was above his head. Swiftly as the grip had flashed about his legs, just as swiftly he brought the revolver down. He was still in the air, his fall in process of completion, when he pulled the trigger. The explosion was deafening in the confined space. The smoke filled the hole so that he could see nothing. He struck the bottom on his back, and like a cat's, the pocket-miner's body was on top of him. Even as the miner's body passed on top, the stranger crooked in his right arm to fire; and even in that instant the miner, with a quick thrust of elbow, struck his wrist. The muzzle was thrown up and the bullet thudded into the dirt of the side of the hole.

The next instant the stranger felt the miner's hand grip his wrist. The struggle was now for the revolver. Each man strove to turn it against the other's body. The smoke in the hole was clearing. The stranger, lying on his back, was beginning to see dimly. But suddenly he was blinded by a handful of dirt deliberately flung into his eyes by his antagonist. In that moment of shock his grip on the revolver was broken. In the next moment he felt a smashing darkness descend upon his brain, and in the midst of the darkness even the darkness ceased.

But the pocket-miner fired again and again, until the revolver was empty. Then he tossed it from him and, breathing heavily, sat down on the dead man's legs.

The miner was sobbing and struggling for breath. "Measly skunk!" he panted; "a-campin' on my trail an' lettin' me do the work, an' then shootin' me in the back!"

He was half crying from anger and exhaustion. He peered at the face of the dead man. It was sprinkled with loose dirt and gravel, and it was difficult to distinguish the features.

"Never laid eyes on him before," the miner concluded his scrutiny. "Just a common an' ordinary thief, hang him! An' he shot me in the back! He shot me in the back!"

He opened his shirt and felt himself, front and back, on his left side.

"Went clean through, and no harm done!" he cried jubilantly. "I'll bet he aimed all right all right; but he drew the gun over when he pulled the trigger—the cur! But I fixed 'm! Oh, I fixed 'm!"

His fingers were investigating the bullet-hole in his side, and a shade of regret passed over his face. "It's goin' to be stiffer'n hell," he said. "An' it's up to me to get mended an' get out o'here."

He crawled out of the hole and went down the hill to his camp. Half an hour later he returned, leading his pack-horse. His open shirt disclosed the rude bandages with which he had dressed his wound. He was slow and awkward with his left-hand movements, but that did not prevent his using the arm.

The bight of the pack-rope under the dead man's shoulders enabled him to heave the body out of the hole. Then he set to work gathering up his gold. He worked steadily for several hours, pausing often to rest his stiffening shoulder and to exclaim:

"He shot me in the back, the measly skunk! He shot me in the back!"

When his treasure was quite cleaned up and wrapped securely into a number of blanket-covered parcels, he made an estimate of its value.

"Four hundred pounds, or I'm a Hottentot," he concluded. "Say two hundred in quartz an' dirt—that leaves two hundred pounds of gold. Bill! Wake up! Two hundred pounds of gold! Forty thousand dollars! An' it's yourn—all yourn!"

He scratched his head delightedly and his fingers blundered into an unfamiliar groove. They quested along it for several inches. It was a crease through his scalp where the second bullet had ploughed.

He walked angrily over to the dead man.

"You would, would you!" he bullied. "You would, eh? Well, I fixed you good an' plenty, an' I'll give you decent burial, too. That's more'n you'd have done for me."

He dragged the body to the edge of the hole and toppled it in. It struck the bottom with a dull crash, on its side, the face twisted up to the light. The miner peered down at it.

"An' you shot me in the back!" he said accusingly.

With pick and shovel he filled the hole. Then he loaded the gold on his horse. It was too great a load for the animal, and when he had gained his camp he transferred part of it to his saddle-horse. Even so, he was compelled to abandon a portion of his outfit—pick and shovel and gold-pan, extra food and cooking utensils, and divers odds and ends.

The sun was at the zenith when the man forced the horses at the screen of vines and creepers. To climb the huge boulders the animals were compelled to uprear and struggle blindly through the tangled mass of vegetation. Once the saddle-horse fell heavily and the man removed the pack to get the animal on its feet. After it started on its way again the man thrust his head out from among the leaves and peered up at the hillside.

"The measly skunk!" he said, and disappeared.

There was a ripping and tearing of vines and boughs. The trees surged back and forth, marking the passage of the animals through the midst of them. There was a clashing of steel-shod hoofs on stone, and now and again a sharp cry of command. Then the voice of the man was raised in song:—

> "Tu'n around an' tu'n yo' face
> Untoe them sweet hills of grace
>   (D' pow'rs of sin yo' am scornin'!).
> Look about an' look aroun'
> Fling yo' sin-pack on d' groun'
>   (Yo' will meet wid d' Lord in d' mornin'!))."

The song grew faint and fainter, and through the silence crept back the spirit of the place. The stream once more drowsed and whispered; the hum of the mountain bees rose sleepily. Down through the perfume-weighted air fluttered the snowy fluffs of the cottonwoods. The butterflies drifted in and out among the trees, and over all blazed the quiet sunshine. Only remained the hoof-marks in the meadow and the torn hillside to mark the boisterous trail of the life that had broken the peace of the place and passed on.

The Banks of the Sacramento

Jack London

This second California gold rush story by Jack London originally appeared in a 1904 issue of *The Youth's Companion*. It is quite an exciting and dramatic tale of danger, featuring a young caretaker of an abandoned mine near the Sacramento River, which runs from the Klamath Mountains—north of Mount Shasta at the northern end of the Sacramento Valley—south into San Francisco Bay and eventually out through the Golden Gate into the Pacific Ocean. Descriptive clues in the story appear to indicate that it takes place in Northern California, probably somewhere along the river between the towns of Mount Shasta and Redding—roughly fifty to a hundred miles from the Oregon border.

> "And it's blow ye winds, heigh-ho,
>   For Cal-i-for-ni-o;
> For there's plenty of gold, so I've been told,
>   On the banks of the Sacramento!"

It was only a little boy, singing in a shrill treble the sea chantey which seamen sing the wide world over when they man the capstan-bars and break the anchors out for "Frisco" port. It was only a little boy who had never seen the sea, but two hundred feet beneath him rolled the Sacramento. "Young" Jerry he was called, after "Old" Jerry, his father, from whom he had learned the song, as well as received his shock of bright-red hair, his blue, dancing eyes, and his fair and inevitably freckled skin.

For Old Jerry had been a sailor, and had followed the sea till middle life, haunted always by the words of the ringing chantey. Then one day he had sung the song in earnest, in an Asiatic port, swinging and thrilling round the capstan-circle with twenty others. And at San Francisco he turned his back upon his ship and upon the sea, and went to behold with his own eyes the banks of the Sacramento.

He beheld the gold, too, for he found employment at the Yellow Dream mine, and proved of utmost usefulness in rigging the great ore-cables across the river and two hundred feet above its surface.

After that he took charge of the cables and kept them in repair, and ran them and loved them, and became himself an indispensable fixture of the Yellow Dream mine. Then he loved pretty Margaret Kelly; but she had left him and Young Jerry, the latter barely toddling, to take up her last long sleep in the little graveyard among the great sober pines.

Old Jerry never went back to the sea. He remained by his cables, and lavished upon them and Young Jerry all the love of his nature. When evil days came to the Yellow Dream, he still remained in the employ of the company as watchman over the all but abandoned property.

But this morning he was not visible. Young Jerry only was to be seen, sitting on the cabin step and singing the ancient chantey. He had cooked and eaten his breakfast all by himself, and had just come out to take a look at the world. Twenty feet before him stood the steel drum round which the endless cable worked. By the drum, snug and fast, was the ore-car. Following with his eyes the dizzy flight of the cables to the farther bank, he could see the other drum and the other car.

The contrivance was worked by gravity, the loaded car crossing the river by virtue of its own weight, and at the same time dragging the empty car back. The loaded car being emptied, and the empty car being loaded with more ore, the performance could be repeated—a performance which had been repeated tens of thousands of times since the day Old Jerry became the keeper of the cables.

Young Jerry broke off his song at the sound of approaching steps. A tall, blue-shirted man, a rifle across the hollow of his arm, came out from the gloom of the pine-trees. It was Hall, watchman of the Yellow Dragon mine, the cables of which spanned the Sacramento a mile farther up.

"Hello, yonker!" was his greeting. "What you doin' here by your lonesome?"

"Oh, bachin'," Jerry tried to answer unconcernedly, as if it were a very ordinary sort of thing. "Dad's away, you see."

"Where's he gone?" the man asked.

"San Francisco. Went last night. His brother's dead in the old country, and he's gone down to see the lawyers. Won't be back till to-morrow night."

So spoke Jerry, and with pride, because of the responsibility which had fallen to him of keeping an eye on the property of the Yellow Dream, and the glorious adventure of living alone on the cliff above the river and of cooking his own meals.

"Well, take care of yourself," Hall said, "and don't monkey with the cables. I'm goin' to see if I can't pick up a deer in the Cripple Cow Cañon."

"It's goin' to rain, I think," Jerry said, with mature deliberation.

"And it's little I mind a wettin'," Hall laughed, as he strode away among the trees.

Jerry's prediction concerning rain was more than fulfilled. By ten o'clock the pines were swaying and moaning, the cabin windows rattling, and the rain driving by in fierce squalls. At half past eleven he kindled a fire, and promptly at the stroke of twelve sat down to his dinner.

No out-of-doors for him that day, he decided, when he had washed the few dishes and put them neatly away; and he wondered how wet Hall was and whether he had succeeded in picking up a deer.

At one o'clock there came a knock at the door, and when he opened it a man and a woman staggered in on the breast of a great gust of wind. They were Mr. and Mrs. Spillane, ranchers, who lived in a lonely valley a dozen miles back from the river.

"Where's Hall?" was Spillane's opening speech, and he spoke sharply and quickly.

Jerry noted that he was nervous and abrupt in his movements, and that Mrs. Spillane seemed laboring under some strong anxiety. She was a thin, washed-out, worked-out woman, whose life of dreary and unending toil had stamped itself harshly upon her face. It was the same life that had bowed her husband's shoulders and gnarled his hands and turned his hair to a dry and dusty gray.

"He's gone hunting up Cripple Cow," Jerry answered. "Did you want to cross?"

The woman began to weep quietly, while Spillane dropped a troubled exclamation and strode to the window. Jerry joined him in gazing out to where the cables lost themselves in the thick downpour.

It was the custom of the backwoods people in that section of the country to cross the Sacramento on the Yellow Dragon cable. For this service a small toll was charged, which tolls the Yellow Dragon Company applied to the payment of Hall's wages.

"We've got to get across, Jerry," Spillane said, at the same time jerking his thumb over his shoulder in the direction of his wife. "Her father's hurt at the Clover Leaf. Powder explosion. Not expected to live. We just got word."

Jerry felt himself fluttering inwardly. He knew that Spillane wanted to cross on the Yellow Dream cable, and in the absence of his father he felt that he dared not assume such a responsibility, for the cable had never been used for passengers; in fact, had not been used at all for a long time.

"Maybe Hall will be back soon," he said.

Spillane shook his head, and demanded, "Where's your father?"

"San Francisco," Jerry answered briefly.

Spillane groaned, and fiercely drove his clenched fist into the palm of the other hand. His wife was crying more audibly, and Jerry could hear her murmuring, "And daddy's dyin', dyin'!"

"Look here kid," he said, with determination, "the wife and me are goin' over on this here cable of yours! Will you run it for us?"

Jerry backed slightly away. He did it unconsciously, as if recoiling instinctively from something unwelcome.

"Better see if Hall's back," he suggested.

"And if he ain't?"

Again Jerry hesitated.

"I'll stand the risk," Spillane added. "Don't you see, kid, we've simply got to cross!"

Jerry nodded his head reluctantly.

"And there ain't no use waitin' for Hall," Spillane went on. "You know as well as me he ain't back from Cripple Cow this time of day! So come along and let's get started."

No wonder that Mrs. Spillane seemed terrified as they helped her into the ore-car—so Jerry thought, as he gazed into the apparently fathomless gulf beneath her. For it was so filled with rain and cloud, hurtling and curling in the fierce blast, that the other shore, seven hundred feet away, was invisible, while the cliff at their feet dropped sheer down and lost itself in the swirling vapor. By all appearances it might be a mile to bottom instead of two hundred feet.

"All ready?" he asked.

"Let her go!" Spillane shouted, to make himself heard above the roar of the wind.

He had clambered in beside his wife, and was holding one of her hands in his.

Jerry looked upon this with disapproval. "You'll need all your hands for holdin' on, the way the wind's yowlin'."

The man and the woman shifted their hands accordingly, tightly gripping the sides of the car, and Jerry slowly and carefully released the brake. The drum began to revolve as the endless cable passed round it, and the car slid slowly out into the chasm, its trolley-wheels rolling on the stationary cable overhead, to which it was suspended.

It was not the first time Jerry had worked the cable, but it was the first time he had done so away from the supervising eye of his father. By means of the brake he regulated the speed of the car. It needed regulating, for at times, caught by the stronger gusts of wind, it swayed violently back and forth; and once, just before it was swallowed up in a rain-squall, it seemed about to spill out its human contents.

After that Jerry had no way of knowing where the car was except by means of the cable. This he watched keenly as it glided round the drum. "Three hundred feet," he breathed to himself, as the cable markings went by; "three hundred and fifty, four hundred, four hundred and . . ."

The cable stopped. Jerry threw off the brake, but it did not move. He caught the cable with his hands and tried to start it by tugging smartly. Something had gone wrong. What? He could not guess; he could not see. Looking up, he could vaguely make out the empty car, which had been crossing from the opposite cliff at a speed equal to that of the loaded car. It was about two hundred and fifty feet away. That meant, he knew, that somewhere in the gray obscurity, two hundred feet above the river and two hundred and fifty feet from the other bank, Spillane and his wife were suspended and stationary.

Three times Jerry shouted with all the shrill force of his lungs, but no answering cry came out of the storm. It was impossible for him to hear them or to make himself heard. As he stood for a moment, thinking rapidly, the flying clouds seemed to thin and lift. He caught a glimpse of the swollen Sacramento beneath, and a briefer glimpse of the car and the man and woman. Then the clouds descended thicker than ever.

The boy examined the drum closely, and found nothing wrong with it. Evidently it was the drum on the other side that had gone wrong. He was appalled at the thought of the man and woman out there in the midst of the storm, hanging over the abyss, rocking back and forth in the frail car and ignorant of what was taking place on the shore. And he did not like to think of their hanging there while he went round by the Yellow Dragon cable to the other drum.

But he remembered a block and tackle in the tool-house, and ran and brought it. They were double blocks, and he murmured aloud, "A purchase of four," as he made the tackle fast to the endless cable. Then he heaved upon it, heaved until it seemed that his arms were being drawn out from their sockets and that his shoulder muscles would be ripped asunder. Yet the cable did not budge. Nothing remained but to cross over to the other side.

He was already soaking wet, so he did not mind the rain as he ran over the trail to the Yellow Dragon. The storm was with him, and it was easy going, although there was no Hall at the other end of it to man the brake for him and regulate the speed of the car. This he did for himself, however, by means of a stout rope, which he passed, with a turn, round the stationary cable.

As the full force of the wind struck him in mid-air, swaying the cable and whistling and roaring past it, and rocking and careening the car, he appreciated more fully what must be the condition of mind of Spillane and his wife. And this appreciation gave strength to him, as, safely across, he fought his way up the other bank, in the teeth of the gale, to the Yellow Dream cable.

To his consternation, he found the drum in thorough working order. Everything was running smoothly at both ends. Where was the hitch? In the middle, without a doubt.

From this side, the car containing Spillane was only two hundred and fifty feet away. He could make out the man and woman through the whirling vapor, crouching in the bottom of the car and exposed to the pelting rain and the full fury of the wind. In a lull between the squalls he shouted to Spillane to examine the trolley of the car.

Spillane heard, for he saw him rise up cautiously on his knees, and with his hands go over both trolley-wheels. Then he turned his face toward the bank.

"She's all right, kid!"

Jerry heard the words, faint and far, as from a remote distance. Then what was the matter? Nothing remained but the other and empty car, which he could not see, but which he knew to be there, somewhere in that terrible gulf two hundred feet beyond Spillane's car.

His mind was made up on the instant. He was only fourteen years old, slightly and wirily built; but his life had been lived among the mountains, his father had taught him no small measure of "sailoring," he was not particularly afraid of heights.

In the tool-box by the drum he found an old monkey-wrench and a short bar of iron, also a coil of fairly new Manila rope. He looked in vain for a piece of board with which to rig a "boatswain's chair." There was nothing at hand but large planks, which he had no means of sawing, so he was compelled to do without the more comfortable form of saddle.

The saddle he rigged was very simple. With the rope he made merely a large loop round the stationary cable, to which hung the empty car. When he sat in the loop his hands could just reach the cable conveniently, and where the rope was likely to fray against the cable he lashed his coat, in lieu of the old sack he would have used had he been able to find one.

These preparations swiftly completed, he swung out over the chasm, sitting in the rope saddle and pulling himself along the cable by his hands. With him he carried the monkey-wrench and short iron bar and a few spare feet of rope. It was a slightly up-hill pull, but this he did not mind so much as the wind. When the furious gusts hurled him back and forth, sometimes half-twisting him about, and he gazed down into the gray depths, he was aware that he was afraid. It was an old cable. What if it should break under his weight and the pressure of the wind?

It was fear he was experiencing, honest fear, and he knew that there was a "gone" feeling in the pit of his stomach, and a trembling of the knees which he could not quell.

But he held himself bravely to the task. The cable was old and worn, sharp pieces of wire projected from it, and his hands were cut and bleeding by the time he took his first rest, and held a shouted conversation with Spillane. The car was directly beneath him and only a few feet away, so he was able to explain the condition of affairs and his errand.

"Wish I could help you," Spillane shouted at him as he started on, "but the wife's gone all to pieces! Anyway, kid, take care of yourself! I got myself in this fix, but it's up to you to get me out!"

"Oh, I'll do it!" Jerry shouted back. "Tell Mrs. Spillane that she'll be ashore now in a jiffy!"

In the midst of pelting rain, which half-blinded him, swinging from side to side like a rapid and erratic pendulum, his torn hands paining him severely and his lungs panting from his exertions and panting from the very air which the wind sometimes blew into his mouth with strangling force, he finally arrived at the empty car.

A single glance showed him that he had not made the dangerous journey in vain. The front trolley-wheel, loose from long wear, had jumped the cable, and the cable was now jammed tightly between the wheel and the sheave-block.

One thing was clear—the wheel must be removed from the block. A second thing was equally clear—while the wheel was being removed the car would have to be fastened to the cable by rope he had brought.

At the end of a quarter of an hour, beyond making the car secure, he had accomplished nothing. The key which bound the wheel on its axle was rusted and jammed. He hammered at it with one hand and held on the best he could with the other, but the wind persisted in swinging and twisting his body, and made his blows miss more often than not. Nine-tenths of the strength he expended was in trying to hold himself steady. For fear that he might drop the monkey-wrench he made it fast to his wrist with his handkerchief.

At the end of half an hour Jerry had hammered the key clear, but he could not draw it out. A dozen times it seemed that he must give up in despair, that all the danger and toil he had gone through were for nothing. Then an idea came to him, and he went through his pockets with feverish haste, and found what he sought—a tenpenny nail.

But for that nail, put in his pocket he knew not when or why, he would have had to make another trip over the cable and back. Thrusting the nail through the looped head of the key, he at last had a grip, and in no time the key was out.

Then came the punching and prying with the iron bar to get the wheel itself free from where it was jammed by the cable against the side of the block. After that Jerry replaced the wheel, and by means of the rope, heaved up on the car till the trolley once more rested properly on the cable.

All this took time. More than an hour and a half had elapsed since his arrival at the empty car. And now, for the first time, he dropped out of his rope saddle and down into the car. He removed the detaining ropes, and the trolley-wheels began slowly to revolve. The car was moving, and he knew that somewhere beyond, although he could not see, the car of Spillane was likewise moving, and in the opposite direction.

There was no need for a brake, for his weight sufficiently counterbalanced the weight in the other car; and soon he saw the cliff rising out of the cloud depths and the old familiar drum going round and round.

Jerry climbed out and made the car securely fast. He did it deliberately and carefully, and then, quite unhero-like, he sank down by the drum, regardless of the pelting storm, and burst out sobbing.

There were many reasons why he sobbed—partly from the pain of his hands, which was excruciating; partly from exhaustion; partly from relief and release from the nerve-tension he had been under for so long; and in a large measure from thankfulness that the man and woman were saved.

They were not there to thank him; but somewhere beyond that howling, storm-driven gulf he knew they were hurrying over the trail toward the Clover Leaf.

Jerry staggered to the cabin, and his hand left the white knob red and bloody as he opened the door, but he took no notice of it.

He was too proudly contented with himself, for he was certain that he had done well, and he was honest enough to admit to himself that he had done well. But a small regret arose and perished in his thoughts—if his father had only been there to see!

Scorpion Gulch

Nathan Urner

Nathan Urner was a short story writer, journalist, and the city editor of the *New York Tribune*. This pulp-fiction adventure story appeared in the January 1866 issue of *Beadle's Monthly,* just a few years after the time it is supposed to have taken place.

California in the scorching mid-summer of 185—.

Joel Hereford, my fast comrade, and myself, had been working a lonely claim on the Red Bar of the Dry Fork of Feather River for over six weeks; and, in the mountain coolness of one evening, soon after sunset, we found ourselves sitting at the door of our little shanty, seriously discussing whether we should continue or abandon the claim, and "prospect" for richer diggings. We had another partner in our present claim, a Mexican or native Californian—I never knew which—named Miguel Gonzago. He resided, with his wife and little daughter, at an insignificant ranch some miles below us, on the Yuba, and near the miniature commonwealth of Ophir, which then consisted of five log edifices, all drinking saloons, an equal number of cattle corrals, and several miners' tents. Gonzago had gone home for the night. Before going, however, he had strongly urged the abandonment of the Bar, and a resort to the richer deposits of the mountains.

The profits of our claim had been steadily decreasing, and both Hereford and myself, at length, came to the conclusion that we would, at all events, "sink the claim," as the phrase went; but in what direction next to turn our gold-seeking steps, we were at a loss to determine. We were always sanguine. That the Eldorado of our golden dreams would, sooner or later, be reached, we never for a moment doubted. For two hardy, adventurous years, we had wandered from gully to gully, from stream to stream, ditching, dredging, cradling, sifting, had made money, lost some also, and now possessed sums of tolerable magnitude in bank at Sacramento. But we had followed the glittering bauble too long to be satisfied with any but colossal results. "Shall we go home?" was never a question with us, but invariably, "Where shall we go next?"

Our present contemplated change of base, however, involved a new consideration. We had long had vague apprehensions about the trustworthiness of our swarthy partner, Miguel, or "Don Miguel," as we jocosely termed him.

We had now fallen into a reverie, when Hereford suddenly broke the silence with:

"George, aren't you somewhat afraid of the Don?"

"Yes," I replied, starting a little at the question, for, at the very moment he spoke, the sinister features of the Mexican were floating darkly through my thoughts.

"I don't like him at all," said my comrade. "If he wasn't so shrewd, I would go in for turning him out of the concern.

"Do you know," he continued, "when I was down at Marysville last week, I heard Jack Hays describing the appearance of that infernal robber and murderer, Gonzago, whom the Vigilance Committee chased for miles up the San Joaquin valley, without being able to catch him."

"What of that?"

"Nothing, only the description fitted our Don to a dot."

"Pshaw!"

"Besides that," persisted Hereford, "I believe he hates me like a fiend. The man has got it into his head, one way or another, that I have been making love to his wife."

I laughed; for I had, "in one way or another," got the same thing into my head.

Except that we would quit the claims, at all events, we came to no conclusion, whatever, and soon retired to our bunks, to sleep the thing through, and see what the morning would bring forth.

We rose betimes, while the sky was yet rosy in the east, as our preparations for departure would occupy several hours. After a hasty meal of biscuit and salt junk, Hereford proceeded to gather our mining implements together, while I stuffed the provisions into rude panniers of canvas cloth, wherewith to pack our mule for the journey. Our visits to Marysville or Sacramento were necessarily unfrequent. We were, therefore, in the habit of secreting our earnings, when of considerable amount, generally by burying them in the ground, until opportunity was afforded one of as to convey them to the nearest depot. Upon this occasion, we had accumulated upward of a hundred ounces of the precious dust, and concluded that the safer plan would be to bury it in the near vicinity of our "ranch," by which name we dignified the dilapidated eight-by-ten log-hut which we had erected among the golden rods and rank grasses at the water's edge.

Other preparations being complete, we sewed up our dust in a little sack, and went into the underbrush to find a suitable place for secreting it. Men are always somewhat nervous upon such occasions. We had hardly entered the thicket before there was a rustling sound behind us; and we both wheeled swiftly, with instinctive alarm.

"Did you see her?" exclaimed Hereford.

"I saw nothing."

"But I did. I think it was that monkey-faced girl of the Don's. She slipped through the bush like a ghost."

"What of it?" said I. "She runs through the mountains at will, and has frequently been here before."

"Not at daybreak," grumbled Hereford, uneasily. "Do you know, George, I suspect the Don sent her as a spy upon us."

This seemed entirely unreasonable to me, and, without replying, I led the way deeper into the thicket. We heard another rustle, but saw nothing to warrant suspicion, and, soon selecting a suitable place—a little hillock, completely surrounded by a dense, bristling growth of the Spanish Bayonet [yucca]—we put our treasure underground, blazed the trees on either side to mark the spot, and then retraced our steps.

We had barely reached the bar again, before we heard a familiar volley of mongrel maledictions fired at some beast of burden. A moment afterward, Don Miguel broke out of the undergrowth on the opposite shore of the stream, driving a laden donkey before him. He was immediately followed by his wife—Donna Maria, as we called her—who was throned upon the back of another donkey, which was about the smallest adult specimen of his species I ever saw. How he supported the weight of his handsome but buxom mistress was a marvel, to which I can only liken the phenomenon of a tiny ant shouldering the carcass of a bluebottle fly to his winter-quarters. The Don's little bare-legged girl was trotting merrily beside her mother as they came through the brush.

"Good-morning, señors," said the Don, who spoke tolerable English when he wished.

We returned his salutation, and, as he had every appearance of migrating somewhere, asked him where he was going.

"*Caramba!* No you going to *vamose los rio?*" said he in great surprise.

"Yes," replied Hereford; "but we didn't know that you were."

"*Si, si, señor! Caramba!* We must dig more dust. Plenty up the mountains! Oh, plenty! plenty!" he earnestly exclaimed, illustrating his idea of "plenty" by describing with his arms a mighty curve, the continuation of which would probably have taken in about three-fourths of the starry heavens.

But, as nearly every barren bar, stream, or gully to which he had heretofore piloted us had been described in much the same manner, we had grown somewhat skeptical. Nevertheless, we had great faith in Gonzago's skill as an explorer, and, after a few minutes' consultation, agreed to accompany him. To my surprise, Hereford was now more earnestly in favor of it than myself. I soon, however, discovered that it was all owing to the shrewdness of the Mexican, who had brought his wife to accompany us; for the black eyes of the fair señora were alluring lights in that then comparatively womanless wilderness. She was from Sonora, barely twenty-five, and possessed much beauty, so far as it is to be found among the humbler classes of Mexico. Besides, she was very lively, rattled off a jargon of Anglo-Spanish very musically, and now looked prettier than ever, as she sat picturesquely perched upon her diminutive donkey, with the smoke-wreaths of her cigarette curling lazily up from her pretty lips.

The Don was a man of forty, dusky-featured, gloomy-browed and sunken-eyed, romantically dressed in the most approved ranchero style of slouched sombrero, white-fringed buckskin trowsers, and enormous spurs—upon the whole, half-ruffianly in his appearance, but polite and suave withal.

The little girl, Inez, was probably ten years old, perhaps eight, and possibly twelve. She ran at large, half-naked, picked up rattlesnakes and bloated spiders with charming impunity, and laughed like an idiot at everything she saw.

Hereford, having gone to the forest, returned with our mule, which had been picketed there. It occurred to me, for the second time, to ask the Don where he proposed to go.

"Oh, plenty dust! plenty! plenty!" he replied, again describing an arc of the heavens, to indicate the limitless extent of affluence to which he was about to lead us. But, upon being pressed to explain himself more minutely, he threw some light upon our understandings by mentioning the single name:

"Los Scorpion Gulch!"

I started back in surprise, and Hereford mechanically paused from arranging the pack on our mule. But the Don and his wife laughed immoderately at our astonishment, and the little Inez chimed in as a matter of course.

"*Caramba!*" said Miguel. "Gulch only sixty miles off! Gulch full of gold!"

"True; but fuller of snakes, tarantulas, and every other poisonous pest!" cried Hereford; "and I, for one, have no inclination to pursue lucre in such company."

The place in question was far up in the Sierras, somewhere in the neighborhood of Antelope Creek. A few miners, who were supposed to have been there, had spread marvelous reports throughout the mines of the treasures there concealed, but most effectually guarded by indescribable swarms of deadly insects and reptiles, as well as being almost unapproachable from the topographical nature of the neighboring country. I, for one, however, had come to regard these stories as altogether fabulous, or, at best, ridiculously exaggerated—a sort of bugbear, resorted to by the old miners, for the purpose of frightening new-comers. Hence,

I rather liked the adventure, although the proposition had somewhat startled me at first. Hereford was induced, with a little persuasion, to fall in with the scheme.

An hour after sunrise, we started for the gulch, crossing Feather River, and striking through the mountains northwest by north. We had a difficult journey before us, which would probably occupy five days, as most of the way lay through the rough, frowning Sierras, increasing in height at every step, over stony and very indistinct hunting-trails, where it seemed to the inexperienced eye that a wild goat could scarcely climb with safety. Nevertheless, with our hardy experience, and our bright visions of the promised land perpetually before us, to our eyes the distance hourly lessened, and we counted it not by footsteps. Our black-eyed señora would cook the game we killed, twice a day, and, as the country we traversed was well watered, we could almost nightly encamp beside a pleasant stream, where, after the breathless heat of those scorching days, the cold, clear gushes from the mountain's heart were an unspeakable blessing.

On the evening of the third day, we reached Antelope Creek, and Donna Maria's faithful little donkey dropped down and died at the brink. It was the first instance in my experience of a donkey actually perishing from exhaustion. I had theretofore been led to suppose that you could drive them any distance whatever, and feed them on a sheep-skin for an indefinite period of time.

Otherwise than that the remainder of the journey would have to be performed on foot, the señora was by no means concerned at the loss of the faithful animal. The next day, Hereford played the gallant in giving her the support of his arm over the more difficult portions of the way. These were numerous. For now we were in the very midst of the loftiest mountains of Shasta county, including peaks surpassed by few in California or Oregon for sublimity of scenery—a region even yet unknown in many of its secret features, to the steps of civilized man.

At about midday on Thursday, the fourth day out from Red Bar, we readied a most delightful plateau. It was covered with ample pasturage for our animals, and kissed at its eastern brink by an ice-cold torrent, which ran swiftly by, ere making the grand plunge of four hundred feet, which it accomplished about half a mile beyond. Here Don Miguel announced to us that we were within a mile of our destination, and proposed to make the plateau our encampment, while we prospected the gulch. This we acceded to. Leaving Donna Maria and her little changeling of a child to prepare the meal by our return, we set out for the infinite "plenty, plenty," of which our guide had so confidently assured us.

As we turned from the comparatively level plateau upon a narrow path, which wound deviously around an awful chasm between two lesser crags, Hereford and myself instinctively paused, and sent forth a great shout of surprise and admiration at the grandeur and magnificence of the scene so suddenly disclosed above, beneath, and around us. Far to the northward rose a single cone, of whose sublime isolation and splendor we had frequently heard from the elder miners, who had given it the nautical but significant title of "sky-scraper." Now we beheld it for ourselves—

> "Not with the frenzy of a dreamer's eye.
> But soaring snow-clad through its native sky,
> In the wild pomp of mountain majesty."

In the interval between our perilous stand-point and this giant of the waste were lesser peaks, looking more gloomy and somber as they lay in the mighty shadow of their superior; and broad, green cañons bordering flashing streams, which rushed to the verge of some near chasm, visible or unseen, while the thunderous music of their fall was borne to our ears on the free, fresh air. One cliff rose with peculiar grandeur far away to the left of the grand cone, and over its rugged crest we could see one torrent slide through the pine-tops below, like a smooth, broad sheet of cold, blue steel. We were familiar with mountains, but the magnificence of this glorious scene was a picture to be recalled through the vicissitudes of a lifetime.

After lingering for many seconds upon its marvelous beauty, we followed the Mexican, who piloted us silently around the narrow brink of the chasm. Attaining firmer ground, we climbed a sharp ridge, through a twilight of dense pines, then down again over more level ground, but still through the trees, until we came suddenly upon the steep, sloping verge of an abyss so black, so terrible, that it seemed grotesque and unnatural—the phantasm of some haunting dream.

"Come, Don! hurry us around this infernal hole!" said Hereford impatiently. "It looks like the mouth of the bottomless pit! Come, let us go on to the gulch!"

"*Caramba!*" exclaimed the Mexican, with a complacent chuckle. "*Caramba!* this *is* the gulch."

We looked at him in amazement.

"*Si, si,*" he continued. "Los Scorpion Gulch! plenty gold! plenty! plenty!"

"Suppose you go down first, and fetch up a few specimens," said Hereford, with some bitterness.

In spite of our disappointment, we both laughed heartily at the ludicrous figures we cut on the outer verge of that yawning, horrible pit, whose very brink was almost unapproachable, without the certainty of being precipitated into unknown depths.

Gulch, until lately, was an obsolete word of Scandinavian origin, signifying, as a verb, to swallow or devour greedily; hence, as a substantive, a greedy swallower or devourer; and, therefore, was almost synonymous with *gulf* or *abyss*. I only know that I found the word in California when I went there; and it is a most excellent one, if we wish to preserve an analogy between the meaning of a thing and the sound of the term expressing it.

Scorpion Gulch, as it was called, was an enormous, irregular rift or crater, covering a surface of probably two acres and a half. The outer edge, upon which we stood, was fringed with dark and lofty pines on every side, with the shadows of a dozen far loftier mountains upon them. The ground sloped from this outer edge, at a steep decline—say that of sixty degrees—down to the proper verge or edge of the abyss, which, from them, dropped into perpendicular blackness; while a little rill of water leaped flashingly down one corner of the slope, and entered the pit with a very slight, shrill, ringing sound, which, as it came up from below, I likened in my mind to the laughter of some maniac giant confined forever in the gloomy depths. Aside from this there was a strange and oppressive stillness. The sound of the distant cataracts was here shut away by the dense woods on all sides, and, owing to the close vicinity of the mountain wall, a strong breeze seldom stirred the trees, which rendered the midday heat almost unbearable. The trees were also so lofty that, on the one side or the other, their deep shadows almost covered the pit, so that the sunlight could seldom reach its mouth with an illuminating ray, but merely stole round the outer skirt—in a pallid, frightened way, it seemed to me. The sloping sides—between the bordering pines and the inner brink—were covered with a thick growth of the pale, tufty grass of those regions, known as Buffalo grass, interspersed with the sharp, stout, bristling prongs of the Spanish Bayonet, prickly pear, and other species of cacti. As we stood wonderingly at the edge of the timber, instinctively keeping hold of the trees, a rattle-snake, about four feet in length, slipped boldly out from behind a cactus clump, eyed us malignantly for a few seconds, then glided glimmeringly down to the gulch, passed cautiously over, and was lost to our sight.

I turned away with a shudder. My comrades followed me, and we began to retrace our steps.

"To-morrow we come with ropes and crowbars, and prospect way down to the bottom," said Don Miguel.

The idea of returning to that pit of evil struck Hereford and myself as so preposterous that we laughed immoderately at the proposition. But, all the way, and about the camp-fire in the evening, the Mexican urged so earnestly and vigorously for an exploration of the gulch that we went to sleep half persuaded to attempt it.

In the morning we were fully so. A hearty meal and a long, refresh-ing slumber are wonderful antidotes to morbid thoughts. When the sun was about three hours high, we started again with crowbars, picks and spades, while the Don carried a brand new three-quarter inch Manilla rope, about a hundred and twenty-five feet in length, which he took from among the effects with which his beast had been laden. Donna Maria gave us a charming God-speed in Spanish, bestowing a bright look on Hereford with her large black eyes; little Inez ran for a considerable dis-tance screaming and laughing after us; and we saw in everything auspi-cious signs of success.

Arriving once more at the gulch, it did not look quite so gloomy and forbidding as on the evening before. We allowed our guide to make the preliminary preparations, which he quickly performed with a practiced hand. Our apprehensions were further modified by the fearlessness with which he approached the yawning chasm.

Fastening one end of his stout rope to a tree on the side which sloped most gradually to the verge, he took the cord in his hand and boldly walked down to the inner brink. He then called out to us to let the crowbar slide down to him. This we did, and, supporting himself with the rope, he soon succeeded in inserting the huge bar deep into the soil. He then made fast the rope to the bar, thus forming a very ingenious rail, by which one could descend to the mouth of the pit with comparative security. According to his directions, we now rolled him down some pine-branches and several large stones, which he dexterously caught and proceeded to build round the crowbar into a little pyramid, selecting and fitting the stones with such nicety that they made a bulwark of considerable strength. Then, flinging the remainder of the line over the verge of the chasm, he suddenly caught it with a seemingly careless grip, flung himself over it, and, in an instant, was lost to view.

His disappearance was so sudden that it startled us considerably. At the same time, it gave us a much higher opinion of our swarthy confrère than we ever before had entertained.

He must have gone down pretty far, for, although we could hear him swearing at the obstacles he was encountering, his voice came up very indistinctly. Then there was a silence for many seconds. We began to fear that some accident had befallen him, when suddenly the rope was tugged more vigorously, indicating that he was now ascending, and pretty soon his huge sombrero appeared above the mouth of the pit. With an agile leap, he was again standing on the edge.

"Gold! gold! plenty! plenty!" he cried, and, taking off his hat, he took from its depths, and tossed us up, two fragments of dirty quartz, weighing two or three pounds each.

Hereford and I uttered joyful exclamations as we cracked one of these open with a pick. Absolutely one-eighth of the mass was pure, glittering metal. The second fragment proved even richer than the first. Surely, we had found our Eldorado at last.

But sin is a frequent accompaniment of wealth. "See!" said Hereford, pointing to the earth that was clinging to one of the fragments; and, as I looked, I saw a scorpion about three inches in length, spring from it, and glide with incredible rapidity down the slope.

"Pluto, the god of riches, was also the deity of hell," I moralized.

But we were by no means despondent. We now thought little of the horrors of that rift in the bosom of the hills, but only of the yellow treasures which its black maw must contain.

Miguel now came up to us. After witnessing our delight with his usual equanimity, he intimated that the gulch should now be explored upon a more extensive scale. He said that he had not gone down more than thirty feet, and his powers of language were entirely inadequate to express the "plenty" of gold which he had seen shining on the walls. He thought that one of the party had better be fastened to the rope, and lowered down to its full length, it being his theory that the quartz was richer further down. Hereford and I were so elated at the prospect of filling our pockets on the instant, as well as of making preparations for future cartloads of the precious mineral, that there was some contention between us as to which should first go down. At length we tossed up a half-dollar to decide, and I was elected.

Strapping a small pick to my belt, and providing myself with pine-knots and matches, to illuminate the depths when I should get to the extent of the line, I concluded my preparations by stuffing in my belt a small meal-bag, in which the Donna had placed my lunch. The bag I confidently expected to fill with gold before returning to the surface. Then, permitting Miguel to fasten the rope under my arm-pits, I was swung over the chasm, my two comrades meanwhile keeping a tight grip on the rope, which had also a twist round the crowbar.

A feeling of horror took possession of me as I felt myself slowly descending into the unknown depths of that fearful abyss. I raised my hand, feeling of the tightly drawn rope above my head, and was astonished that it had not before [been] noticed how very frail it was. My sensitiveness was so great that it seemed to be a mere thread. I was filled with a vague horror that it might, at any moment, snap, and launch me to destruction. Nevertheless, I conquered my fears by a great effort of volition, controlling myself sufficiently to call up at intervals, "All right!" to my companions above. Upon examining the wall of the chasm nearest me, I was also exceedingly encouraged to perceive, in the uncertain light, the yellow glitter which I knew so well how to appreciate. The rock was literally seamed and clothed with golden ore. I was about to realize all I had dreamed—I was penetrating the bosom of the mountains, the golden heart of the Sierras, at whose gloomy exteriors I had so often moodily gazed, longing to pierce them with clairvoyant vision. Nevertheless, the darkness soon became so dense that I could not see my hand before my face, and my golden visions were slowly darkened by the actual terrors by which I was surrounded.

At length I felt that the extremity of the rope must be reached, as the regular jerks above my head suddenly ceased. I had left the broad, sunny daylight behind me; but now, turning my gaze upward through the apparently diminutive aperture at the top, the outline of which I could faintly distinguish, I saw the stars shining brightly in the heavens. I must now surely be deep enough. Feeling out for the wall, I luckily found it close at hand, and, to my joy, discovered a broad, firm ledge, which I immediately gained, giving a sigh of relief as I loosened the tight pressure of the cord from across my lungs. The wall was moist, but I managed to strike a match, and soon kindled a flaring torch from one of my pine-knots, placing it in a niche just above my head. I was disappointed at the amount of light emitted by the flame, which I attributed to the dampness of the atmosphere. Nevertheless, a broad portion of the opposite side of the chasm was made visible, the sight of which dissipated any uncertainty which may have existed in my mind as to whether the glittering particles I had seen were truly gold. The glorious metal cropped out in huge, pure masses at my very feet. The entire circumference of the abyss was auriferous ore! I was almost wild with conflicting emotions. Where I stood, the quartz was exceedingly friable. It was possible, with a little diligence with my pick, to detach masses, seventy-five per cent of which was clean, genuine gold.

I was suddenly interrupted in my operations by a great noise, as of contention, far above my head. I could hear curses and yells, and now and then fragments of the little pyramid, which Gonzago had piled about the crowbar, would come hurtling down before my face. I held my breath in an excess of terror. An indistinct premonition that something frightful was about to happen took possession of me, and I quaked from head to foot. Just then there was a great shout at the top; then as a mass—rendered shapeless by the velocity of its fall—came rushing by me to the depths below, a shriek, an awful howl of horror smote my ears with an emphasis which will continue to echo through them till my dying day. That mass was a human form, that howl a human voice.

Whose?

My heart stood still as I put to it that frightful query. I listened, with a sense of hearing sharpened by my extremity into an acuteness of abnormal intensity. Far, far down below went the sullen boom of that falling body, striking the ledges as it went, until at length it died away; and then, far up above, I heard a fierce shout, and caught the expression: "Accursed Americanos." Then, with horrible rapidity—like the events of a lifetime that pass in panorama through the brain of the drowning man—link by link, I worked together the incidents of the few previous days. Our instinctive fear of Gonzago—his silent, sinister ways—his little girl spying us as we buried our treasure—his jealousy and hatred of Hereford—and, last of all, his luring us to that remote and almost impenetrable crater; all these reflections rushed through my mind in an instant, and I knew that my friend was, ere this, in the other world.

In a few seconds, I was aroused from my horror by feeling a tug at the rope from above. Instinctively loosening it from my person, I wound the end securely around a massive fragment close at hand. Scarcely was this done, when the crowbar and rope came rattling and clanging by me. Down, down, clanked the iron bar, but was soon brought to a stop by the fastening which I had made secure. The fiend at the top was evidently in doubt as to whether he had succeeded in launching me after my comrade, for he hung around the mouth of the abyss, sending down a jargon of oaths and yells, but without eliciting any response from me. At length all was silent. I concluded he had gone away; and, sitting down upon the ledge, and bowing my head upon my knees, I gave myself up to the host of emotions which oppressed my brain.

Need I say that I considered myself lost beyond redemption? The awful extremity of my own situation soon ameliorated the grief and horror into which the death of my friend had plunged me. I must have sat thus for hours, for, when I again scanned the walls of the abyss, I saw them but indistinctly, for the torch, which I had lighted, was nearly consumed.

Even while I looked, it burnt from its fastening and fell into the unknown depths below. The bare idea of being left in that subterranean darkness was so horrible that my hand fluttered at my belt for a match immediately.

But I paused. I only had three more pine-knots. Should I not be sparing of them for an emergency? Emergency! What one could arise more perilous than my present situation? The air was so moist that I began to shake with cold.

No sound through that realm of darkness—no sound but the shrill small voice of that little torrent, dripping somewhere downward through the gloom. When far above, in the blissful regions of light and warmth, I had imagined that sound to be the chuckling laughter of a fiend! With what fearful fancies did it now impress me! I could have sworn that it was a voice, a demoniac voice. There was a weird, ghostly significance in its hollow but ringing laugh. Now it would chuckle in a wicked, self-satisfied way, then it would ring long and dear in silvery peals, with a joy so exultant and wild that I feared it would make me insane, and closed my ears with my fingers, which gave to it a muffled, ill-defined murmur, as of half-suppressed mirth, which was more horrible still. The awful blackness of that quintessence of midnight darkness lay upon me with the weight of an iron globe. I shut my eyes, and would yet feel it, pressing upon head and bosom, until I could scarcely breathe. But sufferings of the imagination, like those of the body, must cease in time; and, after an interval, I resigned myself to my fate, and passed into a kind of torpor of despair. From this I was awakened by a clammy hand—so it seemed—a corpse-like, death-dewy, shuddering hand, passing across my neck. Flinging it off with a stifled shriek, I hastily lit another torch, and perceived that the ledge upon which I stood was swarming with the great, black, loathsome lizards peculiar to California, one of which must have given me that clammy touch which had so appalled me. The sudden gleam of the torch was reassuring, and I again began to examine the walls in a mechanical way. To my disgust, they were alive with large scorpions, while, from several ledges, I noticed, hanging and swinging, several of those hideous, black, bloated spiders, the tarantula—whose very aspect curdles the blood of the stranger. The bite of this insect is exceedingly venomous and sometimes fatal, and the sting from the tail of the scorpion—doubly dangerous from the fact that it moves with incredible velocity—is scarcely less painful.

Again I viewed the glittering gold-crusted walls of my prison-house with gloomy reflections. Above, around, beneath my feet was opulence outvying that of kingdoms and principalities—wealth enough to equip vast armies and cover the seas with mighty navies—all this within my clutch—all this, and yet not enough to purchase me a gulp of God's pure atmosphere; not enough, perhaps, to save me from a lingering, miserable, unwept-for tomb. I covered my face with my hands, and burst into a torrent of bitter, scalding tears. But dark as may be the vicissitudes of fortune, often there are little things which may afford momentary relief.

I found that the little rivulet, whose silvery voice had at first so frightfully affected my morbid sensibility, dripped from the rocks so near me that, by cautious crawling, I could reach a little plashing basin, which it formed on the right hand extremity of the ledge where on I rested. I drank a deep draught, and bathed my head in its refreshing currents. That, at least, was sweet and pure, and fresh from the free air of the mountains above. It had no longer a demon's voice for me, but tinkled merrily down like a chime of fairy-bells. That hearty draught and ablution was like a resumption of the connection with the upper world, which I had almost resigned forever. Naturally of a disposition exceedingly sanguine, the reaction from despair to hope was almost like the work of enchantment. I began to eye the walls, not with the dull stare of hopelessness, but with the swift glance of enterprise.

The ledge upon which I stood was a broad, deep platform of mingled earth and quartz, and it shook as I stamped it with my heavy heel. It must, therefore, be also comparatively thin as well as broad. Advancing to the outer edge as near as I dared, I cast the light of my torch up and down the opposite wall, and saw that the conformation of all sides was in no instance smoothly perpendicular, but composed entirely of ledges or galleries, at quite regular intervals, probably varying in width from six to ten feet. Above and below, as far as I could throw the light of my torch, I saw this singular formation, and concluded that it must be so all the way to the surface. It struck me at once as a kind of ogre's amphitheater, as if there, in other days, they had held their hideous orgies.

I was encouraged to find myself planning and devising, with a busy brain, some method of ascent, however ridiculously impossible. Anything was preferable to the torpidity of despair. To ascend by climbing up the edges of these projections, outside, over their appalling brinks, was not to be thought of for a moment. Even if the horror of the unfathomable depths had not been a sufficient objection, the fact that these edges were crumbly and insecure was an insurmountable one. I retired to the center of the platform I occupied, and looked up. The ceiling of the ledge immediately above was about two feet above my head. The only possible mode of ascent seemed to be by digging one's way up through the successive platforms or tiers. When I reflected that I must be nearly or quite one hundred feet below the crater's rim, the old qualms of despair almost repossessed me, but I managed to become myself again.

At least I would die trying to escape. Choosing several large fragments, I loosened them with my pickax, and built a little hillock on the ledge, by which I was enabled to step up to within a few inches of the ceiling; and, avoiding the loathsome insects as much as possible, I commenced pegging away at the rocky roof with all my might. It was very slow and arduous work; still I made headway in the friable stone made porous by the filtrations of ages and the corrosions of nameless centuries. Once I came very near losing my pick. It flew from my hand by accident, and almost rolled over the ledge. Regaining it, I proceeded to avoid a similar accident by securing it to my wrist with a thong, which I cut from my buckskin trowsers. While doing this, I perceived the rope dangling over the ledge. I had forgotten all about that, yet there it was, with the crowbar probably attached to its other end. I was overjoyed at this discovery, as the crowbar would be a most valuable auxiliary to the furtherance of my project. Quickly drawing up the line and loosening the still secure bar, I set to work again, with a degree of cheeriness which surprised me. I pried off great fragments, which went booming down the abyss, making a most appalling, long-echoing din. In about an hour, to my great joy, I felt the crowbar go through to the surface above. With a little more hard work, I effected a large breach in the yielding rock, through which, after increasing the elevation of the artificial stool on which I stood, I could thrust my head and shoulders. Very greatly encouraged, I put all my implements up through the aperture, and then crawled up myself, torch in hand.

After gaining the new ledge, I found to my alarm, that my torch was more than half consumed. I had only made my way up about ten feet, according to my calculation—estimating eight feet, from floor to ceiling, with two for the thickness of the ledge through which I had forced a breach. At that rate it would require the light of more than a dozen pine-knots—of which I now had but two and a half—to light me up to life again.

Nevertheless, I resolved to do the best I could with the materials at hand. The next ledge, immediately overhead, was thicker than the first, but not so far above me, which rendered it easier of access; and I made a breach in about the same time. In this way, after consuming another of my precious pine-knots, I forced through five ledges in all, when I was so exhausted that I concluded to call it a full day's or night's work (I could not tell which,) and knock off for a dose of nature's sweet restorer. I was very hungry, and then, for the first time, examined into the contents of the little meat-bag slung at my side. Meat there was none—only a few broken pieces of hard-tack. I had seen the Donna place meat within the bag. It must have been removed by that monster in human shape, who would thus consign me to a death by starvation—thus to insure my destruction. How precious now became these pieces of hard-baked and stale crackers!

With a full knowledge of their value, I took a handful of the crumbs, crawled to the tumbling rill which I yet held within reach, and there made a supper whose delicious relish passes all words to express. This done, deeply refreshed and thankful, I crawled back to my working place, extinguished the torch and composed my weary limbs for repose, satisfied that I was forty feet nearer the surface than when my labor commenced.

Notwithstanding the dampness of the air, and the tormenting lizards, I slept well, and arose strong and hopeful for another struggle to gain the upper air. Before lighting my torch, I was greatly encouraged to perceive that the darkness was not so densely black as it had been. I could see the larger auriferous particles glittering on the wall. To my still greater satisfaction, on creeping to the verge of the ledge, and looking upward, I noticed that the stars in the sky were not so distinct as upon my former observation. I correctly ascribed these phenomena partially to the fact that my sight had improved on longer acquaintance with the darkness, and partially because I was approaching the regions of light. I also argued that I must have passed a portion of one day and an entire night in the abyss. When I first observed the stars, from the lower ledge, it was shortly after my descent, and, therefore, broad day in the upper regions; whereas now, if it were night, I should perceive the stars quite as distinctly as if viewing them from the earth's surface.

Much encouraged, though with a visible sense of hunger, I lit my torch, and set to work with a will. The present roof which I was attempting to force was more difficult than any of the others, being thicker, harder, and more compact. Fully twelve inches of the way was through quartz, unmixed with earth or sandstone, although it was veined, seamed, and crusted in every direction with pure metal. How the huge masses glittered and shimmered as they rolled, like flashes of yellow light, over the giddy brink!

I was now so confident of ultimately reaching the upper world, that, before proceeding to the work of my deliverance, I spent upward of an hour in hewing out the most valuable pieces of quartz I could select, and filling my little meal-sack, first carefully gathering every crumb of the cracker, which I placed in my side-pocket. All, save one piece, which would find its way to my mouth!

When, at length, the little bag was filled, by its weight I judged it to contain pure bullion to the value of nearly twenty thousand dollars. This I resolved to carry with me to the upper world, if possible; and, not daring to burden myself with more, I now proceeded to attack the roof.

I here, however, met with a misfortune which impressed me more severely than any incident that yet had befallen me. Scarcely had I resumed my labors with the crowbar, when it accidentally slipped from my hands and rolled over the ledge. I stood, for a few seconds, perfectly petrified with grief and despair. The ringing clang of the bar, as it bounded from ledge to ledge to the seemingly depthless abyss, sounded like the knell of expiring hope. I looked upon the event as a judgment upon my cupidity in gathering together wealth in such a place, when time was so precious, and burst into tears. All men learn to weep in the course of an average lifetime—I graduated in the accomplishment during my residence in that shadow of the valley of death.

I still had my pick, and again I dashed away despair by a resort to my unfailing and sympathizing little friend, the torrent. Judgment or no Judgment, gold-seeking was my trade, and, grasping my remaining implement with an iron hand, I resolved to cleave to my bag of bullion, if the heavens fell.

I soon found that I had somewhat exaggerated the misfortune sustained in the loss of the crowbar. Although fully four hours were consumed in breaching the ledge, at length I succeeded, and passed through with all my effects. I was well rewarded for my perseverance. For here I found the uniformity of the system of ledges destroyed by a long, natural gallery, upward of thirty feet in height, while the ledges continued on the opposite side of the abyss in unbroken order.

I immediately attacked the sloping and irregular side of the gallery, to hew a staircase around and up to the highest ledge I could see on the opposite side. This, however, required many hours of arduous toil; and when at last I reached the ledge, and had carried up my effects, I was almost utterly exhausted. Just then, my last pine-knot torch expired. But this now gave me little concern, for I had reached a point barely twenty feet below the top of the crater's rim, and could see quite distinctly, as the sun had not yet gone down.

I had left the little rivulet far behind in my devious ascent; so, wearily retracing my steps, I found it again, and placing in my mouth the last crumb of the cracker, I took a deep draught from the limpid flood. Then, regaining my lofty perch—not, however, without being severely stung by a scorpion on the way—I prepared for sleep.

That night I had a horrible dream. I thought that I rolled from the ledge into the abyss. Down, down, indefinitely down, I felt myself plunging, while a great sound of thunder was in my ears. At length, of all the impossible freaks of dream-land, I landed safely on a ledge, with a moderate bump which merely awoke me. I was lying on my back, and started up in alarm for I could see no stars above me. All was inky blackness. Good heavens! The dream must be true. Surely the heavens had fallen in, with a vengeance. In my first confusion, I argued that, perhaps I had fallen so far that the stars were out of sight; but just then a crash of thunder and a vivid flash of lightning apprised me that the blackness overhead was only a temporary freak of the elements.

After awaking from another and longer nap in a drenching rain, I was further alarmed to find my left hand so swollen from the sting of the scorpion that I could use it only with the greatest difficulty. I also discovered, after due toil at the rocky roof overhead, that it would be impossible to effect an aperture sufficiently large to admit the passage of my body. The rock through this was like adamant. After great effort I succeeded in piercing with my steel-pointed pick a small hole, and pushed through it all my effects, but could not follow. The only way of making the ascent was to project the rope through, so that it would hang over the ledge; then to secure it by the handle of the pick under the hole, then climb up over the brink of the ledge, by means of the suspended cord. It was a fearful thing to contemplate, dangling again over that frightful pit, while, in my present weary and faint condition, with a disabled hand, it seemed almost impossible. Nevertheless, it was the only chance, and I nerved myself for the attempt. Slinging the rope through and securing it, I swung over the gulch with a prayer for deliverance on my lips. By great effort and indescribable pain from my suffering hand, I succeeded in climbing to the coveted ledge, where I sunk down moaning and breathless.

But I was now so high up that I could look over the verge of the pit almost to the roots of the encircling trees. To my amazement, I discovered that I had emerged almost at the very spot where I had left poor Hereford and the perfidious Mexican at the time of my descent into the pit, in which I had remained three days and four nights. From the fact that I knew my ascent had not been made in a straight line, I argued that I must have performed the complete circuit of the crater once, perhaps twice, in the course of my devious windings. The spot, whence I had been lowered down, bore many indications of the terrible struggle, which must have ensued before Gonzago had succeeded in overcoming and flinging his victim into the abyss.

Now, leaving my implements behind me, by a great effort I threw my heavy bag of gold far up and beyond the smooth, treacherous green slope; then I clambered up, with a profound shudder at the horrors I was leaving behind. I had not crawled more than halfway up the brief funnel-shaped slope, when I heard a fierce "*Caramba!*" behind me, and, turning my head while I clung to a cactus with both hands, I saw the infernal Don at the edge of the opposite pine-skirt, taking deliberate aim at me with his rifle. With the instinct of a guilty soul, he had been unable permanently to leave the scene of his fearful crime, but had, probably, haunted the gulch like a specter, fearing that the ghosts of the dead within would rise and bear witness against him.

He fired, but, in his excitement or terror, missed me entirely. My belt still retained its never-absent knife and revolver, and the presence of that infernal wretch nerved me with the new incitement of vengeance.

By a desperate effort, I scrambled up before he could get another shot at me, but the bloodthirsty ruffian was around the pit and confronting me as soon as I gained the skirt of trees. Emaciated and disabled as I was, without a moment's hesitation, and without a word, I caught my knife, and closed with him. He was a man of prodigious muscular power, but vengeance nerved me with superhuman strength. Neither party expected mercy. We were at such close quarters that neither of us could, for the instant, use a weapon. Brief, but unspeakably terrible, was that struggle on the verge of the bottomless abyss. At length I felt his fresh and well-fed muscle overcoming my wasted frame. I felt him lifting and bearing me to the horrid edge. The agonizing thought of being again precipitated into that perdition of darkness inspired me with electric volition and thews [strength] of steel. With a yell, which must have been heard for miles, I got my swollen left hand on his windpipe and closed it with a deathly grip. Then, as he relaxed his clutch, I got in a blow with my knife, then another, and he rolled from me toward the verge of the chasm. Regaining my own balance only with the utmost difficulty, I saw him stay his descent for one instant by clutching a prickly-pear bush, while he glared at me with eyes in which hatred and horror commingled. Then, as the weight of his grasp tore the shrub from its tendrils, he disappeared.

Faint with hunger, and overcome by my extraordinary experiences, I sought my rifle, which I had left in the thicket before my descent into the pit. I found it, together with poor Hereford's, and managed to shoot a great wood grouse. This served to appease my raging hunger; and then

I lay down, overcome, to sleep a sleep of many hours. It was full, blazing day when I awoke.

I never heard what became of Gonzago's wife and child. They were not at the plateau, where I had left them, though the donkey and mule were, and they were never seen at Ophir again. Like enough the villain murdered them both.

Reaching Marysville, at length, in safety, I passed a few days in rest, but never uttered a word of my adventure. To make my way home—to leave behind me the horrors of that gulch, and never to lure thither, by tales of its treasures, other victims—was my set purpose: so I passed from the mountains to the coast, a silent man; nor was my silence, on that one theme, again broken, until to tell to poor Hereford's mother the awful story of her son's burial in the Scorpion Gulch.

"May no man ever touch its horrid confines again," is my oft-repeated invocation!

The Luck of Roaring Camp

Bret Harte

Bret Harte was friend of Mark Twain's, and it was Harte who talked Twain into writing down the story that brought Twain to national attention—"The Notorious Jumping Frog of Calaveras County." (The "Notorious" was later changed to "Celebrated.") The stars of Twain and Harte rose at about the same time, and in the late 1800s, Harte was almost as well known as Twain.

"The Luck of Roaring Camp" is the story that made Bret Harte famous, but it almost didn't make it into print. At the time, Harte was the young editor of the *Overland Monthly*, a new San Francisco magazine that focused on the West Coast. He wrote the story to add some local color to the magazine's first issue. The young woman assigned to proofread the story was so horrified after the first few pages that she refused to read any more of the "wicked and immoral" tale, threatening to quit her job. The printer also declared it "immoral and indecent." Harte explained, "I read it over again in proof, at the request of the publisher, and was touched, I am afraid, only with my own pathos. I read it to my wife—I had married in the meantime—and it made her cry also. I am told that Mr. Roman [the publisher] also read it to his wife, with the same diabolically illogical result." (Apparently people were a bit more sensitive to the written word back then, or perhaps we're a bit more jaded, for it's doubtful that the story will have that effect today.) The publisher finally gave in after Harte, refusing to make any alterations to the story, offered to resign as editor.

Fortunately the story survived the do-gooders' attempts to quash and censor it. It was featured in the magazine's August 1868 issue and was immediately denounced by various religious groups. The local press criticized it for making the West Coast look bad, insisting it could harm immigration. On the East Coast it was given a warm reception, and a Boston book publisher quickly offered "to publish anything he chose to write, upon his own terms." Once it became known that the East Coast loved it, the story became popular on the West Coast as well, and eventually around the world. His tales were very enthusiastically received in Britain, where there was a particular fascination with the American West.

There was commotion in Roaring Camp. It could not have been a fight, for in 1850 that was not novel enough to have called together the entire settlement. The ditches and claims were not only deserted, but "Tuttle's" grocery had contributed its gamblers, who, it will be remembered, calmly continued their game the day that French Pete and Kanaka Joe shot each other to death over the bar in the front room. The whole camp was collected before a rude cabin on the outer edge of the clearing. Conversation was carried on in a low tone, but the name of a woman was frequently repeated. It was a name familiar enough in the camp: "Cherokee Sal."

Perhaps the less said of her the better. She was a coarse and, it is to be feared, a very sinful woman. But at that time she was the only woman in Roaring Camp, and was just then lying in sore extremity when she most needed the ministration of her own sex. Dissolute, abandoned, and irreclaimable, she was yet suffering a martyrdom—hard enough to bear even in the seclusion and sexual sympathy with which custom veils it— but now terrible in her loneliness. The primal curse had come to her in that original isolation, which must have made the punishment of the first transgression so dreadful. It was, perhaps, part of the expiation of her sin, that at a moment when she most lacked her sex's intuitive sympathy and care, she met only the half-contemptuous faces of her masculine associates. Yet a few of the spectators were, I think, touched by her sufferings. Sandy Tipton thought it was "rough on Sal," and in the contemplation of her condition, for a moment rose superior to the fact that he had an ace and two bowers in his sleeve.

It will be seen, also, that the situation was novel. Deaths were by no means uncommon in Roaring Camp, but a birth was a new thing. People had been dismissed from the camp effectively, finally, and with no possibility of return, but this was the first time that anybody had been introduced *ab initio* [from the beginning]. Hence the excitement.

"You go in there, Stumpy," said a prominent citizen known as "Kentuck," addressing one of the loungers. "Go in there, and see what you kin do. You've had experience in them things."

Perhaps there was a fitness in the selection. Stumpy, in other climes, had been the putative head of two families; in fact, it was owing to some legal informality in these proceedings that Roaring Camp—a city of refuge—was indebted to his company. The crowd approved the choice, and Stumpy was wise enough to bow to the majority. The door closed on the extempore surgeon and midwife, and Roaring Camp sat down outside, smoked its pipe, and awaited the issue.

The assemblage numbered about a hundred men. One or two of these were actual fugitives from justice, some were criminal, and all were reckless. Physically, they exhibited no indication of their past lives and character. The greatest scamp had a Raphael face, with a profusion of blond hair; Oakhurst, a gambler, had the melancholy air and intellectual abstraction of a Hamlet; the coolest and most courageous man was scarcely over five feet in height, with a soft voice and an embarrassed timid manner. The term "roughs," applied to them, was a distinction rather than a definition. Perhaps in the minor details of fingers, toes, ears, etc., the camp may have been deficient, but these slight omissions did not detract from their aggregate force. The strongest man had but three fingers on his right hand; the best shot had but one eye.

Such was the physical aspect of the men that were dispersed around the cabin. The camp lay in a triangular valley, between two hills and a river. The only outlet was a steep trail over the summit of a hill that faced the cabin, now illuminated by the rising moon. The suffering woman might have seen it from the rude bunk whereon she lay—seen it winding like a silver thread until it was lost in the stars above.

A fire of withered pine boughs added sociability to the gathering. By degrees the natural levity of Roaring Camp returned. Bets were freely offered and taken regarding the result: Three to five that "Sal would get through with it;" even, that the child would survive; side bets as to the sex and complexion of the coming stranger. In the midst of an excited discussion an exclamation came from those nearest the door, and the camp stopped to listen. Above the swaying and moaning of the pines, the swift rush of the river, and the crackling of the fire, rose a sharp querulous cry—a cry unlike anything heard before in the camp. The pines stopped moaning, the river ceased to rush, and the fire to crackle. It seemed as if Nature had stopped to listen too.

The camp rose to its feet as one man! It was proposed to explode a barrel of gunpowder, but, in consideration of the situation of the mother, better counsels prevailed, and only a few revolvers were discharged; for, whether owing to the rude surgery of the camp, or some other reason, Cherokee Sal was sinking fast. Within an hour she had climbed, as it were, that rugged road that led to the stars, and so passed out of Roaring Camp, its sin and shame forever. I do not think that the announcement disturbed them much, except in speculation as to the fate of the child.

"Can he live now?" was asked of Stumpy. The answer was doubtful. The only other being of Cherokee Sal's sex and maternal condition in the settlement was an ass. There was some conjecture as to fitness, but the experiment was tried. It was less problematical than the ancient treatment of Romulus and Remus, and apparently as successful.

When these details were completed, which exhausted another hour, the door was opened, and the anxious crowd, which had already formed themselves into a queue, entered in single file. Beside the low bunk or shelf on which the figure of the mother was starkly outlined below the blankets, stood a pine table. On this a candle-box was placed, and within it, swathed in staring red flannel, lay the last arrival at Roaring Camp. Beside the candle-box was placed a hat. Its use was soon indicated.

"Gentlemen," said Stumpy, with a singular mixture of authority and *ex officio* complacency—"Gentlemen will please pass in at the front door, round the table, and out at the back door. Them as wishes to contribute anything toward the orphan will find a hat handy." The first man entered with his hat on; he uncovered, however, as he looked about him, and so, unconsciously, set an example to the next. In such communities good and bad actions are catching. As the procession filed in, comments were

The Luck of Roaring Camp, by Henry Bacon

audible—criticisms addressed, perhaps, rather to Stumpy, in the character of showman: "Is that him?" "mighty small specimen;" "hasn't mor'n got the color;" "ain't bigger nor a derringer."

, The contributions were as characteristic: A silver tobacco-box; a doubloon; a navy revolver, silver mounted; a gold specimen; a very beautifully embroidered lady's handkerchief (from Oakhurst, the gambler); a diamond breastpin; a diamond ring (suggested by the pin, with the remark from the giver that he "saw that pin and went two diamonds better"); a slung shot; a Bible (contributor not detected); a golden spur; a silver teaspoon (the initials, I regret to say, were not the giver's); a pair of surgeon's shears; a lancet; a Bank of England note for £5; and about $200 in loose gold and silver coin. During these proceedings Stumpy maintained a silence as impassive as the dead on his left—a gravity as inscrutable as that of the newly-born on his right. Only one incident occurred to break the monotony of the curious procession. As Kentuck bent over the candle-box half curiously, the child turned, and, in a spasm of pain, caught at his groping finger, and held it fast for a moment. Kentuck looked foolish and embarrassed. Something like a blush tried to assert itself in his weather-beaten cheek.

"The damned little cuss!" he said, as he extricated his finger, with, perhaps, more tenderness and care than he might have been deemed capable of showing. He held that finger a little apart from its fellows as he went out, and examined it curiously. The examination provoked the same original remark in regard to the child. In fact, he seemed to enjoy repeating it. "He rastled with my finger," he remarked to Tipton, holding up the member, "The damned little cuss!"

It was four o'clock before the camp sought repose. A light burnt in the cabin where the watchers sat, for Stumpy did not go to bed that night. Nor did Kentuck. He drank quite freely and related with great gusto his experience, invariably ending with his characteristic condemnation of the new comer. It seemed to relieve him of any unjust implication of sentiment, and Kentuck had the weaknesses of the nobler sex. When everybody else had gone to bed he walked down to the river and whistled, reflectingly. Then he walked up the gulch, passed the cabin, still whistling with demonstrative unconcern. At a large redwood tree he paused and retraced his steps, and again passed the cabin. Half way down to the river's bank he again paused, and then returned and knocked at the door. It was opened by Stumpy.

"How goes it?" said Kentuck, looking past Stumpy toward the candle-box.

"All serene," replied Stumpy, "Anything up?"

"Nothing." There was a pause—an embarrassing one—Stumpy still holding the door. Then Kentuck had recourse to his finger, which he held up to Stumpy. "Rastled with it—the damned little cuss," he said and retired.

The next day Cherokee Sal had such rude sepulture as Roaring Camp afforded. After her body had been committed to the hill-side, there was a formal meeting of the camp to discuss what should be done with her infant. A resolution to adopt it was unanimous and enthusiastic. But an animated discussion in regard to the manner and feasibility of providing for its wants at once sprung up. It was remarkable that the argument partook of none of those fierce personalities with which discussions were usually conducted at Roaring Camp. Tipton proposed that they should send the child to Red Dog—a distance of forty miles—where female attention could be procured. But the unlucky suggestion met with fierce and unanimous opposition. It was evident that no plan which entailed parting from their new acquisition would for a moment be entertained.

"Besides," said Tom Ryder, "them fellows at Red Dog would swap it and ring in somebody else on us." A disbelief in the honesty of other camps prevailed at Roaring Camp, as in other places.

The introduction of a female nurse in the camp also met with objection. It was argued that no decent woman could be prevailed to accept Roaring Camp as her home, and the speaker urged that "they didn't want any more of the other kind." This unkind allusion to the defunct mother, harsh as it may seem, was the first spasm of propriety—the first symptom of the camp's regeneration. Stumpy advanced nothing. Perhaps he felt a certain delicacy in interfering with the selection of a possible successor in office. But when questioned he averred stoutly that he and "Jinny"— the mammal before alluded to—could manage to rear the child. There was something original, independent and heroic about the plan that pleased the camp. Stumpy was retained. Certain articles were sent for to Sacramento.

"Mind," said the treasurer, as he pressed a bag of gold-dust into the expressman's hand, "the best that can be got—lace, you know, and filigree work and frills—damn the cost!"

Strange to say, the child thrived. Perhaps the invigorating climate of the mountain camp was compensation for material deficiencies. Nature took the foundling to her broader breast. In that rare atmosphere of the Sierra foot-hills—that air pungent with balsamic odor; that ethereal cordial, at once bracing and exhilarating, he may have found food and nourishment, or a subtle chemistry that transmuted asses' milk to lime and phosphorus. Stumpy inclined to the belief that it was the latter and good nursing.

"Me and that ass," he would say, "has been father and mother to him! Don't you," he would add, apostrophizing the helpless bundle before him, "never go back on us."

By the time he was a month old, the necessity of giving him a name became apparent. He had generally been known as "the Kid," "Stumpy's boy," "the Cayote"—(an allusion to his vocal powers)—and even by Kentuck's endearing diminutive of "the damned little cuss." But these were felt to be vague and unsatisfactory, and were at last dismissed under another influence. Gamblers and adventurers are generally superstitious, and Oakhurst one day declared that the baby had brought "the luck" to Roaring Camp. It was certain that of late they had been successful. "Luck" was the name agreed upon, with the prefix of Tommy for greater convenience. No allusion was made to the mother, and the father was unknown.

"It's better," said the philosophical Oakhurst, "to take a fresh deal all around. Call him Luck, and start him fair."

A day was accordingly set apart for the christening. What was meant by this ceremony the reader may imagine, who has already gathered some idea of the reckless irreverence of Roaring Camp. The master of ceremonies was one "Boston," a noted wag, and the occasion seemed to promise the greatest facetiousness. This ingenious satirist had spent two days in preparing a burlesque of the church service, with pointed local allusions. The choir was properly trained, and Sandy Tipton was to stand godfather. But after the procession had marched to the grove with music and banners, and the child had been deposited before a mock altar, Stumpy stepped before the expectant crowd.

"It ain't my style to spoil fun, boys," said the little man, stoutly, eyeing the faces around him, "but it strikes me that this thing ain't exactly on the squar. It's playing it pretty low down on this yer baby to ring in fun on him that he ain't going to understand. And ef there's going to be any godfathers round, I'd like to see who's got any better rights than me."

A silence followed Stumpy's speech. To the credit of all humorists be it said that the first man to acknowledge its justice was the satirist, thus estopped of his fun.

"But," said Stumpy quickly, following up his advantage, "we're here for a christening, and we'll have it. I proclaim you Thomas Luck, according to the laws of the United States and the State of California—So help me God."

It was the first time that the name of the Deity had been uttered aught but profanely in the camp. The form of christening was perhaps even more ludicrous than the satirist had conceived, but strangely enough, nobody saw it and nobody laughed. "Tommy" was christened as seriously as he would have been under a Christian roof, and cried and was comforted in as orthodox fashion.

And so the work of regeneration began in Roaring Camp. Almost imperceptibly a change came over the settlement. The cabin assigned to "Tommy Luck"—or "The Luck," as he was more frequently called—first showed signs of improvement. It was kept scrupulously clean and whitewashed. Then it was boarded, clothed, and papered. The rosewood cradle—packed eighty miles by mule—had, in Stumpy's way of putting it, "sorter killed the rest of the furniture." So the rehabilitation of the cabin became a necessity. The men who were in the habit of lounging in at Stumpy's to see "how The Luck got on" seemed to appreciate the change, and, in self-defence, the rival establishment of "Tuttle's grocery" bestirred itself, and imported a carpet and mirrors. The reflections of the latter on the appearance of Roaring Camp tended to produce stricter habits of personal cleanliness. Again Stumpy imposed a kind of quarantine upon those who aspired to the honor and privilege of holding "The Luck." It was a cruel mortification to Kentuck—who, in the carelessness of a large nature and the habits of frontier life, had begun to regard all garments as a second cuticle, which, like a snake's, only sloughed off through decay—to be debarred this privilege from certain prudential reasons. Yet such was the subtle influence of innovation that he thereafter appeared regularly every afternoon in a clean shirt, and face still shining from his ablutions.

Nor were moral and social sanitary laws neglected. "Tommy," who was supposed to spend his whole existence in a persistent attempt to repose, must not be disturbed by noise. The shouting and yelling which had gained the camp its infelicitous title were not permitted within hearing distance of Stumpy's. The men conversed in whispers, or smoked in Indian gravity. Profanity was tacitly given up in these sacred precincts, and throughout the camp a popular form of expletive, known as "Damn the luck!" and "Curse the luck!" was abandoned, as having a new personal bearing. Vocal music was not interdicted, being supposed to have a sooth-ing, tranquillizing quality, and one song, sung by "Man-O'-War Jack," an English sailor, from Her Majesty's Australian Colonies, was quite popular as a lullaby. It was a lugubrious recital of the exploits of "the *Arethusa,* Seventy-four," in a muffled minor, ending with a prolonged dying fall at the burden of each verse, "On b-o-o-o-ard of the *Arethusa.*"

It was a fine sight to see Jack holding The Luck, rocking from side to side as if with the motion of a ship, and crooning forth this naval ditty. Either through the peculiar rocking of Jack or the length of his song—it contained ninety stanzas, and was continued with conscientious delib-eration to the bitter end—the lullaby generally had the desired effect. At such times the men would lie at full length under the trees, in the soft summer twilight, smoking their pipes and drinking in the melodious utterances. An indistinct idea that this was pastoral happiness pervaded the camp.

"This ere kind o' think," said the Cockney Simmons, meditatively reclining on his elbow, "is evingly." It reminded him of Greenwich.

On the long summer days The Luck was usually carried to the gulch, from whence the golden store of Roaring Camp was taken. There, on a blanket spread over pine boughs, he would lie while the men were work-ing in the ditches below. Latterly, there was a rude attempt to decorate this bower with flowers and sweet-smelling shrubs, and generally someone would bring him a cluster of wild honeysuckles, azaleas, or the painted blossoms of Las Mariposas. The men had suddenly awakened to the fact that there were beauty and significance in these trifles, which they had so long trodden carelessly beneath their feet. A flake of glittering mica, a fragment of variegated quartz, a bright pebble from the bed of the creek, became beautiful to eyes thus cleared and strengthened, and were invari-ably put aside for "The Luck." It was wonderful how many treasures the woods and hillsides yielded that "would do for Tommy."

Surrounded by playthings such as never child out of fairyland had before, it is to be hoped that Tommy was content. He appeared to be securely happy—albeit there was an infantine gravity about him—a contemplative light in his round grey eyes that sometimes worried

Stumpy. He was always tractable and quiet, and it is recorded that once, having crept beyond his "corral"—a hedge of tessellated pine boughs, which surrounded his bed—he dropped over the bank on his head in the soft earth, and remained with his mottled legs in the air in that position for at least five minutes with unflinching gravity. He was extricated without a murmur.

I hesitate to record the many other instances of his sagacity, which rest, unfortunately, upon the statements of prejudiced friends. Some of them were not without a tinge of superstition.

"I crep up the bank just now," said Kentuck one day, in a breathless state of excitement, "and dern my skin if he wasn't a talking to a jay bird as was a-sittin on his lap. There they was, just as free and sociable as anything you please, a-jawin at each other just like two cherry-bums." Howbeit, whether creeping over the pine boughs or lying lazily on his back, blinking at the leaves above him, to him the birds sang, the squirrels chattered, and the flowers bloomed. Nature was his nurse and playfellow. For him she would let slip between the leaves golden shafts of sunlight that fell just within his grasp; she would send wandering breezes to visit him with the balm of bay and resinous gums; to him the tall redwoods nodded familiarly and sleepily, the bumble-bees buzzed, and the rooks cawed a slumbrous accompaniment.

Such was the golden summer of Roaring Camp. They were "flush times"—and the Luck was with them. The claims had yielded enormously. The camp was jealous of its privileges and looked suspiciously on strangers. No encouragement was given to immigration, and to make their seclusion more perfect, the land on either side of the mountain wall that surrounded the camp, they duly preempted. This, and a reputation for singular proficiency with the revolver, kept the reserve of Roaring Camp inviolate.

The expressman—their only connecting link with the surrounding world—sometimes told wonderful stories of the camp. He would say, "They've a street up there in 'Roaring,' that would layover any street in Red Dog. They've got vines and flowers round their houses, and they wash themselves twice a day. But they're mighty rough on strangers, and they worship an Ingin baby."

With the prosperity of the camp came a desire for further improvement. It was proposed to build a hotel in the following spring, and to invite one or two decent families to reside there for the sake of "the Luck"— who might perhaps profit by female companionship. The sacrifice that this concession to the sex cost these men, who were fiercely skeptical in regard to its general virtue and usefulness, can only be accounted for by their affection for Tommy. A few still held out. But the resolve could not be carried into effect for three months, and the minority meekly yielded in the hope that something might turn up to prevent it. And it did.

The winter of '51 will long be remembered in the foot-hills. The snow lay deep on the Sierras, and every mountain creek became a river, and every river a lake. Each gorge and gulch was transformed into a tumultuous water-course that descended the hill-sides, tearing down giant trees and scattering its drift and debris along the plain. Red Dog had been twice under water, and Roaring Camp had been forewarned.

"Water put the gold into them gulches," said Stumpy, "It's been here once and will be here again!"

And that night the North Fork suddenly leaped over its banks, and swept up the triangular valley of Roaring Camp.

In the confusion of rushing water, crushing trees, and crackling timber, and the darkness which seemed to flow with the water and blot out the fair valley, but little could be done to collect the scattered camp. When the morning broke, the cabin of Stumpy, nearest the river bank, was gone. Higher up the gulch they found the body of its unlucky owner, but the pride—the hope—the joy—the Luck—of Roaring Camp had disappeared. They were returning with sad hearts when a shout from the bank recalled them.

It was a relief boat from down the river. They had picked up, they said, a man and an infant, nearly exhausted, about two miles below. Did anybody know them, and did they belong here?

It needed but a glance to show them Kentuck lying there, cruelly crushed and bruised, but still holding the Luck of Roaring Camp in his arms. As they bent over the strangely assorted pair, they saw that the child was cold and pulseless.

"He is dead," said one. Kentuck opened his eyes.

"Dead?" he repeated feebly.

"Yes, my man, and you are dying too."

A smile lit the eyes the expiring Kentuck. "Dying," he repeated, "he's a taking me with him—tell the boys I've got the Luck with me, now;" and the strong man clinging to the frail babe as a drowning man is said to cling to a straw, drifted away into the shadowy river that flows forever to the unknown sea.

How I Went to the Mines

Bret Harte

The following story by Bret Harte appears to be based on Harte's experiences as a prospector, but how much is fact and how much fiction is unknown. One of Harte's biographers, Henry Childs Merwin, noted that it "seems to have the ear-marks of an autobiographical sketch. It is regarded as such by his sisters; and the modest, deprecating manner in which the storyteller's adventures are related, serves to confirm that impression." Still, most of it seems like fiction. Harte did work as a schoolmaster and he did try prospecting for gold, but not necessarily in that order. Ultimately, it's left to the reader to speculate which elements are true and which are imaginary.

I had been two years in California before I ever thought of going to the mines, and my initiation into the vocation of gold digging was partly compulsory. The little pioneer settlement school, of which I was the somewhat youthful and, I fear, the not over-competent master, was state-aided only to a limited extent; and as the bulk of its expense was borne by a few families in its vicinity, when two of them—representing perhaps a dozen children or pupils—one morning announced their intention of moving to a more prosperous and newer district, the school was incontinently closed.

In twenty-four hours I found myself destitute alike of my flock and my vocation. I am afraid I regretted the former the most. Some of the children I had made my companions and friends; and as I stood that bright May morning before the empty little bark-thatched schoolhouse in the wilderness, it was with an odd sensation that our little summer "play" at being schoolmaster and pupil was over. Indeed, I remember distinctly that a large hunk of gingerbread—a parting gift from a prize scholar a year older than myself—stood me in good stead in my future wanderings, for I was alone in the world at that moment and constitutionally improvident.

I had been frightfully extravagant even on my small income, spending much money on "boiled shirts," and giving as an excuse, which I since believe was untenable, that I ought to set an example in dress to my pupils. The result was that at this crucial moment I had only seven dollars in my pocket, five of which went to the purchase of a second-hand revolver, that I felt was necessary to signalize my abandonment of a peaceful vocation for one of greed and adventure.

For I had finally resolved to go to the mines and become a gold-digger. Other occupations and my few friends in San Francisco were expensively distant. The nearest mining district was forty miles away; the nearest prospect of aid was the hope of finding a miner whom I had casually met in San Francisco, and whom I shall call "Jim." With only this name upon my lips I expected, like the deserted Eastern damsel in the ballad, to find my friend among the haunts of mining men. But my capital of two dollars would not allow the expense of stage-coach fare; I must walk to the mines, and I did.

I cannot clearly recall *how* I did it. The end of my first day's journey found me with blistered feet and the conviction that varnished leather shoes, however proper for the Master of Madrono Valley School in the exercise of his functions, were not suited to him when he was itinerant. Nevertheless, I clung to them as the last badge of my former life, carrying them in my hands when pain and pride made me at last forsake the frequented highway to travel barefooted in the trails.

I am afraid that my whole equipment was rather incongruous, and I remember that the few travelers I met on the road glanced at me with curiosity and some amusement. The odds and ends of my "pack"—a faded morocco dressing-case, an early gift from my mother, and a silver-handled riding-whip, also a gift—in juxtaposition with my badly rolled, coarse blue blanket and tin coffee-pot, were sufficiently provocative. My revolver, too, which would not swing properly in its holster from my hip, but worked around until it hung down in front like a Highlander's dirk, gave me considerable mortification.

A sense of pride, which kept me from arriving at my friend's cabin utterly penniless, forbade my seeking shelter and food at a wayside station. I ate the remainder of my gingerbread, and camped out in the woods. To preclude any unnecessary sympathy, I may add that I was not at all hungry and had no sense of privation.

The loneliness that had once or twice come over me in meeting strangers on the traveled road, with whom I was too shy and proud to converse, vanished utterly in the sweet and silent companionship of the woods. I believe I should have felt my solitary vagabond condition greater in a strange hostelry or a crowded cabin. I heard the soft breathings of the lower life in the grass and ferns around me, saw the grave, sleepy stars above my head, and slept soundly, quite forgetting the pain of my blistered feet, or the handkerchiefs I had sacrificed for bandages.

In the morning, finding that I had emptied my water flask, I also found that I had utterly overlooked the first provision of camping—nearness to a water supply—and was fain to chew some unboiled coffee grains to flavor my scant breakfast, when I again took the trail.

I kept out of the main road as much as possible that day, although my detours cost me some extra walking, and by this time my bandaged feet had accumulated so much of the red dust that I suppose it would have been difficult to say what I wore on them. But in these excursions the balsamic air of the pines always revived me; the reassuring changes of scenery and distance viewed from those mountain ridges, the most wonderful I had ever seen, kept me in a state of excitement, and there was an occasional novelty of "outcrop" in the rocky trail that thrilled me with mysterious anticipation.

For this outcrop—a strange, white, porcelain-like rock, glinting like a tooth thrust through the red soil—was *quartz*, which I had been told indicated the vicinity of the gold-bearing district. Following these immaculate finger-posts, I came at about sunset upon a mile-long slope of pines still baking in the western glare, and beyond it, across an unfathomable abyss, a shelf in the opposite mountain-side, covered with white tents, looking not unlike the quartz outcrop I have spoken of. It was "the diggings"!

I do not know what I had expected, but I was conscious of some bitter disappointment. As I gazed, the sun sank below the serried summit of the slope on which I stood; a great shadow seemed to steal *up* rather than down the mountain, the tented shelf faded away, and a score of tiny diamond points of light, like stars, took its place. A cold wind rushed down the mountain-side, and I shivered in my thin clothes, drenched with the sweat of my day-long tramp.

It was nine o'clock when I reached the mining camp, itself only a fringe of the larger settlement beyond, and I had been on my feet since sunrise, nevertheless, I halted at the outskirts, deposited my pack in the bushes, bathed my feet in a sluice of running water, so stained with the soil that it seemed to run blood, and, putting on my dreadful varnished shoes again, limped once more into respectability and the first cabin.

Here I found that my friend "Jim" was one of four partners on the "Gum Tree" claim, two miles on the other side of the settlement. There was nothing left for me but to push on to the "Magnolia Hotel," procure the cheapest refreshment and an hour's rest, and then limp as best I could to the "Gum Tree" claim.

I found the "Magnolia," a large wooden building given over, in greater part, to an enormous drinking "saloon," filled with flashing mirrors and a mahogany bar. In the unimportant and stuffy little dining-room or restaurant, I selected some "fish balls and coffee," I think more with a view to cheapness and expedition than for their absolute sustaining power. The waiter informed me that it was possible that my friend "Jim" might be in the settlement, but that the barkeeper, who knew everything and everybody, could tell me or give me "the shortest cut to the claim."

From sheer fatigue I lingered at my meal, I fear, long past any decent limit, and then reentered the bar-room. It was crowded with miners and traders and a few smartly dressed professional-looking men. Here again my vanity led me into extravagance. I could not bear to address the important, white-shirt-sleeved and diamond-pinned barkeeper as a mere boyish suppliant for information. I was silly enough to demand a drink, and laid down, alas! another quarter.

I had asked my question, the barkeeper had handed me the decanter, and I had poured out the stuff with as much ease and grown-up confidence as I could assume, when a singular incident occurred. As it had some bearing upon my fortune, I may relate it here.

The ceiling of the saloon was supported by a half-dozen wooden columns, about eighteen inches square, standing in a line, parallel with the counter of the bar and about two feet from it. The front of the bar was crowded with customers, when suddenly, to my astonishment, they one and all put down their glasses and hurriedly backed into the spaces between the columns. At the same moment a shot was fired from the street through the large open doors that stood at right angles with the front of the counter and the columns.

The bullet raked and splintered the mouldings of the counter front, but with no other damage. The shot was returned from the upper end of the bar, and then for the first time I became aware that two men with leveled revolvers were shooting at each other through the saloon.

The bystanders in range were fully protected by the wooden columns; the barkeeper had "ducked" below the counter at the first shot. Six shots were exchanged by the duelists, but, as far as I could see, nobody was hurt. A mirror was smashed, and my glass had part of its rim carried cleanly away by the third shot and its contents spilt.

I had remained standing near the counter, and I presume I may have been protected by the columns. But the whole thing passed so quickly, and I was so utterly absorbed in its dramatic novelty, that I cannot recall having the slightest sensation of physical fear; indeed, I had been much more frightened in positions of less peril.

My only concern, and this was paramount, was that I might betray by any word or movement my youthfulness, astonishment, or unfamiliarity with such an experience. I think that any shy, vain schoolboy will understand this, and would probably feel as I did. So strong was this feeling, that while the sting of gunpowder was still in my nostrils I moved towards the bar, and, taking up my broken glass, said to the barkeeper, perhaps somewhat slowly and diffidently:

"Will you please fill me another glass? It's not my fault if this was broken."

The barkeeper, rising flushed and excited from behind the bar, looked at me with a queer smile, and then passed the decanter and a fresh glass. I heard a laugh and an oath behind me, and my cheeks flushed as I took a single gulp of the fiery spirit and hurried away.

But my blistered feet gave me a twinge of pain, and I limped on the threshold. I felt a hand on my shoulder, and a voice said quickly: "You ain't hurt, old man?"

I recognized the voice of the man who had laughed, and responded quickly, growing more hot and scarlet, that my feet were blistered by a long walk, and that I was in a hurry to go to "Gum Tree" claim.

"Hold on," said the stranger. Preceding me to the street, he called to a man sitting in a buggy: "Drop him," pointing to me, "at 'Gum Tree' claim, and then come back here," helped me into the vehicle, clapped his hand on my shoulder, said to me enigmatically, "You'll do!" and quickly reentered the saloon.

It was from the driver only that I learned, during the drive, that the two combatants had quarreled a week before, had sworn to shoot each other "on sight," i.e., on their first accidental meeting, and that each "went armed." He added, disgustedly, that it was "mighty bad shooting," to which I, in my very innocence of these lethal weapons, and truthfulness to my youthful impressions, agreed!

I said nothing else of my own feelings, and, indeed, soon forgot them; for I was nearing the end of my journey, and *now,* for the first time, although I believe it a common experience of youth, I began to feel a doubt of the wisdom of my intentions. During my long tramp, and in the midst of my privations, I had never doubted it; but now, as I neared "Jim's" cabin, my youthfulness and inefficiency and the extravagance of my quest of a mere acquaintance for aid and counsel came to me like a shock. But it was followed by a greater one. When at last I took leave of my driver and entered the humble little log cabin of the "Gum Tree Company," I was informed that "Jim" only a few days before had given up his partnership and gone to San Francisco.

Perhaps there was something in my appearance that showed my weariness and disappointment, for one of the partners dragged out the only chair in the cabin—he and the other partners had been sitting on boxes tilted on end—and offered it to me, with the inevitable drink. With this encouragement, I stammered out my story. I think I told the exact truth. I was too weary to even magnify my acquaintance with the absent "Jim."

They listened without comment; I dare say they had heard the story before. I am quite convinced they had each gone through a harder experience than mine. Then occurred what I believe could have occurred only in California in that age of simplicity and confidence. Without a word of discussion among themselves, without a word of inquiry as to myself, my character or prospects, they offered me the vacant partnership "to try."

In any event I was to stay there until I could make up my mind. As I was scarcely able to stand, one of them volunteered to fetch my pack from its "cache" in the bushes four miles away; and then, to my astonishment, conversation instantly turned upon other topics—literature, science, philosophy, everything but business and practical concerns. Two of the partners were graduates of a Southern college and the other a bright young fanner.

I went to bed that night in the absent Jim's bunk, one-fourth owner of a cabin and a claim I knew nothing of. As I looked about me at the bearded faces of my new partners, although they were all apparently only a few years older than myself; I wondered if we were not "playing" at being partners in "Gum Tree" claim, as I had played at being schoolmaster in Madrono Valley.

When I awoke late the next morning and stared around the empty cabin, I could scarcely believe that the events of the preceding night were not a dream. My pack, which I had left four miles away, lay at my feet. By the truthful light of day I could see that I was lying apparently in a parallelogram of untrimmed logs, between whose interstices, here and there, the glittering sunlight streamed.

A roof of bark thatch, on which a woodpecker was foolishly experimenting, was above my head; four wooden "bunks," like a ship's berth, were around the two sides of the room; a table, a chair, and three stools, fashioned from old packing boxes, were the only furniture. The cabin was lighted by a window of two panes let into one gable, by the open door, and by a chimney of adobe that entirely filled the other gable, and projected scarcely a foot above the apex of the roof.

I was wondering whether I had not strayed into a deserted cabin, a dreadful suspicion of the potency of the single drink I had taken in the saloon coming over me, when my three partners entered. Their explanation was brief. I had needed rest, they had delicately forborne to awaken me before. It was twelve o'clock! My breakfast was ready. They had something "funny" to tell me! I was a hero!

My conduct during the shooting affray at the "Magnolia" had been discussed, elaborately exaggerated, and interpreted by eye-witnesses; the latest version being that I had calmly stood at the bar, coolly demanding to be served by the crouching barkeeper, while the shots were being fired! I am afraid even my new friends put down my indignant disclaimer to youthful bashfulness, but, seeing that I was distressed, they changed the subject. Yes! I might, if I wanted, do some "prospecting" that day. Where? Oh, anywhere on ground not already claimed; there were hundreds of square miles to choose from. What was I to do? What! was it possible I had never prospected before? No! Nor dug gold at all? Never!

I saw them glance hurriedly at each other; my heart sank, until I noticed that their eyes were eager and sparkling! Then I learned that my ignorance was blessed! Gold miners were very superstitious; it was one of their firm beliefs that "luck" would inevitably follow the *first* essay of the neophyte or "greenhorn." This was the inexplicable good fortune of the inferior and incompetent. It was not very complimentary to myself, but in my eagerness to show my gratitude to my new partners I accepted it.

I dressed hastily, and swallowed my breakfast of coffee, salt pork, and "flapjacks." A pair of old deerskin moccasins, borrowed from a squaw who did the camp washing, was a luxury to my blistered feet; and, equipped with a pick, a long-handled shovel, and a prospecting pan, I demanded to be led at once to my field of exploit. But I was told that this was impossible; I must find it myself, alone, or the charm would be broken!

I fixed upon a grassy slope, about two hundred yards from the cabin, and limped thither. The slope faced the magnificent canon and the prospect I had seen the day before from the further summit. In my vivid recollection of that eventful morning I quite distinctly remember that I was, nevertheless, so entranced with the exterior "prospect" that for some moments I forgot the one in the ground at my feet. Then I began to dig.

My instructions were to fill my pan with the dirt taken from as large an area as possible near the surface. In doing this I was sorely tempted to dig lower in search of more hidden treasure, and in one or two deeper strokes of my pick I unearthed a bit of quartz with little seams or veins that glittered promisingly. I put them hopefully in my pocket, but duly filled my pan. This I took, not without some difficulty, owing to its absurd weight, to the nearest sluice-box, and, as instructed, tilted my pan in the running water.

As I rocked it from side to side, in a surprisingly short time the lighter soil of deep red color was completely washed away, leaving a glutinous clayey pudding mixed with small stones, like plums. Indeed, there was a fascinating reminiscence of "dirt pies" in this boyish performance. The mud, however, soon yielded to the flowing water, and left only the stones and "black sand." I removed the former with my fingers, retaining only a small, flat, pretty, disk-like stone, heavier than the others—it looked like a blackened coin—and this I put in my pocket with the quartz. Then I proceeded to wash away the black sand.

I must leave my youthful readers to imagine my sensations when at last I saw a dozen tiny star-points of gold adhering to the bottom of the pan! They were so small that I was fearful of washing further, lest they should wash away. It was not until later that I found that their specific gravity made that almost impossible. I ran joyfully to where my partners were at work, holding out my pan.

"Yes, he's got the color," said one blandly. "I knew it."

I was disappointed. "Then I haven't struck it?" I said hesitatingly.

"Not in *this* pan. You've got about a quarter of a dollar here."

My face fell. "But," he continued smilingly, "you've only to get that amount in four pans, and you've made your daily 'grub.'"

"And that's all," added the other, "that we, or indeed *any one* on this hill, have made for the last six months!"

This was another shock to me. But do not know whether I was as much impressed by it as by the perfect good humor and youthful unconcern with which it was uttered. Still, I was disappointed in my first effort. I hesitatingly drew the two bits of quartz from my pocket.

"I found them," I said. "They look as if they had some metal in them. See how it sparkles."

My partner smiled. "Iron pyrites," he said; "but what's that?" he added quickly, taking the little disk-like stone from my hand. "Where did you get this?"

"In the same hole. Is it good for anything?"

He did not reply to me, but turned to his two other partners, who had eagerly pressed around him. "Look!"

He laid the fragment on another stone and gave it a smart blow with the point of his pick. To my astonishment it did not crumble or break, but showed a little dent from the pick point that was bright yellow!

I had no time, nor indeed need, to ask another question. "Run for your barrow!" he said to one. "Write out a Notice, and bring the stakes," to the other; and the next moment, forgetful of my blistered feet, we were flying over to the slope. A claim was staked out, the "Notice" put up, and we all fell to work to load up our wheelbarrow. We carried four loads to the sluice-boxes before we began to wash.

The nugget I had picked up was worth about twelve dollars. We carried many loads; we worked that day and the next, hopefully, cheerfully, and without weariness. Then we worked at the claim daily, dutifully, and regularly for three weeks. We sometimes got "the color," we sometimes didn't, but we nearly always got enough for our daily "grub." We laughed, joked, told stories, "spouted poetry," and enjoyed ourselves as in a perpetual picnic. But that twelve-dollar nugget was the first and last "strike" we made on the new "Tenderfoot" claim!

A man looks on a camp among the oak trees in the foothills.

BIBLIOGRAPHY

Anonymous, "Notes of a Trip through Western Utah: Number III," *Daily Alta California* (San Francisco, CA), October 7, 1860.

Ayers, Col. James J. *Gold and Sunshine: Reminiscences of Early California*, Boston: Richard G. Badger/The Gorham Press, 1922.

Borthwick, J.[ohn] D.[avid]. "Three Years in California," *Hutchings' California Magazine*, September 1857; October 1857.

Buck, Franklin A. *A Yankee Trader in the Gold Rush: The Letters of Franklin A. Buck*, edited by Katherine A. White, Boston: Houghton Mifflin Co., 1930.

The Californian, May 29, 1848.

Coke, Henry J. *A Ride Over the Rocky Mountains to Oregon and California*, London, UK: Richard Bentley, 1852.

Crosby, Elisha Oscar. *Memoirs of Elisha Oscar Crosby; Reminiscences of California and Guatemala from 1849 to 1864*, edited by Charles Albro Barker, San Marino, CA: The Huntington Library, 1945.

Dame Shirley (Louise Clappe), "California in 1851: Letter First, A Trip Into the Mines," *The Pioneer: or, California Monthly Magazine*, January 1854; April 1854; November 1854; December 1854; May 1855; June 1855.

Delano, Alonzo. *Life on the Plains and Among the Diggings*, New York: Miller, Orton & Co., 1857.

——. *Alonzo Delano's California Correspondence: Being Letters Hitherto Uncollected from the* Ottawa *(Illinois)* Free Trader *and the* New Orleans True Delta, *1849–1852*, edited by Irving McKee, Sacramento, CA: Sacramento Book Collectors Club, 1952.

Emerson, Ralph Waldo. *The Conduct of Life*, Boston: James R. Osgood & Co., 1876.

Gibbs, Mifflin Wistar. *Shadow and Light*, Washington, DC: n.p., 1902.

Gilmore, Andrew Hall. Letter to his brother, December 24, 1851–January 8, 1852.

Grant, Ulysses S. *Personal Memoirs of U. S. Grant*, vol. 1, New York: Charles L. Webster & Co., 1885 (1892 ed.).

Harte, Bret. "How I Went to the Mines," *Openings in the Old Trail*, New York: P. F. Collier & Son, 1903.

——. "The Luck of Roaring Camp," *Overland Monthly*, August 1868.

Hittell, John S. "Reminiscences of the Plains and Mines in '49 and '50," *Overland Monthly*, February 1887.

——. *Mining in the Pacific States of North America*, San Francisco: H. H. Bancroft & Co., 1861.

London, Jack. "All Gold Cañon," *The Century Magazine*, November 1905.

——. "The Banks of the Sacramento," *The Youth's Companion*, March 17, 1904.

Marshall, James. "The Discovery of Gold in California," *Hutchings' Illustrated California Magazine*, November 1857.

Mason, Col. Richard; edited by Rodman W. Paul. *The California Gold Discovery*, Georgetown, CA: The Talisman Press, 1967. **Note:** My book includes a mixture of three versions of the report.

Meyer, Carl. *Nach dem Sacramento,* Aarau, Switzerland, 1855, translated by Ruth Frey Axe as *Bound for Sacramento: Travel-Pictures of a Returned Wanderer,* Claremont, CA: Saunders Studio Press, 1938. ***Note:*** Since this is a translation, some corrections have been made to the text, but were made with care not to change the meaning.

Sherman, General William Tecumseh. *Memoirs of General William T. Sherman,* vol. 1, New York: D. Appleton & Co., 1875.

Sutter, General John A. "The Discovery of Gold in California," *Hutchings' California Magazine,* November 1857.

Thoreau, Henry David. His journal, February 1, 1852; *The Writings of Henry David Thoreau,* vol. 9, Boston: Houghton Mifflin & Co., 1906.

Twain, Mark. *Roughing It,* Hartford, CT: American Publishing Co., 1872 (1879).

Urner, Nathan A. "Scorpion Gulch: A Gold-Seeker's Tale," *Beadle's Monthly,* January 1866.

Index

Note: Page numbers in *italics* indicate photos/illustrations. Footnotes are noted with "n" after page number.

About the Author

John Richard Stephens is the author/editor of nineteen books, which include *Commanding the Storm* (Lyons Press), *Weird History 101, Wyatt Earp Speaks!*, and *Kitty Literature.*

Before becoming a writer, Stephens gained experience in a wide variety of occupations ranging from work as a psychiatric counselor in two hospitals and three mental health facilities to being an intelligence officer and squadron commander in the US Air Force.

His books have been selections of the Preferred Choice Book Club, the Quality Paperback Book Club and the Book of the Month Club. His work has been published as far away as India and Singapore, and has been translated into Japanese and Finnish.

Stephens also has the distinguished honor of being quoted around the world next to such luminaries as Abraham Lincoln, Mark Twain, Lord Byron, and Franz Kafka.